POPULISM AND NEOLIBERALISM

Populism and Neoliberalism argues that the roots of populism lay in the contradiction between the democratic ideal, which implies that the people should decide, and neoliberal governance, which seeks to make markets and competition the arbiters of major social developments.

Neoliberalism is not the product of a clearly conceived ideology but rather a set of doctrines based on a few major principles which have been embraced by decision-makers of all kinds with little reassessment along the way. In practice, a certain art of governing that exploited an economic thinking insensitive to social complexity gradually imposed itself by being wrongly identified as the successor to liberalism. The rise of populist movements poses a significant challenge to liberal democracies, yet the causes of these movements remain beyond the understanding of experts. The explanation of populism is often limited to a mere political analysis. Contrary to that, this book investigates the economic and social dynamics of the free-market system and explains how populism emerges from its imbalances. It also aims to explain the emergence of the neoliberal doctrines during the 1930s and to characterise their common features. In light of this, it explores how the rise of inequality and social discontent create a pressing duty to develop another model, and argues that we must now rethink our policies in depth in order to respond to the challenge of authoritarian populism.

This book marks a significant intervention in the debate about the rise and fall of neoliberalism. Its analysis of the links between the failings of neoclassical economics and the failings of neoliberal politics provides essential reading for anyone interested in the damaging impact of neoliberalism, the failings of neoclassical economics, and explanations for the rise of populism.

David Cayla is an Associate Professor of Economics and Vice-Dean of the Faculty of Law, Economics and Management at Angers University, France. His research focuses primarily on the economy of the European Union and the history of economic thought.

POPULISM AND NEOLIBERALISM

David Cayla

Routledge
Taylor & Francis Group

LONDON AND NEW YORK

First published 2021
by Routledge
2 Park Square, Milton Park, Abingdon, Oxon OX14 4RN

and by Routledge
52 Vanderbilt Avenue, New York, NY 10017

Routledge is an imprint of the Taylor & Francis Group, an informa business

© 2021 David Cayla

British Library Cataloguing-in-Publication Data
A catalogue record for this book is available from the British Library

Library of Congress Cataloging-in-Publication Data
A catalog record has been requested for this book

ISBN: 978-0-367-42856-3 (hbk)
ISBN: 978-0-367-42770-2 (pbk)
ISBN: 978-0-367-85559-8 (ebk)

Typeset in Bembo
by Deanta Global Publishing Services, Chennai, India

CONTENTS

FIGURES

TABLES

ABOUT THE AUTHOR

David Cayla is an Associate Professor of Economics and Vice-Dean of the Faculty of Law, Economics and Management at Angers University, France. His research focuses primarily on the economy of the European Union and the history of economic thought. He has published three books in France, most notable of which are *L'Économie du réel* (De Boeck Supérieur, 2018) and *La Fin de l'Union europénne* (Michalon 2017, with Coralie Delaume). An active member of the French heterodox economist association "Les Économistes atterrés", he defends an economic science more open to other social sciences and equipped to understand institutional issues.

ACKNOWLEDGEMENTS

The idea for this book was conceived in the fall of 2018, while I was working on a paper for an academic conference held in Atlanta in January 2019. The preparatory work of reading and reflection lasted almost a year, punctuated by the lectures and administrative responsibilities that I have in charge at the University of Angers. The writing took place between March and July 2020, a period marked by the coronavirus pandemic.

The episode of lockdown imposed by the health crisis affected a French University which has suffered for many years from a continuous deterioration in the working conditions of its teaching and non-teaching staff. We had to urgently transform our practices, adapt to new ways of teaching and evaluating, find solutions for students without means of connection, reassure them, sometimes by telephone from our personal lines, and do the best we could without being able to do as well. My task as a teacher and pedagogical manager for our first-year programme has been considerably increased by this context. Fortunately, I was able to count on the kindness and commitment of my colleagues. I believe that if this book was completed, it is because others worked extremely hard to ensure that everything went well. I would therefore like to thank Christophe Daniel, Dean of the Faculty of Law, Economics and Management, and Michèle Favreau and Philippe Le Gall, co-directors of the Economics Department, for their constant involvement, their attentiveness, their availability and their unfailing support. I would also like to express my gratitude to the Schooling Department, in particular Blandine Blaiteau, Marion Ferrand and Véronique Loret, for their professionalism and commitment in organising the continuity of our work to the students.

I have a special thought for my friend and co-author Coralie Delaume, whose discussions, opinions, and reviews have been invaluable and have contributed a great deal to this book. A deep thank you as well to my other proofreaders

Thibault Laurentjoye, Anne Musson and Cassandre Vielle whose suggestions, corrections, and comments helped me a lot.

Writing a whole book in English has been a challenge for a native French-speaking person like me. Hopefully, I was helped in that task by two precious friends: Anastasia Petrenko and Oriane de Laubrière. Not only did they help me to improve my writing skills, but they also improved the content of the book by continuously insisting on clarifying my thoughts.

At last, I wish to thank Routledge editor Andy Humphries for his constant trust and his great patience.

INTRODUCTION

What's next?

Our world is the consequence of past decisions; tomorrow's world will be the product of the decisions we make today. But how are these decisions made? How can we consider at one time that a good economic policy is based on free trade, while at other times it was considered vital to give generous subsidies to domestic exporters or to protect the economy from international competition?

Most researchers and academics believe in the power of ideas. In 1944, the Austrian-born economist Friedrich Hayek expressed a paradoxical feeling on this subject: "a change of ideas, and the force of human will, have made the world what it is now". But he adds immediately: "though men did not foresee the results" (Hayek 1944, p. 12). The ideas that lead the world do so without knowing where they are going, like a blind man. And, like the blind man, they sometimes collide with concrete reality, with the occurrence of unforeseen crises. They are then forced to change direction, sometimes abruptly, under the influence of other ideas that seem more innovative. The American economist Milton Friedman described these phases of ideological change as follows:

> There is enormous inertia – a tyranny of the status quo – in private and especially governmental arrangements. Only a crisis – actual or perceived – produces real change. When that crisis occurs, the actions that are taken depend on the ideas that are lying around. That, I believe, is our basic function: to develop alternatives to existing policies, to keep them alive and available until the politically impossible becomes politically inevitable.
>
> (Friedman 1982)

Ideas vary in economic policy, but they don't necessarily do so according to the progress of scientific knowledge. This is because economics is a complex discipline that never provides a single solution to a particular issue. Moreover, these solutions have to be implemented on the basis of circumstances, says Rodrik (2015). It can even be argued that all proposals made by economists must be subject to social arbitration, for there is no economic policy measure that does not contradict at least one particular interest. Therefore, in democracies, the only policies that can be pursued are those that are considered good by a large part of the public.

Thus, economics is essentially political. Friedman and Hayek were well aware of this. That is why they both put a lot of effort into defending their ideas, not only academically but also in the public arena. The world they helped to build gradually came into existence from the late 1970s onwards. However, the world their ideas helped build was not necessarily the one they had foreseen.

Forty years after the so-called "neoliberal" revolution, we are going through a major sanitary and economic crisis which may finally mark the end of the prevalence of Hayek and Friedman's ideas. The COVID-19 pandemic has forced world leaders to urgently devise exceptional health and economic responses. The administrative closure of shops, places of worship and culture, restaurants and cafés, and the abrupt halt of international travel and air traffic have profoundly disrupted economic and social life. In the worst affected countries, extreme measures have forced people to remain confined at home for several months. Meetings were held by video, lessons online, dinners or aperitifs were organised remotely. For a time, the social and economic life was put aside.

The economic shock produced by lockdowns was not symmetrical: it affected some sectors much more than others. Some firms continued to operate almost normally, while others had to stop suddenly. The latter saw their rental and financial charges accumulate without being able to cover them with equivalent income. Many were unable to continue paying their employees. Layoffs and business failures were likely to increase. Ultimately, banks and the financial sector would have to bear billions of losses due to multiple defaults, jeopardizing the financial sector as a whole.

To avoid economic collapse, many governments were forced to partially substitute for the private sector. Financial support for the manufacturing industry and airline companies was put in place; banks were required to provide state-guaranteed emergency loans or payment facilities; benefits were sometimes paid directly to households; salaries of laid-off employees were covered; some tax debts were waived or postponed. Central banks also acted by multiplying support programmes to accompany government initiatives.

For a few months, the economies of some countries were partly driven and financed by the public sector. Trade contracted sharply, and the usual rules of capitalism were suspended. The financial sector had been heavily supported by very accommodating monetary policies following the 2008 financial crisis. They embarked on new and extensive buyback programmes to lower the funding costs for the entire economy.[1] The European Central Bank (ECB) was even caught up in a frenzy of purchasing Italian securities on financial markets to prevent a new Eurozone crisis.[2]

What kind of world is unfolding before our eyes? It is certainly not the one Friedman and Hayek dreamt of. Nor is it the Soviet socialism they both feared so much. It is a world in which the state and the central banks have become the global firefighters of the capitalist system, choosing to pour out an impressive amount of money in the hope of avoiding a major fire.

Some would like to see this crisis and the reactions it has imposed as the beginning of a profound ideological change. Just as the crisis of the 1930s sounded the death knell for 19th-century *laissez-fairism*, the pandemic crisis would mark the end of neoliberalism, a doctrine already weakened by the financial crises of the 2000s. The next world, they believe, will bring the return of the state and intervention measures.

But what if it is exactly the opposite? For the economist Olivier Passet, the year 2020 does not mark any real break with the past but, on the contrary, testifies to the acceleration of a logic that has been under way for decades.

> Just what kind of return are we talking about? For the state to return, it would need to have disappeared. This is not the case. There has been a shift over several decades. The producer state has certainly regressed. So has the investor state. The redistributing state has also been challenged to varying degrees in different countries. But overall, the OECD governments have not retreated in financial terms. Almost everywhere, they have been given the role of facilitator of business and major final insurer of economic risks, which has gone from strength to strength. It is this insurance function, in its various forms, that has taken precedence over all others for years.
>
> *(Passet 2020)*

The state's insurance function is not new, says Passet. Above all, it is in no way incompatible with the withdrawal of the state' s productive functions: "The state has maintained itself financially while it has gradually abandoned entire sectors of production that it can't efficiently manage anymore. It has concentrated with stunted means on its sovereign functions: security and justice in particular" (*Ibid.*). The return of the state into the economy is therefore, for the time being, a mere *trompe-l'oeil*. The way it responds to the crisis is symptomatic of the new role it has taken on. It is spending huge sums while the bulk of productive action is being delegated to the private sector. It finances without controlling, if at all, and without engaging in real strategic coordination of productive action.

> Is this a return of the state? There is reason to doubt it. On the contrary, we are experiencing the apotheosis of the insurance state and its resignation from the field of production of common goods. A sort of generalised "flexicurity", pushed to its climax. The rest of the story, however, is written in advance. States will come out discredited from the management of this crisis, having to account for the stocks of masks or respirators that have evaporated, having also gotten over-indebted in order to regain control of

the social or ecological question. Moreover, if the state producing common goods had returned, we would already see that. It would not only mobilise billions, or import masks from China, but it would hire people. Its response would not only be financial, but real. Our companies would be requisitioned to produce the essentials.

(Ibid.)

Passet's analysis shows that short-term responses should not be confused with structural responses. Is the purpose of massive state intervention aimed at changing the system or saving it from bankruptcy? The methods of intervention suggest that, in reality, there has probably been no substantive change in doctrine, even if the measures appear radical in terms of volume.

In fact, the crisis is still ahead of us and we can legitimately wonder what will happen to the world once the strictly health-related episode is over. Will we face economic and financial chaos that will make the 2008 financial crisis look like "child's play" (Farrer 2020)? This is the opinion of economist Nouriel Roubini (2020), who believes that the coronavirus crisis hit a world economy which was already scarred by deep structural imbalances. These imbalances, whether economic, financial, or political, are likely to be reinforced by this crisis. He, therefore, fears that the 2020s will turn into a decade of depression, with political authorities paralysed and unable to implement the vast project of a profound transformation of the economic system.

Although crises are often opportunities to change ideas and push political action towards new directions, there is no proof that they are enough. Indeed, ideas must be "lying around", to use Friedman's formula. But it is these ideas that are missing. Or, more precisely, of the many representations of what should be done, none emerge clearly that would take the economy out of the dominant ideology. There is every reason to fear that, in this situation, routine and the "tyranny of the status quo" will prevail.

The real issue is that everyone may find some confirmation of their own beliefs in the moment we are experiencing. At least, that is the analysis of economist Dani Rodrik in one of his recent articles dedicated to the consequences of the pandemic:

So, those who want more government and public goods will have plenty of reason to think the crisis justifies their belief. And those who are sceptical of government and decry its incompetence will also find their prior views confirmed. Those who want more global governance will make the case that a stronger international public-health regime could have reduced the costs of the pandemic. And those who seek stronger nation-states will point to the many ways in which the WHO seem to have mismanaged its response …

In short, COVID-19 may well not alter – much less reverse – tendencies evident before the crisis. Neoliberalism will continue its slow death. Populist autocrats will become even more authoritarian. Hyper-globalisation will remain on the defensive as nation-states reclaim policy space.

(Rodrik 2020)

In addition to the lack of new ideas, what exactly to change and how to do it, the political situations in many countries do not favour a radical overhaul of public policies. The management of the 2007–2008 crisis, as well as the sharp rise in inequality that most countries experienced since the 1980s, has led to a deep distrust among a section of the population that has resulted in the emergence of populist forces and broad social protest movements. The turn that the political debate has taken since then is not conducive to a thorough rethinking and rebuilding of societies. Instead, populism generates sterile opposition against elites accused of betraying the people and against minorities or foreign populations. Populism is also an "identitarianism". It seeks to rehabilitate popular cultures and identities in response to representations and social hierarchies that fail to give them the consideration they expect.

But populism cannot be reduced to its political dimension. It is, more fundamentally, the expression of a social disorder. The vote for the Brexit and the election of Donald Trump are sometimes considered the most striking populist events of recent years. That is forgetting that populist movements took root in many countries long before they reached the Anglo-Saxon world. Central Europe was, in the early 2010s, the laboratory of a form of populism that managed to gain and maintain power. In Southern Europe, a specific form of populism emerged, shaped by social issues and the Eurozone crisis. In Turkey, Russia and the Philippines, populism has taken an authoritarian dimension that challenges civil rights and democracy itself. The list is long: the key point is that populism, although fairly easy to identify, is embodied politically and socially in very diverse ways. Moreover, its causes are not always clear, and no consensus can be found among those who study it.

For instance, while social and economic inequalities appear to be a decisive factor in the emergence of populism, it is not clear that fiscal redistribution alone would be sufficient to weaken it. Indeed, once populist leaders come to power, they rarely implement equalitarian measures. Behind the nationalist rhetoric many employ, there are frequent injunctions to work and effort instead of waiting for governmental subsidies. Similarly, populist leaders are often businessmen, and some of them are billionaires.

In this book, I wish to explore the link between populism and neoliberalism. Why? Perhaps because the former may be a consequence of the latter, and to understand them, it may be necessary to deal with them together. The idea to study populism and neoliberalism in conjunction is not new. Most authors who have studied populism connect it to the economic disarray that the working classes have fallen into. And those scholars have no difficulty in linking this disarray to economic policies and neoliberalism.

What is more debatable, however, is the nature of the relationship between these two phenomena. In order to characterise it, it is primarily necessary to delve deeper into the origin of the different forms of populism and to understand what it is that unites them despite the apparent heterogeneity of their agendas. Secondly, it is essential to clearly define what neoliberalism stands for. What a curious doctrine whose name is itself a matter of debate! Is it a simple "market fundamentalism" as the Nobel Prize winner in economics, Joseph Stiglitz claims? If that is all there is, then one would conclude that the global economy has already emerged from neoliberalism since states have intervened widely and massively to rescue markets in recent years.

First, let us honestly admit that no one seriously believes in the perfection of markets any more. Everyone now accepts that markets need public institutions to function and, on occasion, strong support from public authorities to rescue them from chaos. But if neoliberalism is not simply market fundamentalism, how shall it be defined and characterised precisely?

This book seeks to answer all these questions. More specifically, I defend two main arguments. The first one is that the roots of populism lie first and foremost in the feeling of distrust that people feel towards a powerless political structure. It is argued that if politics have become impotent, it is mainly because its ability to act in the economic sphere has been taken away. In the name of free competition and free trade, many levers of action have been deactivated by competitive markets in favour of regulation. The state has thus gradually resigned from its role as a producer and economic regulator in favour of merely preserving and repairing the market order. Neoliberalism is therefore not market fundamentalism because it does not rest on the perfection and autonomy of markets. That is why it puts the state at its service. There are, of course, as we shall see, several forms of neoliberalism and different conceptions about the nature of the order that is supposed to ensure the proper functioning of markets. But all neoliberals, including Hayek and Friedman, believe that some form of public intervention is necessary to make markets work in the best possible way.

The second thesis that I wish to defend is that neoliberalism is now deeply embedded in the representations of most economists, including those who claim to oppose a "neoliberalism" conceived as market fundamentalism. As former Harvard University president Lawrence Summers acknowledges, almost all economists have now become Friedmanites.[3] Contemporary economics does not buy into the myth that markets are perfect, rather that they are an imperative necessity. Indeed, it has totally ceased to question the relevance of the market's mechanisms. According to this view, all economic issues can be reduced to problems of allocating scarce resources, and markets – when they function well – are the most efficient instruments available for allocating these resources. The problem is that this conception of economics is extremely simplistic and that economic science has systematically failed – despite investing a lot of energy into it – to demonstrate that markets are efficient devices for doing what is expected from them. The result is a profound bias in most contemporary economic analysis that stands in the way of the emergence of new ideas.

In other words, as economist Joan Robinson stated, a specific economic doctrine, the one who tends to analyse the economy through supply and demand curves, became a strong part of the dominant ideology in such a way that it is now difficult to conceive the economy and its issues without first thinking about how we could better allocate resources through better functioning markets.

> We must go round about to find the roots of our own beliefs. In the general mass of notions and sentiments that make up an ideology, those concerned with economic life play a large part, and economics itself (that is the subject as it is taught in universities and evening classes and pronounced upon in leading articles) has always been partly a vehicle for the ruling ideology of each period as well as partly a method of scientific investigation.
>
> *(Robinson 1962, p. 7)*

This book is divided into three main chapters. The first chapter examines the return of populist movements to the political and social arena. The specific analysis of the European case is intended to show how the establishment of the Single Market in the 1990s has profoundly destabilised the Old Continent. The second chapter deals with neoliberalism. It proposes to make a clear distinction between classical forms of liberalism and contemporary neoliberalism and sets out the specific values and principles on which neoliberal doctrines are based on. Finally, the last chapter examines the proposals put forward by a number of economists who wish to respond to the challenges posed by populism and rising inequality. Despite their relative diversity, the propositions held by most contemporary economists are coloured by a certain conservatism and have difficulties to challenge some neoliberal dogma.

In short, this book intends to propose an in-depth analysis of the dominant ideology for which economics has become the "vehicle". Above all, it intends to show the limits of market mechanisms when they come to organise social life. It is these limits that economists ignore and that political leaders do not see. They are the ones we need to discuss.

Notes

1 In March 2020, the European Central Bank (ECB) announced a new asset purchase programme for a total of €750 billion. In April, the US Federal Reserve announced a similar project with a ceiling of $2,300 billion. Finally, in June, the Bank of England extended its support programme, initiated in the wake of the 2008 crisis, by £300 billion.
2 In particular, in April and May 2020 the ECB bought more Italian government securities than the country issued. See: Reuters, "UPDATE 2-Italian bond yields rise as focus on ECB purchases, meeting", June 2, 2020, online.
3 A few days after Friedman's death (November 16, 2006) Summers wrote for the *New York Times*: "Not so long ago, we were all Keynesians. ("I am a Keynesian," Richard

Nixon famously said in 1971.) Equally, any honest Democrat will admit that we are now all Friedmanites. Mr. Friedman, who died last week at 94 [years], never held elected office but he has had more influence on economic policy as it is practiced around the world today than any other modern figure" (Summers 2006).

References

Farrer, Martin (2020), "Coronavirus credit crunch could make 2008 look like 'child's play'", *The Guardian*, Mar. 20, 2020, online.

Friedman, Milton (1982) [2002], "Preface, 1982", in *Capitalism and Freedom*. Chicago, IL: The University of Chicago Press.

Hayek, Friedrich (1944) [2001], The Road to Serfdom. London: Routledge Classics.

Passet, Olivier (2020), "Du trop d'État à l'État démissionnaire", *Xerfi Canal*, Apr. 28, 2020, online.

Robinson, Joan (1962), *Economic Philosophy*. London: C. A. Watts & Co.

Rodrik, Dani (2015), Economics Rules: The Rights and Wrongs of the Dismal Science. New-York: Norton & Company, Inc.

Rodrik, Dani (2020), "Will Covid-19 remake the world?", *Project Syndicate*, Apr. 4, 2020, online.

Roubini, Nouriel (2020), "The coming greater depression of the 2020s", *Project Syndicate*, Mar. 28, 2020, online.

Summers, Lawrence H. (2006), "The great liberator", *The New York Times*, Nov. 19, 2006, online.

1

THE AGE OF UPRISINGS

The populist menace

Recently, a wealth of literature on the subject of populism has appeared in bookstores and university library shelves. Like any concept, populism has been forged to reflect a specific phenomenon: the sudden appearance of widespread revolt movements, in the polls or in the streets, that wish to overthrow the established order and put an end to a "system" of which the people consider themselves to be the victim.

The year 2016, marked by the victories of Brexit in the United Kingdom and Donald Trump in the United States, has raised awareness that populist phenomena are not reserved for emerging countries or those with fragile democratic institutions. It can just as easily affect old and stable democracies in rich and developed countries. Researchers in political science, sociology, and even economics have been looking at the roots of this new populism. All agree that it cannot be studied without its social context and that it is a symptom of a deeper democratic crisis. But what is the nature of this crisis? Here is where opinions diverge.

Many authors of books and articles on populism, especially economists, try to explain its resurgence on the basis of its most visible characteristics. Populism is not a constituted ideology. It can be left- or right-wing, defend public services, or demand fewer civil servants. What characterises populist movements is that they share a world view based on the opposition between the people and the elite. From this characteristic, it can be deduced that the emergence of neo-populism would be the consequence of growing inequality and economic stagnation of the middle classes.

The economist Dani Rodrik broadly adopts this vision. In an academic article (Rodrik 2018a), he argues that the populist dynamic is linked to the growing inequality and the economic and job transfers produced by the globalisation process. Moreover, the free movement of capital and the perpetual blackmail of offshoring have contributed to strengthening the bargaining power of capital to the detriment of employees. Admittedly, Rodrik acknowledges, technological progress also affects the distribution of income, and probably more significantly than free trade. But, from the citizens' point of view, the negative consequences of globalisation are much less acceptable than those resulting from scientific progress since they emanate from political decisions.

What also contributes to populism, according to Rodrik, is that economists, and more broadly political elites, appear insensitive to the social consequences of globalisation. By overemphasising the overall benefits of free trade and forgetting to mention the fate of the losers and how to cope with it, they fuel mistrust and provide arguments of anti-systemic tendencies for the vindictive rhetoric. Moreover, academic economists tend to not show enough concern for the institutions that structure political and social life. In particular, the nation-state is perceived as "an archaic construct that is at odds with twenty-first-century realities" and generates "transaction costs that block fuller global economic integration" (Rodrik 2018b, pp. 16-18).

For non-economist researchers, while inequality undoubtedly contributes to populism, the existence of deeper dysfunctions in modern democracies must also be considered. Political scientist Yascha Mounk (2018) sees populism as a consequence of a contradiction that has recently arisen between liberal values and democratic principles. By favouring action over institutional checks and balances, populists threaten the principles of the rule of law and some civil liberties. An alternative approach is that of Ivan Krastev (2017), a Bulgarian political scientist, who explains that populism in Central and Eastern Europe is the consequence of identity insecurity linked to migratory tensions and the European Union's institutional fragilities. Finally, the feeling of democratic powerlessness, generated by an economy governed on a global scale and over which politicians have little control, is also an advanced element in understanding democratic dysfunctions (Cox 2017).

But what is crucial to understand is that populism is not simply an electoral phenomenon. It is a social trend before it reaches the polls. This multifactorial aspect implies that its roots are deep and embedded in social life. The Yellow Vests movement in France or the medical debate surrounding the use of hydroxychloroquine in the treatment of COVID-19 were indeed populist moments, even if they did not necessarily have electoral consequences. More fundamentally, the growth of distrust towards institutions, such as the press, political parties, the education system, or medical authorities, is an essential element in the populist dynamic.

My purpose in this chapter is to propose a global analysis of populist phenomena starting from the economic dimension, drawing the sociological identity, and finally political consequences. The idea defended here is that populism is not simply a matter of income or wealth inequality; nor is it the consequence of an inevitable phenomenon generated by modernity; it is more fundamentally the consequence of demographic and sociological transformations which are themselves the consequences of underlying economic dynamics. Yet the economy is a human construct, the product of an institutional framework, and the result of political choices. In this sense, populism is not inevitable.

The analysis of populism I wish to develop is based mainly on the European situation. The European Union is indeed a very interesting model, not only because it is the scene of a specific resurgence of populist movements, but also because it combines having a common institutional framework at the economic level with the fact that it brings together a highly diverse set of countries. This "unity in diversity" makes it a unique laboratory for studying the links among institutional changes, economic developments, and sociological transformations. It also helps to understand how the same institutional framework can give rise to different forms of populism. Nevertheless, most of the dynamics that emerge from this study can be applied to other world regions – especially, as we shall see, to the United States.

Who wants to gag Professor Raoult?

On February 25, 2020, just as the COVID-19 epidemic began to affect the European continent (eleven cities in northern Italy were placed under quarantine three days earlier), a less than two-minute video was released on the official website of the Institut Hospitalo-Universitaire (IHU), a research and hospital facility based in the city of Marseille and dedicated to the study of infectious diseases. Titled "Coronavirus: game over!"[1] the video defended the use of chloroquine medication usually used to treat malaria, to treat the disease. Standing in front of his desk, IHU president Didier Raoult, an internationally renowned French microbiologist, explained in a reassuring tone why the new virus should not worry anyone. At that time, several thousand deaths, most of them in the Hubei province in China, were already to be deplored. But Raoult appeared confident: "It's probably the easiest respiratory infection to cure", he said, promising clinical test results would come soon.

Indeed, clinical test results were not long to come. On March 16, 2020, a new twenty-minute video reported that the treatment with hydroxychloroquine and azithromycin (a broad-spectrum antibiotic) was able to eradicate the virus load of all the six patients following the treatment after six days.[2]

The idea of treating COVID-19 with chloroquine did not go unnoticed. In the Anglo-Saxon world, Gregory Rigano, a 34-year-old man, claimed on March 14 on Twitter that he had found a cure for the coronavirus by disclosing a scientific study he co-authored. Two days later, billionaire Elon Musk shared the paper on his account. Soon, Elon Musk's tweet was relayed tens of thousands of times and attracted the attention of the conservative media. On March 19, Rigano was invited by the influential Tucker Carlson, a star presenter of Fox News. Rigano referred to the work of Professor Raoult's Marseille team, whose results had just been made public, and said: "The president has the authority to authorize the use of hydroxychloroquine against the coronavirus immediately". That message to the president was sharply noticed by Donald Trump, a regular viewer of the show. The same day, in a press conference, Trump stated that he was authorising the use of hydroxychloroquine, a remedy described as a "gift from God", to fight the epidemic then raging in the United States.

Problem: As the *Daily Mail* revealed a few days later,[3] Gregory Rigano was neither a doctor nor a scientist, but a lawyer with a passion for cryptocurrency. The study he posted online was fraudulent and had no scientific basis. Finally, it was discovered that Stanford University, of which he claimed to be an adviser, knew nothing about him and demanded that he remove all references to its name from the study. Eventually, Google removed the whole study from its servers.

But Donald Trump's intervention had been heard all over the world, particularly in France. Since March 16 2020, the information that the research centre in Marseille may have found the solution to stop the epidemic had been circulating at full speed. While residential lockdown had just been imposed in France, Professor Raoult's videos had been being widely shared on social networks. Trump's statement accelerated the phenomenon. Many people began to wonder why that essential information was hidden by the press. Why the French government and medical authorities refused to use the treatment protocol that was advocated by the Marseille institute and approved by the American President in person? Conspiracy theories flourished. Didier Raoult was seen as a maverick. At age 68, he looked like a rebellious rock star, thanks to his long hair. He was reported to be in a conflict with the husband of Agnès Buzyn, the former health minister who implemented the anti-pandemic plan before she resigned in order to run for mayor of Paris. Was the French scientific establishment trying to marginalise that great iconoclastic scientist, whose work was quoted as a reference throughout the world?

The reality was rather simpler. If Didier Raoult's work on chloroquine was in dispute, it was only because the clinical experiment carried out in Marseille was deemed insufficient to decide on the effectiveness of the remedy. The sample size was small and scientific protocols were not scrupulously respected. However, the damage was done. When the government announced the strengthening of the lockdown measures, Raoult, who disagreed with the strategy, announced that he would no longer take part in the Scientific Council in charge of informing governmental decisions. He demanded a lifting of the ban on the use of chloroquine and, without even waiting for an answer from the Ministry of Health, launched a vast study within his institute, promising to test and treat all patients who presented themselves. Soon, hundreds of people began flocking to the institute. To prevent the spread of contagion in the waiting lines, the police asked those crowding in front of the sorting tent to move more than a yard away from each other. Behind the tent, supporters of the "Olympique de Marseille" soccer team erected a banner that proclaimed: "Marseille and the world with Professor Raoult!!!".

Everything about this affair is fascinating, in particular what it reveals about French society at the beginning of 2020. The COVID-19 outbreak surprised everyone, especially the French government. In March 2020, while the number of COVID-19 cases was exponentially increasing every day, France was running out of masks for its medical staff. The requisitioning of stocks and the emergency purchase orders made to China, the only country able to produce a quantity adequate to the needs, were too late. Despite the reassuring speeches of the authorities, orders were not always honoured because of the fierce competition among countries all over the world.[4] Finally, France suffered a shortage of hydroalcoholic gel and could only test a very small proportion of suspected cases.

Officially, masks were declared "useless" for uninfected people. It was therefore recommended that masks should not be worn in order to leave the small stocks for hospital staff and those who had to continue working in essential areas. Government guidelines varied from day to day. On March 12, in a solemn address to the Nation, President Emmanuel Macron declared that schools and universities must be closed, but that borders must be kept open because "the virus has no passport". On March 14, the French Prime Minister announced the closure of all bars, restaurants, and non-essential shops that evening, but invited all voters to go to the polls the next day for the first round of the municipal elections. On March 16, a new presidential allocution announced that the entire population would be confined to their homes. In a state of panic, those who were able to do so abandoned the cities and the Paris region and moved to rural residences, at the risk of spreading the virus. A few days later, air, rail, and road passenger traffic came to an almost complete halt. The country froze under lockdown. Yet, the government called for manufacturing and construction activities to continue despite the acute shortage of protective equipment.[5]

These hesitations, the apparent lack of preparation, and the contradictory instructions addressed to the population in a context of great anxiety came together in an explosive mixture, causing a growing distrust towards the government. In this context, the question of Professor Raoult's work emerged and provided the basis for the most far-fetched conspiracy theories. "The problem with chloroquine is that it doesn't cost enough for the pharmaceutical lobby", read one comment on social networks. "It would kill any profitability for the future vaccine". Sensing the movement's popularity, many politicians in the Marseille region publicly showed their support for Didier Raoult, such as Christian Estrosi, the mayor of Nice, who claimed to have "the feeling of being cured" thanks to the professor's remedy.

But in the medical profession, many doctors and experts were sceptical of the relevance of generalising the use of hydroxychloroquine and expressed their reservations in the media. The calls for caution were met with strong opposition. Within a few days, Facebook groups in support of Professor Raoult multiplied, bringing together hundreds of thousands of members. The scientific and medical debate turned into struggles revealing French political and sociological tensions.

The opposition between pro- and anti-Raoult covered multiple fractures: the rivalry between the "folksy" city of Marseille and the capital city, Paris; the gap between elected officials from the field and members of the government; the opposition between the horizontality of social networks and the verticality of the major media; the common folk voices facing the experts who were discredited because of the overly reassuring comments they had made during the previous few weeks.

Didier Raoult was cast as the hero of the people, the answer to the "arrogance" of the elites. The hydroxychloroquine affair was no longer a medical dispute but a political confrontation that destabilised the scientific authorities, unused to dealing with such protests. Interviewed on national television, Professor Gilbert Deray, head of the department at the Pitié-Salpêtrière, a major Parisian hospital, made the following comments: "The Marseille experience, whatever the effectiveness of this drug – which I hope is real, like everyone else – creates a fracture in society that amazes me. Science, medicine, and therapeutic indications are no longer decided by articles published in journals with experts; they are decided on Facebook and Twitter".[6]

France was divided into two camps that reflected two systems of thought and two political logics. It had become clear to everyone that Trump's intervention and his support for the Marseille team's protocol contradicted the scientific establishment embodied by his own adviser, Anthony Fauci, a man Didier Raoult mocked in a video published mid-February. "He must have gotten senile", he said. Like Donald Trump, Didier Raoult is a fan of abrupt language.[7]

The parallels between the two men do not stop at their ability to find the right insult. Their way of communicating is also very unusual. Trump makes massive use of Twitter, while Raoult has his institute post videos of himself on YouTube. Both choose to speak directly to the public without going through the ordinary channels of information. But what they have most in common is that Raoult and Trump embody a seemingly contradictory stance. One is president of the United States and the most powerful man in the world; the other is the director of a prestigious medical research institute, has received numerous honours for his work, and is one of the most highly cited scientists in the world. Both, however, claim they are "rebellious" and intend to fight the establishment. The multi-billionaire and the great scientist boast of embodying the aspirations of the "people" against the "elites" who are said to live in their bubble without regard for the rest of the population.

This astonishing attitude on the part of people who are among the most notable representatives of the elite is, however, nothing new. What was happening in France, in March 2020, that moment of collective hysteria that precipitated into the tragic events of the time, was a populist moment similar to the one the United States and other countries previously experienced; a moment when the people found themselves an anti-establishment hero whose behaviour escapes the usual logics.

Popular uprisings

Anger rumbles. While a garbage strike paralyses the city and social budgets for the poorest are being cut, a billionaire is running for election. One evening, a spontaneous anti-rich demonstration breaks out, inspired by the criminal act of a deprived person who killed a television presenter on air. Taking advantage of the chaos, a man wearing a clown mask murders the billionaire and his wife in front of their only son as they were on their way home.

Here, in a few words, is the synopsis of a film that was one of the great critical and popular successes of world cinema in 2019. Hollywood has not yet fully transformed itself into an amusement park, as Martin Scorsese deplored.[8] There are still American films that reflect their times, even when they are part of a comic book franchise.

By depicting the revolt of the oppressed in a Gotham City plagued by inequality, *Joker* paints a portrait in the darkness of the Reagan years. But the film is also a perfect illustration of the state of the world at the time of its release, which was no doubt a contributing factor to its success. In October 2019, many countries were in the grip of popular protests. Since March 2019, the Hong Kong youth had been protesting and calling for the removal of Chief Executive Carrie Lam, whose government intended to change the Special Administrative Region's extradition system to allow Hong Kong citizens to be judged in China. The legitimate fear of losing civil liberties by subjecting local law to Chinese justice was only one aspect of the youth protest. It was also coloured by social and economic motives. Hong Kong is an extremely unequal city. Rents are among the highest in the world, while the minimum hourly wage is less than five US dollars. It is estimated that nearly 20% of the population lives below the poverty line.[9]

In Lebanon, too, protests were taking place in October 2019. This time, the spark that ignited the crowd was the government's plan to tax everyday consumer goods: petrol, tobacco, and, above all, the use of mobile communication applications such as WhatsApp. This seemed like a tax against the youth and their favourite means of communication.[10]

The social situation in Lebanon is quite similar to that of Hong Kong: a few families of billionaires coexist with a population that does not always have access to essential services such as health or education. The Lebanese political system, which establishes a subtle distribution of functions according to religious communities, appears sclerotic and corrupt. But unlike Hong Kong, beyond social inequality and political deadlock, Lebanon was also facing a severe economic crisis, with a state on the verge of bankruptcy.[11]

Lebanon and Hong Kong were not the only places where social contestation was a threat to the political institutions. At the end of 2019, throughout the world, many protest zones appeared. The French newspaper *Le Monde* counted a dozen popular uprisings as of November 8, 2019.[12] In addition to Hong Kong and Lebanon, popular movements were developing in Iraq, Indonesia, Ecuador,

Sudan, Egypt, Gaza, Indonesia, Algeria, Pakistan, and Bolivia. Europe was not spared, either. In Catalonia, the severe condemnation by the Spanish justice system of the pro-independence leaders who organised a referendum on independence had led to a new wave of demonstrations. In France, since November 2018, the Yellow Vests have held demonstrations every Saturday and sometimes faced very tough confrontations with the police forces. The decision to undertake a major reform of the pension system reactivated French social protests from December 2019 to February 2020. Strikes were paralysing entire sectors of transport and public services. Everywhere in the world, during many protests, the figure of the Joker was used as an emblem.[13]

The Chilean protests were undoubtedly ones of the most iconic. On October 1, 2019, the public transport authorities in the Santiago metropolitan area decided to raise fares. It was the second increase since the beginning of the year, the first being implemented in January. Although relatively modest, the price change triggered a huge contestation. High school and university students, particularly affected by the measure, were on the front line. On October 18, the protests took an insurgent turn. Barricades were erected throughout the city and demonstrators attacked street furniture and metro stations.

The rising cost of public transport was only a pretext. The causes of popular discontent ran much deeper. The protesters were challenging not only the cost of transport but also the general cost of living, the political elite's corruption, inequality, and, more broadly, the economic policy the country had followed for decades. Indeed, with the military putsch that overthrew Salvador Allende in September 1973, Chile became a model, a laboratory for neoliberal policies, which profoundly transformed the role of the state. Advised by young economists who had returned from the Chicago school, the famous "Chicago boys", and by the most preeminent of the school's teachers himself, Milton Friedman, the government of Chilean dictator Augusto Pinochet undertook a vast reorganisation of its economy. The main idea was to reduce public intervention in favour of market mechanisms. Education, health, transport, and electricity supply services were privatised. Chile reduced its tariffs, cut public spending, and deregulated its financial system, while at the same time engaging in a fierce fight against inflation. Chile was radically pursuing neoliberal policies a few years ahead of schedule and would later be followed by Margaret Thatcher in the United Kingdom and Ronald Reagan in the United States, and later by the rest of the world.

A detailed analysis of neoliberal policies and the principles on which they were based is provided in the next chapter. At this point, it should be noted that, despite the return to democracy in the early 1990s and the victory of a left-wing coalition in 2006, the Chilean neoliberal model, inherited from the dictatorship, had never seriously been questioned. The growth obtained during the "Chilean miracle" of the 1990s did not bring social prosperity. On the contrary, it exacerbated tensions and social inequality.[14]

At the end of 2019, political instability was not only due to street protests. Donald Trump's term of office was marked by extremely polarising political episodes, the most spectacular of which was undoubtedly the long weeks of the "shutdown", the closure for more than a month – between December 2018 and January 2019 – of most of the federal public administrations. A budgetary disagreement between the presidency and the House of Representatives over the financing of the Mexican border wall that Trump had promised to build was at the root of the imbroglio.

Profound political disputes are multiplying in the United States. In large coastal cities, among the educated population, or in *The New York Times* editorials, Trump's presidency was often perceived as illegitimate. For another America, for some white populations in the industrial cities of the Midwest, in conservative and religious circles, among those who felt neglected by the economic upturn and who perceive globalisation and open borders as threats, Trump was often seen as a hero. Those two camps seemed to be at odds about everything: cultural and political values, world views, and the economic management of the country. In Washington, the slightest rift inevitably turned into a stalemate. As a matter of fact, at the end of 2019, American political life was focused on the impeachment procedure launched by the Democrats against the President because of the very personal use he allegedly made of American diplomacy. A procedure which, staged by the Leader of the opposition and Speaker of the House of Representatives Nancy Pelosi, exacerbated political rivalries.

Democratic officials may have been purposely choosing to beef up their criticism against the presidency. Although the impeachment hearing had no chance of succeeding, the most important thing was to unite one's camp, to play one-on-one, to legitimise the opposition to Donald Trump, and to increase voter involvement; that is to say, prepare for next year's victory by galvanising the troops. Democratic supporters were acting along the same line. After some hesitation during the first Primaries, they would overwhelmingly support Joe Biden, not because of his debating skills or his platform, but because he seemed better able to beat Trump than Bernie Sanders, who was deemed too radical to win. What was being played out in the United States was no longer a simple political debate but an identity and cultural confrontation in which the figure of Donald Trump had become the main, if not the only, issue at stake.

On the other side of the Atlantic, in Great Britain, political life was also experiencing a great deal of confusion. Since the victory of Brexit in the 2016 referendum, the United Kingdom had been plagued by endless negotiations with the European Union. Shortly after taking office, Theresa May promised to turn the departure of the United Kingdom from the European Union into an opportunity, raising the idea of building a "Global Britain", opening up to the world and freely negotiating trade agreements by reviving a certain form of the imperial tradition. The idea was widely contested by those who wished to remain in the EU: "The idea that Britain has somehow been liberated by the prospect of Brexit to seize pace-making status in the world is simply false", wrote editorialist Martin Kettle, denouncing a "fantasy" (Kettle 2018).

Like Trump's victory, Brexit's victory has never been accepted by a part of British society. In the United Kingdom, the same divisions exist as in the United

States. For the most educated population, for inner-city dwellers, and for the Guardian's editorialists, the victory of the leave vote was a democratic error based on lies and the deception of labour classes. "Brexit won the election. But it's an ideology, not a policy", Kettle said, pointing out that the referendum was "populist" in its nature (Kettle 2019). This British division was skilfully exploited by the European negotiators who succeeded in imposing an agreement that kept the United Kingdom in commercial dependency with the Union in the name of preserving the Irish peace to the British government.

So long, Global Britain! Many Conservative MEPs felt betrayed by the deal their government agreed to. During the parliamentary debates, supporters of a hard Brexit contributed to the rejection of the project in the House of Commons by joining their voices with those of Labour party members and all those who were opposed to the United Kingdom's departure. As a result, in the spring of 2019, Brexit had reached an impasse and the idea of a second referendum had finally gained ground among some EU supporters.

Then the British were invited to the polls. In the May 2019 European elections, Nigel Farage's Brexit Party won the vote hands down despite the low workers' voter turnout. In July, Theresa May was replaced by Boris Johnson who took over the leadership of the party and of the government, defending an intransigent line and wishing to put Brexit into effect as soon as possible. General elections held in December 2019 gave him the majority he needed. This time, the verdict of the elections was clear. It was the working classes opposed to the European Union that made the victory of the Conservatives. The Labour Party paid for its procrastination with the loss of its workers' strongholds: the "Red Wall" of the Midlands and the north of England had turned blue; the way to Brexit was now clear. In another ironic twist, England's populist moment had made upper-class politician Boris Johnson the hero of the anti-establishment working classes.

The two European crises

To conclude the overview of the world as it was before the COVID-19 pandemic, we need to cross the Channel and have a look at the situation on the European continent.

Brexit is only one element in a larger and deeper crisis, the crisis of the European project itself. Even before the British referendum, two crises had struck the Union. The first was economic. It pitted the countries of the North against those of the South, revealing the structural dysfunctions of the European economy. The second was an identity and political crisis, the consequence of the catastrophic management of the refugee situation in the summer of 2015. This time it opposed the east and west of the continent and contributed to the strengthening of populist regimes in Central Europe.

In a small book published in 2017, Bulgarian political scientist Ivan Krastev, a liberal and proponent of European construction, likens the current European situation to that of the end of the Austro-Hungarian Empire, which disappeared brutally at the end of the First World War, swept away by nationalist forces. "I am someone who believes that the disintegration train has left Brussels's station – and who fears it will doom the continent to disarray and global irrelevance", writes Krastev (2017, p. 10). According to him, the refugee crisis has awakened deep identity anxieties among the populations of the former communist countries.

> The refugee crisis is critical for gauging the prospects of the European Union's chances of survival because it simultaneously reinforces a sense of national solidarity and erodes the chances for constitutional patriotism in the union as a whole. The crisis is thus a turning point in the political dynamics of the European project. It signals a moment when the demand for democracy in Europe has been transformed into a call to defend one's own political community and thus a demand for exclusion rather than inclusion. It also creates a dynamic in which the European project is seen no longer as an expression of liberal universalism but as a sour expression of its defensive parochialism.
>
> *(ibid.)*

This "demand for exclusion rather than inclusion" has led to misunderstandings on the part of Westerners. Indeed, the identity crisis of Eastern Europeans has its own characteristics. The first is linked to the disrupted history of this part of Europe. The construction of nation-states is recent and national autonomy was only achieved there after the disappearance of the Soviet tutelage. Moreover, Eastern Europeans collectively experienced the collapse of communist regimes in the early 1990s. The thought that such a thing could happen again caused them a great deal of anguish. National withdrawals and the creation of new regional collaborations[15] were one way to get ready for a possible failure of the European project. "Witnessing the political turmoil in Europe", Karstev writes, "we have a sinking feeling that we have been through this before – the only difference being that then it was their world that collapsed. Now it is ours" (*ibid.*, p. 13).

The second eastern specificity is the result of the rapid social and demographic changes that took place in those countries with the transition to a market economy and the subsequent accession to the European Union. With poor employment prospects and low esteem for their governments, part of the population had taken advantage of the border opening to settle in the West. They were "lonely revolutionaries" according to Krastev. Instead of helping to change their country's policies or to develop its economy, they chose the road of exile to improve their own living conditions.

These population movements were considerable. Bulgaria has lost 1.9 million inhabitants since the end of communism, more than 20% of its original population, mainly for migratory reasons. Similarly, more than 2 million Poles and 3 million Romanians went into exile. Such migrations were mostly due to the educated and young categories of the population, i.e. those who were likely to produce wealth and children. As a result, a falling birth rate and a feeling of national downgrading affected those who remained in the country. Many feel they were abandoned by their elite who moved to the West for better fortunes.

This migration also had unfortunate consequences for the destination countries by placing eastern migrants, often with low wage demands, in competition in the labour market with Western populations that otherwise faced unemployment or underemployment. In an article published following the Brexit referendum, British journalist Paul Mason noted that foreign workers accounted for 43% of the British workforce in packing and canning factories, and more broadly 33% of the workforce in the manufacturing industry (Mason 2016). However, since 2000, employment in the UK manufacturing industry has fallen by more than 30% (Table 1.2). From the perspective of the working class, not only have employment opportunities declined, but the remaining opportunities have been partly taken up by a foreign workforce, much of which has come from Central and Eastern Europe. This situation would explain, according to Mason, both the victory of Brexit in the June 2016 referendum and the success of Nigel Farage. In short, for Krastev "[t]he biggest beneficiaries of the opening of the borders turned out to be the brilliant individual émigrés, the bad eastern European politicians, and the xenophobic western European parties" (Krastev 2017, p. 53).

This gobal context explains the "moral panic" that gripped Eastern Europeans when a massive influx of migrants and refugees arrived on European shores. The panic, as mentioned above, was exacerbated by the lack of understanding on the part of Western leaders. Angela Merkel's decision to suspend the Dublin agreements and accept all asylum applications put tens of thousands of people on the road, who ended up crossing the Balkans and Eastern Europe to reach Germany from Greece. Faced with the arrival of columns of refugees, Viktor Orbàn, prime minister of Hungary, began building fences hastily along its borders; in Croatia, the authorities chartered buses and trains to take migrants from one border to another, sometimes creating tensions with the Hungarian government,[16] who hurriedly transported their own migrants to the Austrian border. Finally, a few weeks later, the European decision to distribute the requests for asylums among European countries, according to a quota system, aroused not only frank opposition but also a deep distrust of the people vis-à-vis the European institutions.

The second European crisis is the one of its economy, or more precisely of its deficient economic institutions.

The European economy relies on two major institutions: The Single Market and the euro. The Single Market was founded in 1986 when the Single Act Treaty was signed. Although it is a fundamental institution, it is poorly understood by the people of Europe. It is based on the so-called "Four Freedoms" regime which guarantees the free movement of goods, services, capital, and labour. This regime requires a number of supporting institutions that aim to promote the proper functioning of market mechanisms. The competition authorities ensure that competition is "free", i.e., undisturbed by state intervention, monopolistic practices, cartels, and agreements. The liberalisation of national public services, such as electricity, telecommunications, and air and rail transport, created a large European market for services. The directives on posted work or the introduction of a portability system for social rights removed obstacles to the movement of workers. Finally, the free movement of capital was organised by the unification of banking and financial standards and by the creation of the monetary union.

The Maastricht Treaty, signed in 1992, paved the way for the creation of the single currency and thus completed the free movement of capital. It removed currency barriers and allowed the secure circulation of financial flows between debtor and creditor economies. It is now at the heart of European debates and often highly criticised. In an analysis using a disputed methodology, the Centre for European Policy (CEP) – a liberal German think tank – found that the euro had cost Italy on average more than 70,000 euros per capita and France nearly 56,000 euros over the period 1999–2017. The single currency, on the other hand, would have brought in more than 20,000 euros for the inhabitants of Germany and the Netherlands (Gasparotti and M. Kullas 2019).

The study, published to coincide with the 20th anniversary of the single currency, was widely reported in the press and gave rise to a great deal of debate. While most economists have doubts about its reliability, they recognise the accuracy of the underlying intuition, the idea that the main problem with the euro is not that it is bad for everyone, but that it reinforces economic divergences. This is the conclusion drawn by Joseph Stiglitz, the American Nobel Prize laureate in economics, in a book that is highly critical towards the single currency:

> Several features of the eurozone that were thought of as *essential* to its success were actually central to its divergence. Standard economics is based on the gravity principle: money moves from capital-rich countries with low returns to countries with capital shortage. The presumption was that the risk-adjusted returns in such countries would be high. But in Europe under the euro, movements of not just capital but also labor seem to defy the principles of gravity. Money flowed upward.
>
> *(Stiglitz 2016, chap. 5)*

The reasons why a single currency generates divergent forces are quite simple to understand. The existence of the euro imposes two constraints on the Member States' economies.

First, it unifies exchange rates. But to remain competitive and to keep their industries, the most fragile economies need the ability to devalue, which is made impossible by the single currency. In contrast, countries with a powerful industrial sector take advantage of the inability of their European competitors to adjust their currencies and benefit from an exchange rate that remains artificially low and allows them to export more easily.

Second, the existence of a single central bank implies a common monetary policy, i.e. the banks of every country in the zone enjoy the same interest rate to finance themselves and the economy. The problem is that growth and inflation levels are not the same within the Eurozone. Let us say that the interest rate of the European Central Bank (ECB) is 2%. If the inflation rate in a country is also 2%, that means a real interest rate of 0%. This is because the return on the loan only compensates for the loss in the value of the money. In this case, if inflation rises to 3%, then the real interest rate becomes negative. On the contrary, if inflation falls to zero, then the real interest rate will be equal to the nominal interest rate, 2%. Thus, the same interest rate can mean very different things depending on the levels of inflation. For some countries, it means a low (or even negative) cost of debt, while for others, it means a high cost of debt. It all depends on the level of inflation. Inflation in high-growth countries is generally higher than in low-growth countries. As a result, countries with higher growth benefit from lower real interest rates, and therefore have an advantage. In countries without growth, low inflation raises real interest rates, which hampers business investment and reinforces the economic slump. The central bank is thus constantly confronted with having to balance the contradictory needs of different European countries. But regardless of choice, it can only accentuate the imbalances.

The institutional rigidity of the Eurozone, the fact that it prohibits the adjustment of exchange rates and interest rates to meet the needs of each country, has the effect of reinforcing internal disparities. This is one of the keys to understanding the nature of the euro area crisis.

In September 2008, when the investment bank Lehman Brother went bankrupt and the American authorities decided not to save it, the crisis was perceived as peculiar to American financial capitalism. Many expected that Europe would be spared. However, a few years later, the outcome is bitter. The US subprime mortgage crisis has weakened European economies more than the American one. There are two reasons for this paradox. First, European finance was facing the same structural weaknesses as US finance.[17] Secondly, from 2010 onwards, the banking and financial crisis turned into a European public debt crisis that gravely affected the economies of Ireland and Southern Europe.

How do economists and European authorities explain this second crisis? For Jeffry Friedman and Stefanie Walter, "the crisis in the Eurozone is a classic debt and balance-of-payments crisis" (Frieden and Walter 2017, p. 373). At the time of the banking crisis, agents in creditor countries suddenly stopped financing agents in debtor countries due to uncertainty and increased fear of non-repayment. Interest rates then rose sharply in the debtor countries. Not only governments but also banks and companies were deprived of financing, which precipitated their bankruptcy and led to the recession. To get out of this situation and avoid the explosion of the Eurozone, it was necessary to ask creditor countries to act as guarantors for the loans of the countries in crisis.

But why did the crisis touch some countries more while sparing others? In a baseline analysis signed by sixteen economists from the Centre for Economic Policy Research (Baldwin et al. 2015), the following scenario is proposed: in the years following the creation of the single currency, some countries in the core of the euro area (Germany, the Netherlands, Austria, etc.) have accumulated savings.

These savings were used to meet the financing needs of peripheral countries (Ireland, Spain, Greece, etc.). The fall of interest rates and the growth of foreign investment that these peripheral countries benefited from, particularly in the public and real estate sectors, accelerated borrowings and investments. Cheap money also boosted banking activity, which was sometimes insufficiently controlled, leading to excessive risk-taking. As investment expanded, many jobs were created in both the public and private sectors, which led to higher wages and, in turn, higher export prices and a loss of economic competitiveness. External deficits and financing needs eventually widened in the peripheral countries, while in the core countries, external surpluses and savings were being accumulated. Ultimately, the authors of the study believe that the crisis was caused by a "failure to control national debt" and a "failure to control excessive bank leverage" (*ibid.*, p. 15).

This diagnosis prompted the European authorities to propose two types of measures to improve the functioning of the Eurozone. First, they have strengthened the control mechanisms over public budgets by improving surveillance procedures.[18] Second, they proposed and implemented a series of reforms of the European banking sector by introducing direct supervision of systemic banks by the ECB and by gradually establishing a Banking Union to improve the management of bank failures and avoid financial intervention by governments.[19]

In short, the European authorities and the majority of economists believe that the crisis in the Eurozone is the consequence of national failures that were made possible by the incompleteness of European rules. Their political response has therefore been to strengthen and improve the European institutional framework without questioning the existence of deeper structural failures.

But one question remains unanswered. Why are the economies of Southern Europe dependent on Northern financing?

The answer can, of course, be found by attributing the savings of the Northern countries to a Protestant culture that is quick to good management, and the indebtedness of the countries of the South to a Mediterranean culture that is more indolent and ready to get into debt. This psychologisation, which carries a certain amount of prejudices, does not, however, stand up to scientific analysis. There are no cultural traits common to Italy, Spain, or Greece that would make their inhabitants less efficient at work than the Dutch or the Germans. However, there are singular economic dynamics that explain in a much more convincing way the cause of the economic peculiarities observed in Europe.

The real cause of the Eurozone crisis

In *Principles of Economics*, the textbook written by the famous British economist Alfred Marshall and first published in 1890, the following description of the industrial dynamics can be found:

> When an industry has thus chosen a locality for itself, it is likely to stay there long: so great are the advantages which people following the same

skilled trade get from near neighbourhood to one another. The mysteries of the trade become no mysteries; but are as it were in the air, and children learn many of them unconsciously. Good work is rightly appreciated, inventions and improvements in machinery, in processes and the general organization of the business have their merits promptly discussed; if one man starts a new idea, it is taken up by others and combined with suggestions of their own; and thus it becomes the source of further new ideas. And the presently subsidiary trades grow up in the neighbourhood, supplying it with implements and materials, organizing its traffic, and in many ways conducing to the economy of its material.

(Marshall 1920, p. 225)

As a close observer, Marshall notes that industrial activity tends to be geographically concentrated. The proximity among companies brings many benefits: better access to skilled employment and technology, lower logistics costs through the construction of a more efficient transport infrastructure, and greater ease in negotiating with customers and suppliers. Manufacturing, unlike services, does not need to be located close to customers. A commodity can be produced thousands of miles away from where it is sold if transportation costs are low enough. By the end of the 19th century, however, the transport revolution had cut the cost of transporting goods tenfold compared to the preindustrial era. As a result, the European industry concentrated in very specific geographical areas which led to the development of territorial advantages. For instance, the industrial clusters of the Rhine valley or Saxony, two areas that are rich in coal and iron ore, made Germany's industrial success in the second half of the 19th century.

This process of so-called "industrial agglomeration" took place within the states for years. Some regions expanded industrially through proximity effects, while others became deindustrialised and eventually depopulated. As a result, national economies had developed and structured themselves based on inner divergent forces, which had been offset by labour mobility and public spending to support declining regions.

During the 20th century, transport costs continued to fall, and world-class industrial poles emerged. But this concentration remained limited due to national barriers. Not only tariffs but also limits on the movement of capital and labour helped to preserve many smaller industrial poles that were less efficient than those in the more developed countries. With the acceleration of the import duties reduction and the gradual disappearance of restrictions on the movement of capital, the situation changed from the 1980s onwards. On the European continent, it was the Single Act of 1986 which, as we have seen, "freed" the circulation of capital and labour. Until then, only goods had moved freely in Europe, which limited the natural tendency of industry to concentrate in the most dynamic European regions.

During the 1990s, with the gradual construction of Single Market, the European Union became a large unified market where capital, labour, and goods could circulate without restriction. Yet the European Economic Area was far from being territorially homogeneous. Throughout their history, industrially powerful regions developed specific institutions and infrastructures which made them more attractive for industrial investment. That was the case of the countries of northern Europe, which had considerable geographical advantages: efficient industrial hubs inherited from the accelerated industrialisation phase during the second half of the 19th century, a skilled and abundant industrial workforce, and numerous and diversified transport infrastructures, particularly in the maritime sector.

The importance of maritime trade for industrial activity is well known. A company cannot import raw materials and export its production without access to a major world-class port either directly or by a river. But the four largest European ports are all located on the North Sea, along a coastal strip of about 500 km.[20] In addition, Northern Europe is crisscrossed by navigable rivers and wide-gauge canals that connect these ports to the industrial poles of the continent's interior as far as Bavaria and Austria. Thus, when the limits to the capital movement ceased to exist in Europe, industrial investment concentrated on those central territories which were directly connected to the world economy and left behind the less industrialised peripheral territories which did not have the same territorial advantages.

The maps in Figure 1.1 show how the industrial polarisation of the European continent came about with the creation of the Single Market. The evolution of the volume of labour in manufacturing production provides an effective picture of industrial dynamics.

It must be noted that due to robotisation and productivity gains, employment in the manufacturing industry has been declining structurally in Europe since 2000. This does not mean that industrial production is regressing.[21] But what is most important here is to compare the evolution of labour in the manufacturing industry and to note the differences in trajectories from one country to another.

The circles represent the industrial poles of attraction. During the 2000–2007 period, these poles were relatively diversified. Geographically peripheral Europe – Greece, Bulgaria, Spain, the Baltic States, and Italy – benefited from a certain attractiveness due to lower wages, whereas for Spain, Greece, and Italy, it was the low-interest rates resulting from belonging to the Eurozone that mostly explains the economic boom. Other regions such as the United Kingdom and Portugal, and to a lesser extent France, the Netherlands, Ireland, Romania, and Hungary were losing industrial employment. In 2008–2011, European industrial activity massively deserted the peripheral regions, while core Europe was preserved. Finally, during the recovery period, the core region and Eastern Europe were particularly dynamic, as well as Ireland, which did a little better than recovering the activity lost during the crisis. However, the countries in the South, after they suffered from a major deindustrialisation during the recession, were recovering almost nothing.

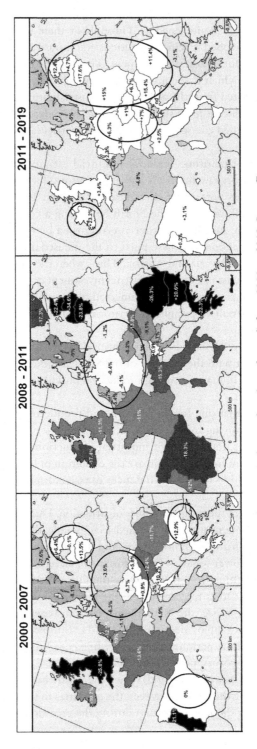

FIGURE 1.1 Change in manufacturing employment (volume of work performed) from 2000 to 2019. Source: Eurostat.

Table 1.1 shows industrial employment over the entire period. To understand this table, it is necessary to consider the increase in labour productivity linked to the progress of mechanisation. As a first estimate, it can be considered that most of the countries whose industrial employment fell by less than 10% have strengthened industrially, while countries with more than 20% job losses deindustrialised. Except for Ireland, for very specific reasons,[22] all the territories that deindustrialised are distant from the industrial core of Europe. By contrast, the dynamics of agglomeration have largely benefited the core countries, as well as the countries of Central Europe which are close to Germany. Poland, which combines geographical advantages with low labour costs, appears to be the main winner in terms of gains in industrial activity.

This rapid deindustrialisation of peripheral economies is the hidden explanation for the European public debt crisis. By losing their industrial infrastructure over the period 2000–2011, the farthest countries from Germany gradually lost export capacity; their external imbalances and financing needs increased, as did their financial dependence on the core countries.

To conclude this section, two complementary elements are worth highlighting. The first is that membership or non-membership of the euro area does not seem to be the most relevant explanatory factor for understanding the causes of industrial divergence. France (euro area) and the United Kingdom (non-euro area) deindustrialised at roughly the same pace over the period; Sweden (non-euro area) and Finland (euro area) followed similar paths, as did the Czech Republic (non-euro area) and Slovakia (euro area). The agglomeration effect, however, is greatest for Poland, which does not belong to the euro area. All these data tend to reinforce the Marshallian explanation: it is the free movement of capital and labour over an economically heterogeneous territory that is at the heart of the divergence phenomenon, with agglomeration effects reinforcing the dynamism of the favoured regions to the detriment of regions less well endowed with territorial factors of production.

TABLE 1.1 Cumulative change in manufacturing employment (volume of work performed) from 2000 to 2019 (countries with more than five million inhabitants)

The losing "Peripheral" countries		The winning "Core" countries	
Name	Change (in %)	Name	Change (in %)
United Kingdom	-31.9	Poland	+9.5
Portugal	-30.4	Austria	+3.2
Finland	-29.4	Germany	-0.8
Romania	-27.6	Slovakia	-2.7
France	-26.8	Czech Republic	-7.9
Greece	-24.7	Hungary	-8.0
Sweden	-20.6	Ireland	-9.1

Source: Eurostat.

The second point that we must stress is that, although the Scandinavian countries escaped the euro crisis, they do belong to the peripheral sphere of the continent. Finland has become more deindustrialised than Greece, and Sweden has lost more industrial jobs than Italy. It must be noted that their economic prosperity and Protestant culture have not protected them from the continent's industrial dynamics and the forces of polarisation. This phenomenon is worrying because it has not been clearly identified by the European authorities or even, it seems, by the leaders of these countries themselves.

The demographic and social upheavals of the Single Market

In February 1905, a newspaper for young girls, *La Semaine de Suzette*, published the illustrated adventures of *Bécassine*. It narrated a story of a young peasant girl from Brittany who had gone to Paris to work as a servant in a Parisian family. The French comic strip was very popular until World War II when its publication was banned by the German occupying forces. The girl, depicted as a naive and clumsy character from a peasant background, illustrated the kind of xenophobia that prevailed at the time against the French internal migrants who were victims of the deindustrialisation of the countryside.

Such attitudes can be found in many countries. In Italy, migrants from Puglia were no better received in Piedmont than Breton peasants were in Paris. At the beginning of the 20th century, economic unification and lower transport costs helped to reshape the internal geography of advanced economies and led to large population movements. Social tensions were fuelled by those movements.

This is a recurring phenomenon, a constant in history. Economic transformations reshape relationships between populations, generate new social hierarchies, and mould local identities. European economic polarisation is by no means an isolated phenomenon. One need only look at the voting map of American elections to understand that this phenomenon also affects the United States.[23] However, it is opposite geographically in comparison with the European example. In the United States, the centre (the Midwest, the Great Plains, etc.) is economically on the periphery while the large coastal cities on the eastern and western seaboard form the dynamic core of the country. This economic structuring generates similar migration trends and social relations. Undoubtedly, it is the feeling of disenfranchisement shared by voters who live in regions economically and culturally dominated by the coastal states that explains a good part of the Trump vote.

From this perspective, the two European crises, the one opposing East and West against the migratory crisis and the one opposing North and South against the economic crisis, are two sides of the same coin: they are both consequences of the free movement of factors of production. In the first case, people migrate in the hope of better living conditions; in the second, they follow capital movements and industrial dynamics.

TABLE 1.2 Cumulative migration balances in Europe[a]

Migration losses in Central and Eastern Europe (2000–2018)		Migratory losses in Western Peripheral Europe (2010–2015)		Migration gains in the western core of Europe (2010–2018)	
Name	Net migration	Name	Net migration	Name	Net migration
Baltic States	- 820,241	Spain	-354,506	Germany	+ 4,299,288
Bulgaria	- 424,708	Greece	-251,668	Austria	+ 486,932
Poland	-185,025	Ireland	-71,322	Belgium	+ 418,193
Romania	- 2,135,802	Portugal	-134,534	Netherlands	+ 431,633

Source: Eurostat.

[a] Net migration plus statistical adjustment. Accessed on April 10, 2020.

Table 1.2 presents a summary of European migrations. It combines three overlapping migratory logics.

- Migration balances of non-European origin. The latter accounts for about half of the immigrants in the western core countries since 2013.
- Migration balances from Central and Eastern European countries expatriations, most of them being due to the educated youth seeking better wages to the West.
- Migration balances following the European crisis of 2010–2015 that are linked to the economic recession and the deindustrialisation of peripheral areas.

It is worth noting that some logics can cumulate or pull in opposite directions. For instance, Romania, Bulgaria, and the Baltic States are suffering demographic losses due to the unattractive nature of their economies and the deindustrialisation dynamic that is the consequence of their geographically peripheral location. In Poland, by contrast, there has been an improvement in the migratory balance, which became positive from 2016 onwards. Although the country continues to see part of its young people emigrate to the West, it is also increasingly attracting Ukrainian and Lithuanian workers who work in its factories or meet the needs of its agriculture. In the other central European countries (Hungary, Czech Republic, Slovakia) the demographic balances have been positive for more than ten years, which shows that the industrial dynamism in these countries more than compensates for expatriation trends. Finally, in Italy and Spain, the migration flow from outside Europe tend to mask expatriation of nationals for economic reasons. For example, Italy benefited from a positive migratory balance of almost 4.6 million people over the period 2000–2018. But this balance is partly the consequence of non-European migrants and the arrival of refugees from Libya after the fall of Gaddafi's regime.[24]

What do these population movements tell us? Firstly, they show that labour mobility has become an adjustment variable during crises. The large European labour market dreamed of by some economists is becoming a concrete reality. Hundreds of thousands of people move from one country to another every year, sometimes to settle there permanently, other times on temporary posting. These changes can be extremely brutal. Thus, countries with high immigration such as Spain or Ireland became countries of high emigration in just a few months after the bursting of the financial and real estate bubble in 2008–2009. Similarly, Germany, which had a virtually zero net migration in the early 2000s, began to hire foreign workers massively from the early 2010s, when its unemployment rate began to fall.

But these figures also tell a social and political story. It is not trivial for a country like Poland to see, on the one hand, its brilliant youth going to Germany or the United Kingdom and, on the other hand, its countryside and factories employ more and more Ukrainian workers. What these population movements demonstrate is that a European division of labour is taking shape and that Poland, driven by this economic dynamic, is becoming a gigantic low-cost production centre. Polish factories are being transformed into sub-contracting units for German industrialists who have chosen to locate the production of certain components with low added value beyond the Oder River. Stuck in this specialisation, it makes sense that the Polish economy attracts low-skilled workers who are likely to accept low wages. It also makes sense that this economic system can only drive away the most qualified workers, engineers, researchers, and intellectuals. They have everything to gain from being hired in Germany where they are paid three to four times more than in their own country.

In a book published in 1914, *The Great Society*, British social psychology professor Graham Wallas wondered about the organisation of industrial capitalism based on the principle of the division of labour and its consequences for the human species. Far from being happy about it, and despite the material benefits that rationalisation of the productive system would inevitably bring, Wallas wondered about the social capacities of human beings to adapt to a global economy.

> Fifty years ago, the practical men who were bringing the Great Society into existence thought, when they had time to think at all, that they were thereby offering an enormously better existence to the whole human race. Men were rational beings, and, having obtained limitless power over nature, would certainly use it for their own good. [...]
>
> The Great Society, even if it should deprive men of some of the romance and intimacy of Life, must, they thought, at least give them such an increase of security as would be far more than an equal return. Famine would be impossible when any labourer could buy flour and bacon from the world-market in his village shop. Wars would be few and short if they meant disaster to an international system of credit.

Now, however, that the change has come, hardly any one thinks of it with the old undoubting enthusiasm. Actual famine has, it is true, disappeared from the Great Society, but there remains the constant possibility of general and uncontrollable depressions of trade. The intervals between great wars are apparently becoming longer, but never has the expenditure on armaments been so great or the fear of war so constant. [...] The deeper anxiety of our time arises from a doubt, more or less clearly realised, whether that development is itself proceeding on right lines.

(Wallas 1914, pp. 5–6)

According to Wallas, the brutal immersion of human societies in a large world market would inevitably produce great social anguish by disintegrating traditional collective identities. But what we see today is that market forces do not only cause annihilation, they also build new identities and hierarchies within and among nations. As the European Single Market deepens and organises economic specialisation, it creates new social relationships among countries. In the manufacturing industry, executives and engineers tend to conglomerate in Germany while the industrial army of low-skilled workers from the continent converges in Poland and the Czech Republic. This reorganisation of the European economy does not bring solidarity or more cordial understanding among countries, but rather strengthens competition and rivalries among people, sometimes generating a type of implicit class struggle. In this new economic arrangement, the Polish situation is far from being the worst. Some countries that lack even the slightest economic advantage are emptying themselves and losing their vital substance. Their destiny is, then, to specialise in beach tourism as the size of their cities shrinks and their population goes into exile.

The current market dynamics, as predicted by Wallas, forces entire societies to engage in a perpetual adaptation for which they are sometimes poorly equipped, but which leads them to profound social transformations. Hence it is not very surprising if, in the course of this never-ending process of adjustment, they wonder "whether that development is itself proceeding on right lines".

As we have seen, this socio–economic dynamic is not unique to the European continent. A similar process is being played out on a global scale and within certain countries. In the United States, as in Europe, the movements of capital and workers, and the accompanying phenomenon of polarisation, tend to create winners and losers, dominant cities and disadvantaged hinterlands. This can lead to entire societies falling into deep decline.

No one has better described how industrial and economic relegation led his home state of Kansas to embrace an ultra-conservative and paranoid view of the world than journalist Thomas Frank. In the epilogue to his book *What's the Matter with Kansas?*, Frank describes the working-class city of his childhood as a lost and depopulated paradise. The shopping malls are abandoned, the churches decrepit, and the youth have disappeared from the streets.

But beyond the physical decrepitude of his native suburbs, what interests Frank is how the mentality of its inhabitants has been transformed. They now cultivate a tenacious hatred for the progressive ideology embodied by left-wing personalities as described by *People* magazine:

> Singers who were big in the seventies express their concern with neatly folded ribbons for this set of victims or that. Minor TV personalities instruct the world to stop saying mean things about the overweight or the handicapped. And beautiful people of every description don expensive transgressive fashions, buy expensive transgressive art, eat at expensive transgressive restaurants, and get edgy with an expensive punk sensibility or an expensive earth-friendly look.
>
> Here liberalism is a matter of shallow appearances, of fatuous self-righteousness; it is arrogant and condescending, a politics in which the beautiful and the wellborn tell the unwashed and the beaten-down and the funny-looking how they ought to behave, how they should stop being racist or homophobic, how they should be better people.
>
> *(Frank 2004, Epilogue)*

How can we fail to see that the way social relations are described above are a modernised and Americanised version of *Bécassine*? Are not the Kansas rednecks or the colourful characters of *Tiger King* like the naive and clumsy young Breton girl, symbols of this new social hierarchy that pits the progressive winners living in the big ocean-front metropolises against the losers who could not adapt to the new division of labour? The difference with the situation in France at the beginning of the 20th century is that now the two worlds no longer coexist together. By taking on a Breton maid, the bourgeois could look at this alien creature with a mixture of benevolence and condescension. Today, New Yorkers have almost no chance to meet a Kansas worker other than through the distorting image of a Netflix series.

The roots of neo-populism

If the COVID-19 crisis proved one thing, it is that the spirit of European solidarity was not the first reflex of the EU states. The beginning of the pandemic was managed in a panic. Each national government urgently began to follow its own strategies without consultation and concern for the fate of its neighbours. The first spontaneous reactions were the disorganised closure of borders, the hijacking of protective masks, and the lack of financial solidarity. In an editorial written at the end of a long and tedious negotiations within the Eurogroup to find common answers, the British journalist Simon Jenkins agreed with the obvious: "The European Union is not a real union ... Political unions are specific things – a marriage of regions, provinces, states in one national unit – based on a sufficiency of shared identity and shared responsibility", he writes (Jenkins 2020).

Sadly, this shared identity and shared responsibility are sorely lacking in Europe. When a crisis emerges, the spontaneous reaction of nations is to address their own governments and not Brussels or the World Health Organisation. Some observers attribute this inclination to the disintegration of the European spirit and wonder whether this spirit has given way to a new national tribalism. The explosion of populist movements in recent years is said to have fuelled nationalist impulses by playing on people's basic fears and flattering national identities to the detriment of universal values, human rights, and European solidarity. It was clear in the first major crisis that the undermining work carried out by demagogues was producing deleterious effects.

The sudden explosion of the pandemic undoubtedly amplified these feelings of anguish. The turn taken in France by the debate over the figure of Professor Raoult clearly shows that moments of crisis can degenerate into sudden and irrational collective passions. But the Raoult episode and the tensions that arose during the pandemic crisis must be rethought in a broader context. There is no doubt that the political landscape in Europe changed considerably over the last ten years. Is it possible to link the multiplication of populist movements to the economic and social dynamics that have transformed the whole continent?

In a collective book published in 2018, Bertrand Badie and Dominique Vidal studied the "return of populism". While they believe that populism is an ancient phenomenon that can affect many societies, the authors note that the epicentre of the current resurgence of populism is on the European continent. Worldwide, 33 countries were governed either alone or in a coalition by populist forces between 2014 and early 2018, but 15 of these countries were European and 11 were members of the European Union (Badie and Vidal 2018).[25] Yascha Mounk, for his part, has calculated that the share of votes in favour of European anti-establishment parties rose from less than 10% to almost 20% between 2004 and 2017 (Mounk 2018, p. 34). But it is not enough to note or deplore populism. The causes of populism must be understood, and the question must be raised as to why the European Union is more affected than other regions of the world.

For Badie and Vidal "populism is more political than ideological" (Badie and Vidal 2018, p. 10). In other words, populism is rather related to political practices and to a way to conquer power than to structured ideologies. Hence there is not just one form of populism, but of a multitude of them, each variant taking roots in a particular social situation at a specific moment. From the agrarian populisms of the late 19th century in both Russia and the United States to the 20th Argentinean Peronism, Italian Fascism, and the pan-Arabism of Gamal Abdel Nasser, populist movements have emerged in successive waves in the wake of economic or institutional crises that have led to a growing sense of mistrust among the population with regard to political powers.

This pluralism of incarnations makes populism difficult to grasp and may even lead to doubts about the relevance of the concept. And yet there are common features between these movements. The first is, of course, the appeal to the people. Populism aims to embody popular expression that would be neither heard nor considered. From this first characteristic stems a second: anti-elitism or anti-systemism. If the people are not listened to, it must be because democracy is corrupted by a caste that uses its institutions for its sole benefit. The third characteristic is the presence of a charismatic leader or even the cult of the leader. Populist movements are often led by a personality who intends to represent the people's voice. This third characteristic (which is not systematic) is the consequence of the second. By being directly represented by a man or a woman, popular expression avoids the institutional mediation of the party or intermediate bodies (press, trade unions, administrations, etc.) suspected of being elements of the system they claim to fight. Finally, populism is sovereignism or nationalism. It claims to defend the interests of the nation, which is the incarnation of the people, by fighting against external forces. Sovereignty and intransigence towards international institutions are the consequence of the *imperative mandate*[26] the populist leader derives from his ambition to embody the people.

In his essay "What is Populism?", German political scientist Jan-Werner Müller argues that anti-elitism is a necessary but not sufficient characteristic to define populism. According to him, the specificity of populist movements is not the appeal to the people (which is more or less what all political figures do), but the fact that they claim to be the sole representative of it:

> In addition to being antielitist, populists are always *antipluralist*. Populists claim that they, and they alone, represent the people. Think, for instance, of Turkish President Recep Tayyip Erdoğan declaring at a party congress in defiance of his numerous domestic critics, "We are the people. Who are you?" Of course, he knew that his opponents were Turks, too. The claim to exclusive representation is not an empirical one; it is always distinctly *moral*. When running for office, populists portray their political competitors as part of the immoral, corrupt elite; when ruling, they refuse to recognize any opposition as legitimate. The populist logic also implies that whoever does not support populist parties might not be a proper part of the people – always defined as righteous and morally pure.
>
> *(Müller 2016, p. 3)*

In populist political mythology, there is necessarily a "true people" and, consequently, a "false people". But on what criteria can the distinction between "true" and "false" be made? One solution is to rely on a nativist doctrine, and that is what most populists do. But ethnic criteria are necessarily insufficient because a person who has been "ethnically" part of the national community for many generations may well make claims that oppose those of the populist movement. Yet this expression must be considered illegitimate in order to maintain the illusion that populists are the only ones defending the interests of the people. Hence it is important to be able to identify a community of "traitors". This is what the elite is supposed to embody in the eyes of populists. It is, however, an elite whose frontiers may spill over into the middle and lower classes. They will be described as "useful idiots of the system" at best and as "complicit agents" at worst.

"Populism, I suggest, is a *particular moralistic imagination* of politics, a way of perceiving the political world that sets a morally pure and fully unified – but, I shall argue, ultimately fictional – people against elites who are deemed corrupt or in some other way morally inferior", writes Müller (*ibid.*, pp. 19–20). The inability of populist movements to conceive pluralism is based on the illusion of the fundamental homogeneity of the people and the presumed clarity of their interests. Consequently, any contradictory expression would necessarily be tainted by corruption: "since chloroquine is a miracle drug, all those who dispute this truth must necessarily be paid by the pharmaceutical laboratories"; "since the European Union was built to weaken nations, it is obvious that all the partisans of European construction are bribed by the interests of Brussels"; "since the elites in Washington are a parasitic class, anyone who defends the growth of federal spending necessarily has a financial interest in it", etc. In short, populism needs conspiracy theory to justify a constant war against the "traitors". Populists thus establish the political divide between the people driven by moral values and the oppositional class associated with the elite whose only interests are financial and economic.

Conspiracy theories are also used to create mythologies of their own that allow them to "recognise" themselves and affirm their identities. In his book cited above, Ivan Krastev relates how, in 2015, Jarosław Kaczyński, president of the Law and Justice Party, the main Polish populist party, exploited the dramatic death of his twin brother in a plane crash in Russia five years earlier to promote a conspiracy theory which claimed that the accident was an attack by the Russian secret service. Although this theory was not based on any proven facts, its promotion by the ruling party helped create a common vision among its supporters, forging a strong sense of identity.

Faced with such practices, anti-populist parties or defenders of European values are powerless, says Krastev, who believes that "the rise of conspiracy theories highlights another major vulnerability of EU designed democratic politics: its failure to build political identities" (Krastev 2017, p. 80).

There may be some truth in the discourse stating that the rise of populism in Europe was one of the causes of the lack of European solidarity at the COVID-19 crisis outbreak. The political emergence of populist movements has indeed contributed to strengthening feelings of national belonging and identity where, in practice, European policies were unable to strengthen pro-European feelings. But this analysis, purely political, is not enough. It would run the risk of confusing cause and effect. While populist movements, whether or not they are in power, tend to exacerbate nationalism, the sudden emergence in almost all European countries of populist movements, which have sometimes led to the collapse of large, strongly established political parties, is not yet explained. A sense of identity is as much a cause as an effect of populism. It is, therefore, necessary to examine the particular vulnerability of the European Union to identity-based passions.

To explain this, let's return to the socio-economic dimension. A collective identity does not emerge spontaneously. It is built-in history, in the feeling of sharing certain values, but also in the awareness of common interests. In *The Eighteenth Brumaire of Louis Napoleon*, Karl Marx shows how the French peasantry, which supported Bonaparte's coup, cannot be considered a real social class because of its atomised configuration and the lack of community spirit.

> Thus the large mass of the French nation is constituted by the simple addition of equal magnitudes – much as a bag with potatoes constitutes a potato-bag. In so far as millions of families live under economic conditions that separate their mode of life, their interests and their culture from those of the other classes, and that place them in an attitude hostile toward the latter, they constitute a class; in so far as there exists only a local connection among these farmers, a connection which the individuality and exclusiveness of their interests prevent from generating among them any unity of interest, national connections, and political organization, they do not constitute a class. Consequently, they are unable to assert their class interests in their own name, be it by a parliament or by convention. They cannot represent one another, they must themselves be represented.
>
> *(Marx 1852, p. 98)*

In the Marxist approach, social class is built around class consciousness, which means that a common economic interest can be transformed into a common political identity. Thus, Marxists tend to value class identity to the detriment of national identity which is perceived as reactionary. Conversely, to gain power and establish themselves in the long run, populists must rely on a collective identity to characterise the people they intend to defend. But what happens if, in the construction of a large unified market, class and national logics are pulling in the same direction? When the Polish territory as a whole becomes the assembly plant of German companies, isn't there the risk to create a national sentiment that is all the more powerful because it relies also on a form of class consciousness that sets Polish "workers" against German "bosses"? The euro crisis led to national confrontations (for instance between Greece and Germany), but these confrontations were reinforced by a debtor or creditor character of their economies. It is therefore conceivable that if populism has been singularly reinforced on the European territory and was able to implement a successful political strategy that contributed to exacerbating national feelings, it is also because it could use national economic interests, which have been fuelled by the logic of the European division of labour. In sum, the European populist movements were able to extract from the polarising forces generated by the Single Market part of the identity substance on which they feed.

Populists and markets (the beginning)

This is not to say that the populist activists are suspicious of the market. The opposite is often the case. If, in the populist discourse, the political world is perceived as one of lies and pretence, the market system is most often naturalised and seen as emanating from a transcendental force that can reveal true values. While the political elite would profess "false values", the market would objectively evaluate through the game of supply and demand and a form of purchasing democracy. Populists see the market as a place of "veridiction" (truthfulness), to use the expression of the French philosopher Michel Foucault:

> [I]t is the natural mechanism of the market and the formation of a natural price that enables us to falsify and verify governmental practice when, on the basis of these elements, we examine what government does, the measures it takes, and the rules it imposes. In this sense, inasmuch as it enables production, need, supply, demand, value, and price, etcetera, to be linked together through exchange, the market constitutes a site of veridiction, I mean a site of verification-falsification for governmental practice. Consequently, the market determines that good government is no longer simply government that functions according to justice. The market determines that a good government is no longer quite simply one that is just. The market now means that to be good government, government has to function according to truth.
>
> *(Foucault 2008, p. 32)*

The idea that there is a market truth combined with the cult of efficiency leads many populist leaders to conceive their action as that of a corporate executive and to use a language and an imagination taken from the business world. Silvio Berlusconi, Donald Trump and the Czech billionaire Andrej Babiš have not been afraid to highlight their economic success in order to legitimise their political skills, making the promise to run their country like one of their companies. They conceive their political action as the execution of a "contract" that would be based on market logic. The Swiss businessman and political leader Christoph Blocher stated: "The decisive factor in doing business is the execution of the contract, the fact that success is achieved. The only thing that counts is the task defined in the contract - and here I am thinking of the task I have set myself. Therefore, it is the contract that always guides the successful conduct of business".[27]

The end of great ideologies, the weakening of states and their capacity to act in a globalised economy, the reduction of politics to the art of "good management" has led to the emergence of a hybrid institution: the *company-state*. This is, at least, the thesis defended by the French researcher Pierre Musso. According to him, the comparison with a business venture allows the state to regain its legitimacy in the conduct of its action. But the transition from the "sovereign state" to the "company-state" also generates a crisis in political representation. The disappearance of the sacred dimension of the state generates a symbolic vacuum in the sense that the representatives of the people lose all forms of transcendence. The result is the mirror game between the people and their representatives in which the politicians are called upon to be a reflection of their electors, something that is obviously impossible, even with the artifices of contemporary communication.

To resolve this contradiction, the crisis in politics tends to reveal new actors who claim to embody a big company (Berlusconi, Trump) or a start-up (Macron). These actors, Musso explains, have hybrid characters (half-entrepreneurs, half-politicians) based on the glorification of action. But in reality, they embody a form of anti-politicism in the sense that, in the name of managerial efficiency, they challenge the very meaning of political action, that is to arbitrate between contradictory values and interests. Interest struggles are thus denied, as are ideological considerations. To maintain the masses, who are themselves perceived as consumers rather than citizens, "pragmatism" or "left-right overcoming" is promoted and news based on storytelling is created (Musso 2019).

This attempt to make politics disappear in favour of management takes advantage of the fertile ground created by a broad depoliticisation of the voters themselves. Ivan Krastev makes a similar observation to that of Musso. Without going so far as to use the term "company-state", he asserts that how the relationship between the people and populist leaders is organised and is more a question of commerce than of politics.

> The disappearance of an internationally minded working class signals a major realignment in European politics. No longer is it surprising that the new postutopian populism fails to plot on conventional left-right axes. Unlike the Catholic Church or the communists of old, the new populism lacks any catechetical or pedagogical ambitions. New populist leaders don't fantasize about changing their societies. They don't imagine people in terms of what they might become; they like them just the way they are. Empowering people without any common project is the ambition of the new populism. In this sense, the new populism is perfectly suited to societies where citizens are consumers above all else and view their leaders as waiters who are expected to move quickly in fulfilling their wishes.
>
> *(Krastev 2017, p. 35)*

How did this depoliticisation of politics come about? Most authors who study populism agree that the development of anti-establishment movements is the consequence of an underlying institutional and democratic crisis. According to political scientist Yascha Mounk, political science has long considered that democracy and liberalism were inseparable and that all countries in the world were destined to become full-fledged liberal democracies in the long run. This is the "end of history" thesis defended by Francis Fukuyama (1992). However, Mounk (2018) notes that the model of liberal democracies is now in crisis due to the emergence of tensions between democratic and liberal values. Instead of going together, the two principles come to oppose each other.

In some countries, the emergence of populist movements tends to produce a shift towards illiberalism. This is the Hungarian situation. In Hungary, while democratic principles are being preserved, individual freedoms are on the decline. The illiberal state that Prime Minister Viktor Orbán intends to establish attacks the principles of the separation of powers and calls into question the foundations of the rule of law, such as the independence of justice and the independence of the press. In the name of popular will and an exacerbated vision of democracy, Hungary is attacking the rights of migrants and minorities, thus becoming a regime that tends towards the "dictatorship of the majority".

Other Western countries are experiencing a symmetrical drift towards a system which tends to establish a kind of attenuated democracy while preserving individual freedoms. "The politics of the Eurozone", writes Mounk, "are an extreme example of a political system in which the people feel as though they have less and less say over what actually happens. But they are far from atypical. Unnoticed by most political scientists, a form of undemocratic liberalism has taken root in North America and Western Europe" (*ibid.* pp. 12–13). To explain the nature of this liberal regime, which contradicts democracy, Mounk mentions the Greek experience. In January 2015, parliamentary elections brought a radical left-wing coalition – Syriza – to power. Its leader, Alexis Tsipras, intended to question the austerity policies imposed by the European trusteeship and negotiate a partial remission of its public debt. Despite an indisputable electoral victory and a successful referendum, he faced a stubborn refusal from his European partners and was forced to capitulate.[28]

It should be noted that, during that struggle, the action of the ECB, an independent administrative authority that is supposed to have no political role, was decisive, as the essayist Coralie Delaume (2015) has explained so well. In this form of liberal and anti-democratic regimes, it therefore appears that fundamental decisions affecting the future of citizens and their ability to govern themselves are not decided by universal suffrage but delegated, to a large extent, to independent authorities that are not subject to democratic arbitration.

So, what has fundamentally changed in our world to make democracy and the rule of law, which appeared to be inextricable, come to be separated? Mounk believes that three conditions are necessary for liberal democracy to function properly: the growth of middle-class incomes and a contained level of inequality; the harmonious management of a multi-ethnic society in which a collective identity would prevail; and a means of taming social networks and making traditional vertical communication systems coexist with the horizontal communication of networks without the latter conveying misleading information or becoming likely to distort the quality of political debate.

According to Mounk, liberal democracy is in crisis in Western countries because these three conditions can no longer be met today.

The problem with this thesis is that it tends to neglect certain fundamental economic parameters. Social networks have developed all over the world, but they have not led to populist movements everywhere. Poland is one of the most ethnically homogenous countries in the world and the level of inequality there is not higher than elsewhere. Moreover, the income of its middle class has been structurally increasing since its accession to the European Union. Yet populism is particularly well rooted there. It is obvious that the electoral success of some populist movements can be explained in part by their misuse of social networks and by an exacerbation of identity tensions. But all of this does little to explain the underlying crisis of democracy, in particular people's fear of being dispossessed of their right to govern themselves. It is because they are torn by this fear that they are prepared to give themselves over to demagogic leaders who can threaten their fundamental freedoms.

Populism is the defensive side of a system that has another side structurally attacking the political choices of voters. The elephant in the room that Yascha Mounk refuses to study in all its implications is that this way to question democracy is almost always done in the name of safeguarding the economy. When Margaret Thatcher says "there is no alternative", she does not do so in the name of defending minority rights or preserving an independent justice system. Thatcher's goal is not to protect the rule of law. What she means is that in order to create jobs and growth, the British will have no choice but to submit to the "law" of the market. What she explains is that the "laws" of the economy – as she understands them – do not allow for the choice of any model of society other than that of neoliberalism.

Therefore voters favour illiberal regimes and politicians because they are caught in an impossible choice between the economic necessities of preserving jobs and incomes (about this, they are told, they have no choice in the manner it should be done) and the need to be able to decide their own destiny (this part presupposes they have a choice).

But this immediately raises an objection. As we have just discussed, populist movements have nothing against markets, quite the contrary. There is, therefore, a paradox in this behaviour of voters that needs to be resolved.

Populism and trust

The images spread around the world. The largest avenue in Paris, *Avenue des Champs-Elysées*, which each year sees the finish of the Tour de France, was the scene of unprecedented urban riots. The *Arc de Triomphe* was vandalised. In Le Puy-en-Velay, Auvergne, demonstrators launched an assault on the prefectural government building and set it on fire. The rage was such that, despite the impressive police force deployed throughout the country, tens of thousands of demonstrators managed to overwhelm the police and ransacked everything that stood in their way: street furniture, cars, stores, restaurants, and so on.

In the uptown areas of the capital, nothing escaped the crowd of thugs who prided themselves on wearing their yellow vests, the high-visibility vests that the French government had recently made mandatory to keep in vehicles. Some of the protestors managed to break into private mansions after smashing down the gates that barred access. The west of Paris, known for its embassies and the discreet charm of its Haussmanian apartments, was in flames. On December 1, alone, the Paris fire brigade counted 249 fires, of which more than a hundred were aimed at vehicles parked on the pavements. Eleven of the few stores that remained open were completely looted.

This "Act III" of the Yellow Vests movement will be recorded in the history of France not by the number of demonstrators but by its violence, unprecedented in the recent history of the country. It is no exaggeration to say that the events of that Saturday were a national shock. In France, the ritual of social protest is generally well established. Unions call for a day-long strike and for a demonstration that brings together several hundred thousand people in the country's major cities. The processions, supervised by an efficient security team, are made up of people of all ages, often activists and union members. They march with placards and banners. They may be students, retirees, civil servants, or employees of large national corporations. In the evening, the Prime minister speaks out, sometimes giving up a few symbolic concessions, but more often he states that "the message of the French people was heard", a reply that does no harm.

The Yellow Vests movement, however, was very different. It began on Facebook pages that were created massively after the decision to raise the tax on diesel. Hundreds of thousands of Internet users gathered virtually on those pages and signed petitions. The movement was spontaneous, the fruit of silent anger that suddenly woke up. In this respect, it was a movement similar to the uprisings in Santiago or Beirut that would come a year later. The tax was modest, but it affected a category of French people who felt ignored by the authorities: peripheral France, which the geographer Christophe Guilly had studied well. In this France of countryside and small towns, where about 60% of the population lives (Guilly 2014, p. 28), a diesel vehicle is an indispensable tool for everyday life. Deprived of local public services and efficient public transport systems, living away from the big dynamic metropolises, the population of those areas feels despised by those in charge. They do not identify with any party, they are not union members, and their income is close to the minimum wage, possibly combined with a few benefits. This is the France of supermarket employees, of workers in small-scale rural industry, a France beautifully described by the French journalist Gérald Andrieu in a book about his walking journey along the country's eastern border during the 2017 presidential election. That France, he wrote, had not been hoping for Macron. In fact, it hadn't been expecting much from its politicians for a long time (Andrieu 2017).

In many ways, the Yellow Vests movement is a populist movement. It claims to embody the people and is opposed to political and media elites. It does not recognise itself in any party, refuses the traditional left-right cleavage, and does not intend to carry a specific ideology. During the demonstrations, trade union representatives were vilified and accused of embezzlement in the same way political leaders were. The heterogeneous nature of the demonstrators and of some claims greatly disconcerted observers. Was it a right-wing manipulated protest action? Was it coming from the radical left? Were there anti-Semitic elements among them? Was it an anti-fiscal initiative? There may have been a bit of everything, but the whole movement could by no means be reduced to such labels. Aware of this limitation, and in order to explain themselves, many groups of Yellow Vests appointed representatives. Platforms of grievances were formed, and some demands emerged. The first was, of course, the cancellation of the planned petrol tax increase. Then came the issue of the minimum wage and small pension raises. Finally, a proposal of institutional nature was unanimously agreed upon: the introduction of the citizens' initiative referendum.

Ultimately, what the Yellow Vests were asking for was mainly two things. On the one hand, they demanded social and fiscal justice and, on the other hand, they requested more democracy in a context of deep distrust towards institutions. These are the fundamental characteristics of a populist movement.

In the previous pages, two causes have been identified to explain European populism. The migration problem, which is at the root of populism in Central Europe; the dynamics of deindustrialisation which explains the euro crisis as well as the populist upsurge in Southern Europe. It has been shown that these two phenomena actually stem from the same European dysfunction. The competition between people and capital organised on a continental scale has generated a European division of labour that has produced both winners and losers. But France is neither Hungary nor Greece. Even though it has undergone strong deindustrialisation since the creation of the Single Market, it has not been subject to the humiliating supervision of the Troika.[29] It can even be considered that the French economy has globally benefited from the euro crisis since its long-term interest rates have followed Germany's downward trend. Moreover, France's net migration has been practically nil since the beginning of 2010. Despite a high unemployment rate (around 9–10% in 2018), France appears neither attractive nor repulsive from an economic point of view. It manages to keep most of the young graduates it trains on its territory and remains relatively attractive socially.

How can we understand the roots of such a revolt, one that differs from traditional social movements and cannot therefore be explained by a simple cultural tropism? In order to do so, it is necessary to look at the economic strategies that have been carried out in France in recent years.

When France was hit by the economic and financial crisis of 2008–2009, it responded with a traditional economic stimulus policy. However, by the end of 2010, due to the euro crisis and the pressure of the European Commission, it was again engaged in an austerity programme to reduce its structural deficit. In May 2012, when François Hollande came to power, the French productive system was in a disastrous situation, affected both by the crisis and by austerity. The profit rate of companies fell and private investment was at its lowest. As the budget margins were narrow and the revival of public investment appeared difficult, the new left-leaning government decided to pursue a supply-side policy aimed at restoring the profitability of the private sector and industry. A plan to support the productive sector was launched at the end of 2012. By the end of Hollande's five-year presidency, it would end up costing an annual amount of more than 40 billion euros, about 2% of French GDP. All those measures, known as the "responsibility package" (pacte de responsabilité), were essentially fiscal in nature. The huge employment subsidy provided by the Competitiveness and Employment Tax Credit (in French: CICE) accounted for almost half of the total amount of expenditure.

Elected in 2017, Emmanuel Macron, a former advisor and Minister for the Economy to President François Hollande, continued with this strategy. His first measures lowered capital and corporate taxes, and transformed the Wealth Solidarity Tax into a less stringent real estate tax. The logic behind those reforms was clear: the aim was to make France more attractive to investors by reducing as much as possible the taxation of mobile assets in order to enhance the fiscal competitiveness of the French economy.

These measures only make sense if perfect competition and capital mobility have been achieved. In the wake of the crisis, many European countries sought to become more attractive, hoping to draw capital and jobs to their territory. This was particularly the case of Spain and Italy, France's southern neighbours. As a consequence, the relative decline in firms' profitability in France led the government to fear that French companies might be sacrificed in the event of a further decline in the global economic activity

Pursuing such a strategy while following European public deficit rules was only sustainable if new tax revenues based on non-mobile assets could be found. As a result, the governments of François Hollande and Emmanuel Macron began to raise taxes on everyday consumer goods such as petrol and tobacco. In addition, major cost-saving plans were initiated in public services (including the health system, with the closing down of many small rural hospitals). In the end, it did not come as a surprise when the inhabitants of the peripheral territories revolted, nor was it a surprise to see that the main objective of their movement was to protest against the increase of the tax on diesel, an essential commodity for the rural population.

Figure 1.2 shows how corporate and household taxation has changed since 1980. The pattern of tax strategy changes is striking. While the austerity phase of 2010–2013 explains the parallel increases in household and corporate taxation, the contradictory evolution of the curves from 2013 onwards is the direct consequence of the fiscal attractiveness strategy pursued in favour of companies. It should be added that this curve does not take into account the effects of the

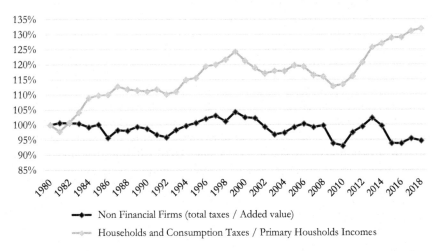

FIGURE 1.2 Comparative change in household and business taxation in France from 1980 to 2018. Source: *INSEE* – National Accounts. Consulted on April 15, 2020.

decline in local authority funding and the sacrifices that have affected local public services everywhere.

In a recent book devoted to the roots of populism, four French researchers explained the emergence of anti-establishment parties as follows (Algan et al. 2019). According to them, society functions thanks to two kinds of trust: trust in institutions, and trust in individuals. But the distrust patterns are not the same depending on whether the loss of trust affects only institutions or both individuals and institutions.

In Eastern European countries, the loss of trust is twofold. According to Krastev, what is blamed on the elites in these countries is above all a lack of loyalty.

> People fear that in times of trouble, the meritocrats will opt to leave instead of sharing the cost of staying. In this sense, meritocratic elites contrast with land-owning aristocratic elites, who are devoted to their estates and cannot take their estates with them in case they want to run away.
>
> *(Krastev 2017, p. 90)*

In a society where young graduates prefer to move abroad rather than seek to improve the situation of the country as a whole, the distrust of the working classes is as much directed at the institutions run by the elite as it is at the individuals.

Conversely, a society that is a victim of the decisions of Brussels or of a government that chooses to favour companies to the detriment of households will reject institutions without necessarily withdrawing its confidence in individuals.

Yet, for the four French researchers, only the generalised loss of trust explains right-wing populism. Radical left-wing movements, for their part, tend to focus their mistrust on institutions alone.

Applied to Europe, this idea partly explains the continent's contradictory political developments. In Central and Eastern Europe, where the identity crisis is the most marked and mistrust is widespread, it is the right-wing populist movements that have emerged whereas in Greece, Italy, Spain, and Portugal, where mistrust touches political leaders and the European institutions, the forces of protest have been better embodied by left-wing political parties or those that put forward social demands.[30] This interpretation grid also makes it possible to explain that, although rejecting any partisan colour, the Yellow Vests movement, which favoured social demands over identity or migration issues was indeed a movement tinged with a left-wing ideal. As for the United States, the situation in Kansas, as recounted by Frank, is characteristic of a generalised distrust of not only cultural and political institutions, but also of the very individuals who make them up. Right-wing populism with paranoid tendencies would be the natural outlet for this form of protest.

Populism and neoliberalism

Why are social institutions getting weaker in Europe and the United States? What common force would explain the widespread increase in mistrust? One hypothesis often put forward is that the emergence of social networks and growing individualism have together led to the development of separated communities that are increasingly isolated from each other. The result is a fragmented society, composed of sub-groups sharing common values but no longer finding themselves in a common entity. Yet community identity, whether local or expressed through social networks, is not necessarily inconsistent with the existence of a broader identity or the acceptance of collective institutions.

To exist and build trust, institutions must be based on a value system. One cannot respect a teacher or member of parliament if one doubts their probity or the usefulness of their position. Most people think schools are useful because they trust the authority of knowledge and the workings of science. They respect their deputy or mayor because they accept the principle of representative democracy. However, the principles of science or those of representative democracy are now being challenged by part of the population, who wishes to debate a widely accepted scientific theory such as global warming as if it were just one opinion among many. Similarly, rather than considering that politicians may be sincerely motivated by the desire to improve their country or municipality, they are treated as if they were pursuing their personal interests.

Social institutions are based on a hierarchical principle. What makes an institution truly social is that it stands on an upper level from the rest of society. Institutions express transcendence. The scientist, the member of parliament, the schoolteacher, or the judge, by the nature of their function, are on a different level from others and stand as arbitrators. This is not because they are superior as individuals but because they perform a social function that transcends the rest of society, the service of common good. Indeed, this distinction between the individual and his or her function is often embodied in a costume or uniform worn in the moment the function is expressed and the individuality fades away.

For law scholar Alain Supiot, the loss of heteronomy which generates the levelling of society, is one of the causes of the weakening of traditional social institutions. To illustrate how such a world works, Supiot refers to a philosophical tale written by the English mathematician Edwin Abbott, *Flatland*. In this story, geometric characters seek to interact and meet each other. But since the world is in two dimensions only, everything becomes extremely difficult (Abbott 1884). More fundamentally, what this flat world expresses, according to Supiot, is the importation of the market value system into society. A market transaction is based on the principle of trade. Everything is exchangeable, calculable, and comparable. Everything is therefore on the same level. The absence of heteronomy means that any asset can be measured in the same monetary value. In other words, the world is flat and devoid of any social institution other than the market. "The neoliberal utopia is precisely this flat world wholly driven by the immanent laws of the market, and in this respect it is much closer to communist utopias than to 'classical' liberalism", summarises Supiot (2017, pp. 106–7).

Let us take the French case again. One could say that what weakens the political institution in this country is that decisions taken by successive governments over the recent period, such as the austerity policy and the strategic choice of fiscal attractiveness, have not benefited the majority. From this fact, two explanations are possible. The first is that French political leaders are allegedly traitors to their country and have knowingly misled their voters by intentionally hijacking the traditional political game to serve the ruling classes. This explanation is, of course, the simplest. It expresses absolute distrust and a world view based on the image of latent social war.

It is also an explanation that has a significant blind spot. Such a manoeuvre is very costly from an electoral point of view and would imply that French politicians have a suicidal attitude. In his book, Yascha Mounk study the evolution of the popularity ratings of the last few French presidents and makes a ruthless observation. Since the early 2000s and the end of Jacques Chirac's second presidency, French presidents have all ended their terms of office with an extremely low popularity rating. Nicolas Sarkozy was thoroughly crushed by François Hollande in 2012, who himself ended his term in such unpopularity that he was unable to stand for re-election. Finally, Emmanuel Macron had his popularity rating fell sharply just a few months after his election, like his predecessors (Mounk 2018, p. 101).

In short, if the simplistic explanation were true, France would be electing presidents selfish enough to serve the interests of their caste at the expense of those of the people, but altruistic enough to accept to sacrifice their own political future in doing so.

The explanation that a Machiavellian political class has been ruling the world for decades is fortunately not the only one. If the leaders of the European Union and those at the head of states come to thwart the aspirations of their people, it is perhaps because their ability to act is constrained by a superior set of economic forces and by legal commitments that limit the scope of what could be achieved. When François Hollande decided to shift the tax burden from companies to households, he did so not simply to help companies as part of a class policy, but also (and perhaps above all) because he sincerely believed that, in the hyper-competitive context of the single European market, this was the only measure that would ultimately make it possible to maintain or create jobs in his country.

In this sense, the democratic problem of the EU member states does not only stem from the existence of institutions of control and counter-powers that limit political action, as Mounk suggests. No institutional constraint prevented François Hollande from pursuing a policy in complete opposition to the one he had chosen. He was free to shift the tax burden from households to companies in order to gain popularity and be easily re-elected. But the dynamics of the European economy prevented him from believing that such a policy could lead to anything other than an acceleration rate of deindustrialisation and a massive rise in unemployment.

In other words, even when they can decide economic policy in a perfectly sovereign manner, most European political leaders have embraced the Thatcherian maxim: "There is no alternative". Therefore, this feeling of powerlessness – rather than a Machiavellian political class opposed to popular aspirations – could well explain the weakening of political institutions. The leaders are legitimate if their actions are decisive, if they can "move the lines" and act by favouring certain interests or values. But the current European context reduces their capacity for action to such an extent that they lose their power to truly perform as leaders. Eventually, their political actions are reduced to the role of news commentators. This puts the leader on the same level as the voters.

Political action is transcendent only if it has weight, and it has weight only if it is capable of ordering bifurcations. Otherwise, its destiny is to become one of the many geometric figures that evolve in Edwin Abbott's flat world.

The British scholar of international relations, Michael Cox, clearly explains how, in his view, Western populism feeds on a generalised feeling of powerlessness:

> I would also wish to suggest that populism is very much an expression in the West of a sense of powerlessness: the powerlessness of ordinary citizens when faced with massive changes going on all around them; but the powerlessness too of Western leaders and politicians who really do not seem to have an answer to the many challenges facing the West right now. Many ordinary people might feel they have no control and express this by supporting populist movements and parties who promise to restore control to them. But in reality it is the established political parties, the established politicians, and the established structures of power as well, which are equally powerless. Powerless to stop the flow of migrants from the Middle

East and Africa. Powerless to control the borders of their own nation states. Powerless when faced with a terrorist threat. Powerless to prevent off-shoring and tax avoidance. And powerless to reduce unemployment to any significant degree across most of the Eurozone.

(Cox 2017, p. 16)

Is populism the consequence of the reactivated class war, or that of the impotence of politics? It all depends on how one interprets current economic policies. Many authors point out the crucial role that neoliberal policies play in the emergence of populism (Bērziņš 2017). Researchers James Montier and Philip Pilkington generalise this thesis:

> From our perspective, the rise of populism has its roots in the same sources that have given rise to so-called "secular stagnation". That is, a broken system of economic governance. This system – which we will hereafter refer to as "neoliberalism" – arose in the mid-1970s and was characterised by four significant economic policies: the abandonment of full employ-ment as a desirable policy goal and its replacement with inflation targeting; an increase in the globalisation of the flows of people, capital, and trade; a focus at a firm level on shareholder value maximisation rather than rein-vestment and growth; and the pursuit of flexible labour markets and the disruption of trade unions and workers' organisations.
>
> *(Montier and Pilkington 2017)*

Neoliberalism would be the ideology of conservative economic policies, the theo-retical framework for austerity measures that seek less public intervention and thus serve the interests of the wealthy. One can admit that an economic policy that favours the interests of a minority is likely to stir up popular opposition, and from this it can be inferred that populism would be the receptacle of this opposition. In a neo-Marxist conception, neoliberalism is basically nothing more than the new clothes of traditional class-oriented politics. This view is shared by many left-wing researchers and intellectuals such as the historian Quinn Slobodian (2018), the geographer David Harvey (2005), and the activist and essayist Naomi Klein (2007).

The thesis of this book is different. It argues that neoliberalism cannot be reduced to the simple implementation of conservative policies or to an ideologi-cal enterprise of domination. First of all, it is not demonstrated that the promot-ers of neoliberalism have the objective of defending the upper classes. Moreover, it is worth noting that some neoliberal principles are shared beyond conservative spheres, especially by left-wing intellectuals and politicians who oppose inequal-ities (we shall see how in Chapter 3). Finally, it is important to point out that some economic policies implemented by conservative leaders such as Donald Trump are, in fact, extremely far from neoliberalism.

It seems truly necessary to redefine more clearly what neoliberalism is. And before doing so, let us note that while populism is a consequence of neoliberalism, the emergence of populism itself cannot be interpreted through the prism of class warfare alone. Populist leaders, while claiming to represent the people, rarely present themselves as heroes of the working class. Their discourse is almost never a class discourse because they claim to defend both the worker and the small business owner. They spare capitalism from criticism and rarely defend raising taxes on the wealthy. Moreover, many of them present themselves as great entrepreneurs. And in spite of this clear identification with the economic elite, they receive massive support from the popular classes. It is decidedly urgent to respond to this paradox.

Populists and markets (the ending)

It has been pointed out previously that European populist uprisings can be partly explained by the construction of the Single Market. The free movement of goods, capital and labour regulated by competition alone created an economic order that has given rise to adaptive behaviours such as labour migration, geographical concentration of industrial investment, and governmental strategies of fiscal attractiveness. All these behaviours have profoundly destabilised European societies and produced deep political disarray.

But, as Michael Cox points out, political disarray does not stem from a difficult economic context only. Rather, it is the product of a collective sense of powerlessness linked to the inability of political leaders to respond satisfactorily to this context. Where does this powerlessness come from and why does it appear so strong in European countries?

History will no doubt provide an answer. In 1939, a promising economist, terrified by the rise of Nazi and communist totalitarianisms and worried about the risks of war, imagined a way to unify the European continent forever while limiting the harmful interventions of governments in the economy. This Viennese economist, Friedrich Hayek, was greatly influenced in his youth by the economic seminars of one of his compatriots, an economist of the Austrian school, Ludwig von Mises. In 1922, Mises published a book that made him known throughout the world: *Socialism: Economic and Sociological Analysis*. In this book, he sought to demonstrate that it was impossible to create an efficient socialist-based economy. For Mises, a centrally planned economy would need a central governmental agency to decide every price and every amount of production. But the economic calculation to do so efficiently would be impossible since an economy is composed of millions of consumers and thousands of factories, each of them having specific needs. Only the market can generate relevant prices and thus solve the problem of the compatibility of economic actions because it operates on the behaviour of individuals who are conscious of their interests. Moreover, Mises believed that any collective intervention, even those concerning the social protection of workers, undermine individual property and are counterproductive for regulating an economic system whose very nature is to be in perpetual change.

Inspired by Mises' work, Hayek was convinced that the market could both unite Europe politically and preserve it from socialism and fascism. In 1939, he published an academic paper devoted to the feasibility of a European economic federation in order to show that it was possible to use the market logic to protect the continent from any collectivisation perspective. In his project, public interventions that would distort the functioning of markets would no longer be possible. On the national scale, interventions that would harm the interests of entrepreneurs and industrialists would make them flee the country, generating an increase in unemployment and a drop in income. In the same way, any intervention at the federal level would also be ruled out because the federal political power would inevitably have little political legitimacy: the only action it could take would be to support free and fair competition between each nation. In short, for Hayek, "the federation will have to possess the negative power of preventing the individual state from interfering with economic activities in certain ways, also it may not have the positive power of acting in their stead" (Hayek 1939, p. 143). This international government would thus find itself, in terms of economic policy, "limited to an essentially liberal program", he concludes (*ibid.* p. 147).

Hayek was not alone in his concern about the rise of fascism. Another intellectual attended von Mises' economic seminars. Of Hungarian origin, Karl Polanyi was also born in Vienna in 1886. While Hayek believed that fascism was the natural consequence of excessive state interventionism, Polanyi was convinced that the emergence of fascism was the result of a deep tension that naturally existed between capitalism and democracy. Indeed, as the spread of industrialisation transformed the peasantry into the working class, democratic principles would strengthen the political weight of those who had an interest in challenging capitalism.

> The extension of democratic principles to economics implies the abolition of the private property of the means of production, and hence the disappearance of a separate autonomous economic sphere: the democratic political sphere becomes the whole of society. This, essentially is socialism.
>
> *(Polanyi 1933, p. 392)*

This situation demonstrates, for Polanyi, the limits of Austrian liberal thinking which, under the pretext of protecting democratic principles, will necessarily find a way to make it inoperative in practice. According to him, it was therefore inevitable that in the ideological battle played out in the 1930s, Mises' supporters ended up siding with the fascists: "Liberals of the Mises school urge that the interference with the price system practiced by representative Democracy inevitably diminishes the sum total of goods produced; fascism is condoned as the safeguard of Liberal economics" (*ibid.*).

This conflict between the principles of the market society and those of democracy is at the heart of Polanyi's thinking and work. In his later book, he returned to the "utopian" model of the liberals. Without accusing Mises' supporters of endorsing fascism this time,[31] he explained why the idea that society as a whole could be organised based on a system of self-regulating markets was socially impossible:

the control of the economic system by the market is of overwhelming consequence to the whole organization of society: it means no less than the running of society as an adjunct to the market. Instead of economy being embedded in social relations, social relations are embedded in the economic system.

(Polanyi 1944, p. 60)

Thus, in *The Great Transformation*, Polanyi defends another interpretation of the rise of fascism. If people turn to reactionary and anti-liberal forces, it is by virtue of a defensive social movement, a "countermovement" that responds to the attempts to embed society as a whole in market mechanisms. Having seen most of their traditional institutions seriously damaged by the liberal utopia, voters turn to the political forces that they deem likely to repair them. Conservatism thus appears as a natural political outlet. In fact, by seeking to manage labour, natural resources, and money as if they were commodities, liberals are endangering society as a whole. And the destruction of social institutions that are deeply rooted in human anthropology leads to deep trauma and social chaos.

Written in the early 1940s, in the midst of the Second World War, *The Great Transformation* seeks to understand the economic, political, and anthropological mechanisms that led to such a human disaster.

Of course, the current situation is different. Contemporary times, though troubled in their democratic principles, though confronted with a world economy that is increasingly difficult to regulate, have not reached such a point of self-destruction, and it is reasonable to hope that, in the age the atomic bomb, they will never reach such an end.

However, Hayek and Polanyi's contradictory views of their times in the 1930s are indeed a useful key to understanding the world we live in today and the reciprocal interactions between neoliberalism and populism. In a nutshell, and before discussing this notion in more details in the following chapter, neoliberalism can be defined, along with the Hayekian project, as the implementation of an institutional framework that aims to limit political action in the economy to preserve as much as possible the proper functioning of market forces and put these forces at the service of achieving an efficient economic order. Populism can also be understood, drawing on Polanyi, as a social response to protect institutions weakened by the neoliberal order that organises the impotence of politics to act upon the economy.

We should beware of simplistic and retrospective readings. The European project, although it has come to resemble, in broad terms, the project defended by Hayek in 1939, is by no means a product of Hayek's thinking. The European Union, as it exists, is not the result of a project determined in the 1930s. With Coralie Delaume, we have shown that the history of European construction is much more chaotic than generally assumed and that it was not necessarily destined to become what it is today when it was created in the 1950s (Delaume and Cayla 2017). Similarly, it is important not to project the infamous image of the fascists and Nazis of the 1930s on today's populisms. As pointed out previously, populist movements are ideologically flexible and can lead to a wide variety of political orientations.

Figure 1.3 below aims to synthetise the main ideas developed in this chapter. It shows that populism is the consequence of a generalised social distrust, which is the result of the weakness of most social institutions. These institutions are themselves fragilised by the functioning of the Single Market created to be in accordance with neoliberal principles.

The main objective of this book is to propose a reinterpretation of Karl Polanyi's intuitions in the light of contemporary upheavals. The fundamental problem that Western societies are going through is that of the contradiction between the preservation of institutions necessary for social life and the functioning of a "total market".[32] With globalisation and the construction of the neoliberal order, the market has become a hegemonic institution. Its power is such that it succeeds in colonising the imagination and the representations that one makes of the future and what should be sought. The market flattens the world, and in doing so, it gradually eliminates the heteronomy necessary for the authority of all other social institutions.

The power of the market imagination is everywhere, especially among the populists themselves. Populist voters who "view their leaders as waiters", to use

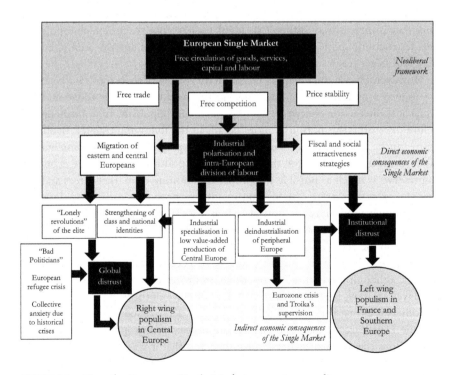

FIGURE 1.3 How the European Single Market generates populism.

Kratev's words, are not immune to consumerist reflexes, quite the contrary! In fact, populists, unlike Marxists or socialists, are far from wanting the abolition of markets. Moreover, they are probably incapable of conceiving how a world that is not subject to market logic could function. It should, therefore come as no surprise if their reflex is to elect billionaire businessmen. For even if they do not want markets to disappear, people are driven by the hope of taking control of them.

The market that becomes hegemonic has wild and destructive power. To put it back into its cage from which it escaped, voters need a tamer. This is precisely what a businessman represents in the collective imagination. Donald Trump, the author of *The Art of the Deal* (1987), is not afraid of the market. With his whip and tweets, he is ready to tame the savage forces of globalisation to save America. Is he convincing? The majority of American voters did not decide so in November 2020. But if we think that Trumpism is a atempt to tame the markets by force of will, then we have to assume that as long as the markets are out of their cages, many people will hope for a new Donald Trump to save them.

Notes

1 The title of this video was later changed to: "Coronavirus: Towards a way out?".
2 This study was published four days later in an academic journal belonging to the Elsevier Group, one of the world's leading publishers of scientific publications (Gautret et al. 2020) "Hydroxychloroquine and Azithromycin as a Treatment of COVID-19: Results of an Open-Label Non-Randomized Clinical Trial", *International Journal of Antimicrobial Agents*.
3 See Daniel Bates, "EXCLUSIVE: 'Gift from God' Coronavirus 'Cure' Touted by Donald Trump is Promoted by a FAKE Stanford University 'Researcher' Who is Actually a Cryptocurrency-Hustling Long Island Lawyer Whose Bogus Science Paper Was Removed by Google", *Mailonline*, March 26, 2020.
4 On the French management of mask supply, read Mediapart's detailed investigation on the subject "Masques: les preuves d'un mensonge d'État", *Mediapart*, April 2, 2020, online.
5 When the crisis started, the indecision and contradictory discourse of authorities is not specific to France. In the Western world, Europe and the United States, and in Latin America governments gave the impression that they were navigating on sight, hesitating between letting the epidemic spread to favour a "group immunity" and imposing a general lockdown at the cost of an economic collapse.
6 During the *C à vous* programme on France 5 on March 27, 2020.
7 On the political polarisation effects of the hydrochloroquine affair see C.O' Connor and J.O. Weatherall, "Hydroxychloroquine and the Political Polarization of Science", *The Boston Review*, May 4, 2020, online.
8 M. Scorsese, "I Said Marvel Movies Aren't Cinema. Let Me Explain", *The New York Time*, November 4, 2019, online.
9 A. Stevenson and J. Wu, "Tiny Apartments and Punishing Work Hours: The Economic Roots of Hong Kong's Protests", *The New York Time*, July 22, 2019, online.
10 "Protests Erupt in Lebanon over Plans to Impose New Taxes", *Aljazeera*, October 18, 2019, online.
11 Lebanon was forced to default on March 7, 2020.
12 "Du déclencheur local à la révolte globale: la convergence des luttes dans le monde", *Le Monde*, November 8, 2019, online.

13 "From Beirut to Hong Kong, the Face of the Joker is Appearing in Demonstrations", *France 24*, October 24, 2019, online.
14 Read the Analysis of British economist Richard Davis (2019) in *The Guardian* columns.
15 The Visegrád Group, founded in 1991 between the Czech Republic, Hungary, Poland, and Slovakia, was reactivated in 2015–2016, at the time of the migration crisis. It is one of the informal groups that structure the diplomatic balance of power within the Union.
16 "Croatian PM: We Sent Train Full of Refugees and Will Send More", *Budapest Business Journal*, September 19, online. This article relates a famous incident. During an operation to transport 850 refugees, 40 Croatian police officers escorting the convoy were allegedly arrested by the Hungarian authorities while on Hungarian territory. The case eventually turned out to be a misunderstanding that was blown out of proportion by the press.
17 See in this respect the comparative analysis of European and American financial dynamics in Cayla 2013.
18 The introduction of the European Semester from 2011 requires member states to communicate their draft budget to the European authorities before it is discussed in national parliaments. In 2012, the adoption of the Treaty on Stability, Coordination and Governance of the European Union (TSCG) strengthened the controls and penalties imposed on states in the event of structural public deficits.
19 While welcoming the principle of the banking union, Joseph Stiglitz points out that the latter is nevertheless incomplete, in particular because it does not provide for European solidarity mechanisms in the event of the collapse of a national banking system. European regulations make the States solely responsible for guaranteeing deposits. See J. Stiglitz (2016), chap. 5.
20 These are the ports of Rotterdam, Antwerp, Hamburg, and Amsterdam.
21 For example, if labour productivity in manufacturing industry increases by 20% over the period 2000–2019, then any decrease in the volume of labour by less than 20% means an increase in industrial output in value terms.
22 The Irish case is an exception that can be explained by a policy of fiscal attractiveness. Ireland's macroeconomic figures are quite unusual and can only be explained by a strategy of parasitic interference in the economic activity of other European countries. On this subject, see D. Cayla (2017) "Ces chiffres miraculeux de l'économie irlandaise", *Libération,* blog Changer l'Europe of Les Économistes Atterrés, online. See also the Wikipedia page dedicated to "Leprechaum Economics" https://en.wiki pedia.org/wiki/Leprechaun_economics, accessed April 8, 2020.
23 See, for example, the map of presidential elections voting in 2016 by county, available on the Brillant Maps website: https://brilliantmaps.com/2016-county-election-map/
24 According to Eurostat, Italy's cumulative net migration in 2012 and 2013 amounts to approximately +1.55 million people.
25 This count does not include the Italian coalition government between the *Lega* and the five-star movement that governed Italy from June 1, 2018, to September 5, 2019.
26 On the notion of imperative mandate see Müller 2016, p. 31.
27 Quoted by Hans Jörg Hennecke 2003, p. 150.
28 The story of these negotiations is related in the book published by the economist and former Greek finance minister Yanis Varoufakis (2017).
29 The Troika represents the three institutions (International Monetary Fund, European Central Bank, European Commission) responsible for overseeing the implementation of structural reforms requested from some European countries in exchange for a financial assistance.
30 The parties mentioned are Syriza (Greece), Podemos (Spain), the five-star movement (Italy), the Left Bloc (Portugal) and the Unitary Democratic Coalition (Portugal).
31 It should be remembered that Mises, who came from a family of Jewish merchants, was tracked down by the German authorities, and his work was blacklisted by the

Nazis. While he was working in Geneva, his apartment in Vienna was looted by the German authorities the same day their troops entered the Austrian capital.
32 An expression taken from Supiot (2012).

References

Abbott, Edwin, A. (1884), *Flatland. A Romance of Many Dimensions, with Illustrations by the Author*, London: Seeley and Co.

Algan, Yand, Elizabeth Beasley, Daniel Cohen and Martial Foucault (2019) *Les origines du populisme. Enquête sur un schisme politique et social*, Paris: Le Seuil, La République des idées.

Andrieu, Gérald (2017), *Le Peuple de la Frontière*, Paris: éditions du Cerf.

Badie, Bernard and Dominique Vidal (2018), *Le retour des populismes, L'État du monde 2019*, Paris: La Découverte.

Baldwin, Richard, Thorsten Beck, Agnès Bénassy-Quéré, Olivier Blanchard, Giancarlo Corsetti, Paul de Grauwe, Wouter den Haan, Francesco Giavazzi, Daniel Gros, Sebnem Kalemli-Ozcan, Stefano Micossi, Elias Papaioannou, Paolo Pesenti, Christopher Pissarides, Guido Tabellini and Beatrice Weder di Mauro (2015), "Rebooting the Eurozone: Step 1 – agreeing a crisis narrative", *CEPR Policy Insight*, 85: 1–15.

Bērziņš, Jānis (2017), "Neoliberalism, austerity, and economic populism", in Andis Kudors and Artis Pabriks (eds.), *The Rise of Populism: Lessons for the European Union and the United States of America*, Rīga: University of Latvia Press, pp. 57–74.

Cayla, David (2013), "European debt crisis: How a public debt restructuring can solve a private debt issue", *Journal of Economic Issues*, 47(2): 427–436. doi:10.2753/JEI0021-3624470216.

Cox, Michael (2017), "The rise of populism and the crisis of globalisation: Brexit, Trump and beyond", *Irish Studies in International Affairs*, 28: 9–17. doi:10.3318/isia.2017.28.12

Davis, Richard (2019), "Why is inequality booming in Chile? Blame the Chicago boys", *The Guardian*, Nov. 13, 2019, online.

Delaume, Coralie (2015), "Où va la banque centrale européenne ?", *Le Débat*, 187: 75–87, Paris: Gallimard.

Delaume, Coralie and David Cayla (2017), *La fin de l'Union européenne*, Paris: Michalon.

Foucault, Michel (2008), *The Birth of Biopolitics: lectures at the Collège de France*, London: Palgrave Macmillan.

Frank, Thomas (2004), *What's the Matter with Kansas?* New York: Metropolitan Books.

Frieden, Jeffry and Setphanie Walter (2017), "Understanding the political economy of the eurozone crisis", *Annual Review of Political Science*, 20: 371–390. doi:10.1146/annurev-polisci-051215-023101.

Fukuyama, Francis (1992), *The End of History and the Last Man*, New York: Free Press.

Gasparotti, Alessandro and Matthias Kullas (2019), "20 years of the Euro: Winners and loser", *CEP*, www.cep.eu.

Gautret, Philippe et al. (2020), "Hydroxychloroquine and azithromycin as a treatment of COVID-19: Results of an open-label non-randomized clinical trial", *International Journal of Antimicrobial Agents*. doi:10.1016/j.ijantimicag.2020.105949.

Guilly, Christophe (2014) [2015], *La France périphérique: Comment on a sacrifié les classes populaires*, Paris: Flammarion, Champs actuel.

Harvey, David (2005), *A Brief History of Neoliberalism*, London: Oxford University Press.

Hayek, Frierich (1939), "The economic conditions of interstate federalism", *New Commonwealth Quarterly*, 5(2): 131–149.

Hennecke, Hans Jörg (2003), "Das Salz in den Wunden der Konkordanz: Christoph Blocher und die Schweizer Politik", in N. Werz (dir.), *Populism: Populisten in Übersee und Europa* , Wiesbaden: VS Verlag für Sozialwissenschaften, pp. 145–162. doi: 10.1007/978-3-663-11110-8_8

Jenkins, Simon (2020), "The coronavirus crisis has exposed the truth about the EU: It's not a real union", *The Guardian*, Apr. 10, 2020, online.

Kettle, Martin (2018), "Theresa May's vision of a global Britain is just a Brexit fantasy", *The Guardian*, Jan. 31, 2018, online.

Kettle, Martin (2019), "At first, I accepted Brexit. Now it's become clear that we must not leave the EU", *The Guardian*, Oct. 16, 2019, online.

Klein, Naomi (2007), *The Shock Doctrine: The Rise of Disaster Capitalism*, Toronto: Knopf Canada.

Krastev, Ivan (2017), *After Europe*, Philadelphia, PA: University of Pennsylvania Press.

Marshall, Alfred (1920) [2013], *Principles of Economics, Eighth Edition*. London: Palgrave Macmillan.

Marx, Karl (1852) [1994], *The Eighteenth Brumaire of Louis Napoleon*, New York: International Publishers.

Mason, Paul (2016), " 'Brexit', les raisons de la colère", *Le Monde diplomatique*, Aug. 2016.

Mises, Ludwig von (1922) [1951], *Socialism: An Economic and Sociological Analysis*, New Haven, CT: Yale University Press.

Montier, James and Philip Pilkington (2017), "The deep causes of secular stagnation and the rise of populism", *GMO White Paper*, March 2017.

Mounk, Yascha (2018), *The People vs. Democracy, Why Our Freedom Is in Danger and How to Save It*, Cambridge, MA: Harvard University Press. doi:10.4159/9780674984776

Müller, Jan-Werner (2016), *What is populism?* Philadelphia, PA: University of Pennsylvania Press.

Musso, Pierre (2019), *Le temps de l'État-Entreprise. Berlusconi, Trump, Macron*, Paris: Fayard.

Polanyi, Karl (1933), "The essence of fascism", in K. Polanyi, J. Lewis and D.K. Kitchin (dirs.), *Christianity and the Social Revolution, 1935*, London: Victor Gollancz, pp. 359–394.

Polanyi, Karl (1944) [2001], *The Great Transformation: The Political and Economic Origins of Our Time*, Boston, MA: Beacon Press.

Rodrik, Dani (2018a), "Populism and the economics of globalization", *Journal of International Business Policy*, 1: 12–33. doi:10.1057/s42214-018-0001-4

Rodrik, Dani (2018b), *Straight Talk on Trade, Ideas for a Sane World Economy*, Princeton, NJ: Princeton University Press. doi:10.2307/j.ctvc779z4

Slobodian, Quinn (2018), *Globalists: The End of Empire and the Birth of Neoliberalism*, Cambridge, MA: Harvard University Press.

Stiglitz, Joseph E. (2016), *The Euro: How a Common Currency Threatens the Future of Europe*, New York: W. W. Norton & Company.

Supiot, Alain (2012), *The Spirit of Philadelphia: Social Justice vs. the Total Market*, London: Verso.

Supiot, Alain (2017), *Governance by Numbers: The Making of a Legal Model of Allegiance*, London: Hart Publishing.

Trump, Donald (1987), *The Art of the Deal*, New York: Random House.

Varoufakis, Yanis (2017): *Adults in the Room: My Battle With Europe's Deep Establishment*, New York: Random House.

Wallas, Graham (1914), *The Great Society: A Psychological Analysis*, London: Macmillan.

2

FIFTY SHADES OF LIBERALISM

Thatcher, Reagan, and the "Washington Consensus"

In the academic world and in the current terminology, the term "neoliberalism" mostly refers to certain economic policies initiated in the 1970s and which marked a break from Keynesian principles. Chile after the 1973 military takeover, the United Kingdom with the election of Margaret Thatcher in 1979, and the United States after Ronald Reagan took office in 1981, are often considered to have been the main laboratories of neoliberal policies.

Two Laureates of the Nobel Prize for Economics, Milton Friedman (1976 Laureate) and Friedrich Hayek (1974 Laureate), inspired these policies. The former contributed to Reagan's program and joined his economic committee after Reagan's election, while Thatcher acknowledged the influence of the latter in her political engagement by confessing that, as a student, she was deeply inspired by Hayek's thought. Both economists met with Augusto Pinochet and supported his economic policy. Other extremely influential institutions such as the Mont Pelerin Society (of which Hayek was elected president during the founding meeting in 1947) and the Chicago School of Economics (of which Friedman was the most eminent representative) actively contributed to the promotion and academic legitimisation of this doctrine[1], which then inspired most of the economic policies conducted in the 1980s and 1990s worldwide.

This neoliberal shift was implemented either autonomously or through international institutions such as the International Monetary Fund (IMF) and the World Bank. When they interven in countries confronted with monetary and financial crises or seeking financing for the development of a country's infrastructure, the IMF and the World Bank impose strict conditionality on the loans they grant. Therefore, once in office, Thatcher and Reagan helped guide the actions of both institutions so that they pursued policies in line with their principles. At the time, a series of debt crises appeared in developing countries, particularly in Latin America. Rising US interest rates and a rising dollar made external debts unsustainable, forcing the affected countries to turn to the IMF. This situation created a specific opportunity that was used to impose a switch in the economic policies. The international economic organisations were able to implement "structural adjustment plans", which were largely inspired by neoliberal principles, as a condition for their help.

Since the 1980s, the reforms demanded by international institutions had been so similar that British economist John Williamson, who worked at the World Bank, described them in 1989 as the "Washington Consensus" in reference to the city in which the institutions were based (Williamson 2008). According to economist Joseph Stiglitz, this consensus betrays the dogmatism and lack of consideration of these international organisations for the specificities and real needs of the economies they were supposed to be assisting. In his book *Globalization and Its Discontents*, he describes his experience as chief economist at the World Bank and relates this symptomatic anecdote:

> The standard IMF procedure before visiting a client country is to write a draft report first. The visit is only intended to fine-tune the report and its recommendations, and to catch any glaring mistakes. In practice, the draft report is often what is known as boilerplate, with whole paragraphs being borrowed from the report of one country and inserted into another. Word processors make this easier. A perhaps apocryphal story has it that on one occasion a word processor failed to do a "search and replace," and the name of the country from which a report had been borrowed almost in its entirety was left in a document that was circulated. It is hard to know whether this was a one-off occurrence, done under time pressure, but the alleged foul-up confirmed in the minds of many the image of "one-size-fits-all" reports.
>
> *(Stiglitz 2002, pp. 63–4)*

Besides the reforms imposed on developing countries, neoliberal policies inspired the "shock therapies" carried out in the former communist world at the time of the transition and of which the IMF was one of the main promoters. These sudden transitions to market economies, organised by means of flash privatisations, usually led to profound disorganisation of economies and societies.[2]

On the European continent, the Single European Act of 1986 and the Maastricht Treaty (1992) set the countries of the European Economic Community (thereafter renamed European Union) on the neoliberal path. As shown in the previous chapter, these treaties established an economic architecture that seriously constrained the Member States' ability to pursue Keynesian policies.

How can we, in a few words, characterise the neoliberal agenda? According to Williamson, the Washington consensus can be defined in ten points (Williamson 2008, pp. 16–17).

The first three points concern budgetary and fiscal policies. The Washington institutions demand budgetary discipline and a reduction of public deficits; taxation must be reformed so as to avoid excessive marginal tax rates and excessive number of exemptions; public spending must focus on what promotes growth, education, and investment, as well as on assistance to the poorest.

The following four points relate to financial regulation and external trade. Interest and exchange rates must be determined by the financial markets; the movement of capital must be liberalised, particularly with regard to foreign investment; the country must open up to foreign trade by removing all quantitative restrictions and imposing low and uniform tariffs.

The last three measures concern structural reforms and the role of the state. They include the implementation of privatisation programmes, the removal of regulations that hinder competition, and the strengthening of property rights.

Curiously, this list of measures does not include any items relating to labour market. Yet labour market reforms are generally one of the most representative components of the neoliberal agenda, even when put forward by the IMF. But perhaps Williamson felt that they did not fall within the scope of the "consensus". In any case, one cannot ignore the crucial part that the war against trade unions played in the policies of Reagan and Thatcher. In 1981, the US President responded with unprecedented severity to an air traffic controllers' strike by ordering the dismissal and banishment from the civil service of more than 11,000 public employees who had refused to return to work despite a court injunction. In the United Kingdom, the year-long strike of British miners in 1983–84, caused by the closure of some twenty coal mines, was an opportunity for the Prime Minister to confront and defeat trade unionism.

More broadly, neoliberal policies aim to allow for a "flexibilisation" of the labour market, i.e. to remove the impediments that prevent the price mechanism (the wage) from adjusting supply and demand. These "impediments" are multiple in nature. In addition to trade unions, which are accused of disrupting the free negotiation of wages, neoliberal proponents intend to abolish administered wages, whether legal minimum wages or wages negotiated collectively under industrial agreements. They also want to reform social security assistance so that excessively high minimum social benefits or overly generous unemployment payments do not "disincentivise" people to return to work. In the early 1990s, the OECD was the main promoter of this type of measures, which had already been widely tested in the Anglo-Saxon countries (OECD 1994). In the 2000s, Germany, headed at the time by Chancellor Gerhard Schröder, also adopted a comprehensive labour market reform package based on these principles.

The previous chapter has shown to what extent the rule of free movement of capital and labour transformed the European economy. It should be remembered that the other side of this policy is to strengthen the regulation of markets through competition mechanisms. Thus, in the 1990s, most of the national public monopolies were gradually liberalised, which meant that they had to accept competition in their activity. Even if the European treaties do not impose the privatisation of public companies, opening up to competition implies prohibiting all state aid in order to avoid giving public companies any advantage over others. This means that the recapitalisation of a public enterprise operating in a competitive market is strictly controlled. To be authorised by the competition supervisor, it is necessary to first be able to demonstrate that any financial support operated by the public authority is done in a strict commercial interest. From the moment a public enterprise is subject to competition, it is expected to act exactly as if it were private. In a competitive market, a state-owned company should therefore pay its shareholder dividends comparable to what a private investor would expect.[3]

The Maastricht Treaty, which presented a plan for the creation of the euro, is also shaped by what are termed "neoliberal principles". It establishes a set of "convergence criteria" which required countries wishing to qualify for the single currency to have a low inflation rate, a public debt of less than 60% and a public deficit of less than 3% of GDP. These budgetary rules were subsequently re-affirmed by the Treaty of Amsterdam (1997) and strengthened in early 2010s. The result is an architecture that imposes a budgetary discipline similar to the one advocated by the Washington Consensus. The other side of the Maastricht Treaty concerns monetary policy. It gives the European Central Bank (ECB) a pre-eminent mandate for price stability and guarantees a very high degree of political independence for the ECB, not only vis-à-vis the Member States of the euro area but also vis-à-vis the European political authorities.

Finally, in its external relationships, the European Treaties promote a free trade policy and free movement of capital, not only between European countries but also to and from third-party countries.[4] Do these decisions, taken together, reflect a politically coherent position? And if so, is it right to call it neoliberal?

Does neoliberalism even exist?

It is not our object to detail all economic policies that have been pursued in the world since the 1980s. Such a list would be tediously long and very boring. What is interesting to note, however, is the close similarity between the structural adjustment reforms that the IMF usually initiates for developing countries and the policies that the European Union often imposes on itself. The fact that two similar sets of reforms may have been undertaken in such different contexts demonstrates that they have common rationales. If proof were needed, one should only look at the huge adjustment plan carried out jointly by the European authorities and the IMF in Greece from 2010 and beyond. In that moment, the harmony between these institutions was remarkable.

The so-called neoliberal policies, therefore, have doctrinal coherence. They emanate from a set of beliefs and a certain vision of the world. But what exactly are they, and what are their principles?

The most common answer is that neoliberalism is the doctrine of those who want to diminish the role of the state in the economy in order to let market mechanisms operate spontaneously. This doctrine presupposes that free markets are naturally efficient while political interventions, because they distort the market order, systematically have negative long-term effects. Thus, in Stiglitz's words, we are dealing with "market fundamentalism":

> Many critics of the views I've put forward in this book combine a skepticism about government with an overarching—and unjustified—faith in markets. Earlier, I referred to the notion of market fundamentalism (sometimes also referred to as neoliberalism): the ideas that unfettered markets on their own were efficient and stable, and that if we just let markets work their wonders and grow the economy, everybody would benefit (called trickle-down economics).
>
> *(Stiglitz 2019, chap. 7)*

Yet if neoliberalism is the belief in efficient markets, why add the prefix "neo" to it? After all, the myth of the "invisible hand" was widely shared by 19th-century economists, and the principle of "laissez-faire" has its roots in the recommendations of French economists dating back to the 18th century. Thus, if neoliberalism boils down to a return to the policies of the 19th-century English liberals, why not call it "economic liberalism", or "liberalism" for short? There is a problem of vocabulary, however. In the United States, the term "liberal" is used to describe left-wing policies that support public intervention in the economy. For instance, Keynesian economist Paul Krugman wrote a book titled *The Conscience of a Liberal*, which was on the *New York Times*'s Best Seller list in 2007. However, it is clear that Krugman is not a "market fundamentalist" at all. Thus, the term "neoliberalism" would have been necessary in the United States to distinguish a purely economic liberalism, inspired by 19th-century policies (neoliberalism), from a social liberalism that promotes a certain state interventionism (liberalism).

This issue becomes even more problematic when one looks at how economists reputed to have inspired neoliberal policies describe themselves. Milton Friedman and Friedrich Hayek call themselves "liberals", although they reject any assimilation with left-wing liberals.

> It is extremely convenient to have a label for the political and economic viewpoint elaborated in this book. The rightful and proper label is liberalism. Unfortunately, "As a supreme, if unintended compliment, the enemies of the system of private enterprise have thought it wise to appropriate its label"[5], so that liberalism has, in the United States, come to have a very different meaning than it did in the nineteenth century or does today over much of the Continent of Europe.
>
> *(Friedman 1962, p. 5)*

If Friedman and Hayek refuse to call themselves neoliberals, at the risk of being confused for pro-intervention economists, it is for two reasons. The first one is, as Friedman's quote illustrates, to reaffirm their affiliation with the tradition of classical liberalism of Adam Smith and 19th-century English economists. However, it is also probably because, in their view, the term "neoliberalism" is associated with a certain liberalism of compromise, which they reject.[6]

In an extensive monograph on the history of neoliberalism, French philosopher Serge Audier (2012b) traces the complex path of the doctrines that were described as neoliberalism in the 20th century. He demonstrates that the concept of "neoliberalism" did not emerge in the American context and that it was thereby not invented to distinguish Paul Krugman's left-wing liberalism from Milton Friedman's conservative liberalism. The term actually originated in the European context of the 1930s and was not used to put forward an affiliation with 19th-century liberals but, on the contrary, to assert a difference from them.

The main conclusion Audier draws from his work is that most of the intellectuals who today speak of neoliberalism often have an essentialist and superficial conception of it. Essentialist, because many of them intend to show that the economic policies of the 1980s were the direct result of a coherent doctrine that had been matured over decades. Superficial, because they rarely agree on what neoliberalism exactly covers and do not perceive that this concept has been used many times in very different ways. For Audier, these naive and often militant visions of neoliberalism do not stand up to in-depth analysis of the texts.

> Most of the works on neo-liberalism that develop an approach based on the history of ideas maintain a very linear and schematic view of the history of neo-liberalism. Some date it back to the 1970s, others to the 1930s, but all offer a view of neo-liberalism that can be said to be *essentialist*. Indeed, it is as if there were a unitary and unequivocal "programme" of neo-liberalism: like a seed planted in the ground, it progressively unfolds its essence, gradually overcoming obstacles. ... Some evoke an apology of laissez-faire and the invisible hand that would spread as far as Reagan and Bush, others a competition policy that found its supreme achievement in the European Constitutional Treaty of 2005 and, previously, in the Treaty of Rome. In any case, there would be an unequivocal meaning, with of course some variations, of neo-liberalism and its socio-economic history. The conviction that emerged from my research is quite different: there is no such thing as neoliberalism, but rather a number of neo-liberalisms, which open up very different concrete policies.
>
> *(ibid. pp. 53–4)*

Hayek and Friedman, who have directly participated in the intellectual history narrated by Audier, are well aware that the legacy of "neo-liberalism" is full of ambiguities. As a result, they refused to call themselves neoliberals not only because they wanted to get rid of a label and align themselves behind the tutelary figure of Adam Smith, but also because they knew the ambivalence of this concept. By asserting themselves as "liberals", the two authors chose to reinvest the roots of liberalism so that they could re-interpret it as they wished.

One might believe the case closed and consider that, under these conditions, "neoliberalism" is nothing more than a militant term for contemporary liberals. After all, if, as Audier argues, neoliberalism refers in practice to very different policies, and if Hayek and Friedman refused to be attached to it, then why seek to maintain the fiction of its existence at all costs?

Because there are good evidences that Hayek and Friedman's liberalism is neither that of Smith nor that of market fundamentalists such as Stiglitz describes them. In his famous book *The Road to Serfdom*, Hayek wrote the reasons why he believed the principles of liberalism did not necessarily meant praising for a minimal state.

> There is nothing in the basic principles of liberalism to make it a station-ary creed, there are no hard-and-fast rules fixed once and for all. The fundamental principle that in the ordering of our affairs we should make as much use as possible of the spontaneous forces of society, and resort as little as possible to coercion, is capable of an infinite variety of applications. There is, in particular, all the difference between deliberately creating a system within which competition will work as beneficially as possible, and passively accepting institutions as they are. Probably nothing has done so much harm to the liberal cause as the wooden insistence of some liberals on certain rough rules of thumb, above all the principle of *laissez-faire*.
>
> *(Haykek 1944, pp. 17–18)*

Friedman made similar statements,[7] demonstrating that both authors did not reject, as a matter of principle, state intervention in the economy. Moreover, as Audier also explains, the theoretical approaches of Hayek and Friedman, while mutually nourishing, are far from perfectly overlapping and may even, on occa-sion, lead to very different proposals. In other words, while there is a plurality of neoliberalisms, this does not necessarily contradict the existence of common political commitments or the common influence these theories may have had in the emergence of a particular political agenda.

The objective of this chapter is to shed light on the nature of neoliberal poli-cies. In order to do so, three pitfalls need to be avoided. The first would be to consider that the policies that have been pursued over the last forty years are the result of a perfect transposition of neoliberal principles. Anyone familiar with political science knows perfectly well that the implementation of any reform is always subject to a particular political, historical, and institutional reality. There is therefore always a gap between a theory and its applications, and it would be hard to find an example of a perfectly neoliberal economy if one were to look for it. The country of true neoliberalism does not exist, as well as the country of true socialism. Concepts and doctrines belong to the world of ideas and they are never purely embodied in the real world.

The second pitfall would be to consider neoliberalism as a unified and coherent ideology. Neoliberal doctrines are a collection of theories based on common values and principles rather than a unified political program based on a single theoretical and methodological approach. The coherence of neoliberalism lies more in the field of values and in the common logic of practical proposals and reforms rather than in the theoretical framework that justifies them. Neoliberalism is thereby not a theory but a "governmentality", to use Michel Foucault's expression. It is a specific way of conceiving and exercising power that is based on a set of doctrines and theories whose coherence lies above all in a few major unifying principles.

Finally, the third pitfall would be to deny the existence and influence of these major principles and of this structured system of beliefs on which a varied set of theories inspiring neoliberal policies is based.

"The proof of the pudding is in the eating", as they say in England. The proof of the existence of neoliberalism and the relevance of the concept is in the strongly consistent policies presented worldwide over the past forty years. We must admit that, if we find similar ideas in an IMF report that tries to respond to the economic situation in Argentina and in the Broad Economic Policy Guidelines (BEPG) produced by the European Commission, it is not because the experts in Brussels who wrote the European report and those in Washington who designed the IMF recommendations worked together. Nor should it be thought that this means the situation of the Argentinean economy is in any way comparable to that of any European country. If the analyses and recommendations are similar, it is because the beliefs that prevail in these two institutions (as well as in many others) are common. It is this belief system called "neo-liberal system" we must understand.

To demonstrate the existence of a neoliberal system, two things have to be accomplished. The first is to determine precisely the principles and beliefs on which it is based; the second is to show how these principles and beliefs are specific and distinct from previous liberal doctrines. To do so, I will start by showing that classical liberalism is not merely a monolithic pro-market doctrine, and particularly that it is not Smith's. Next, I will explain why laissez-faire liberalism experienced a deep crisis at the beginning of the 20th century and how some intellectuals sought to renew it. Finally, I will characterise the main principles of this renewed liberalism and show how it differs from the classical liberalism of Adam Smith or John Stuart Mill in many respects.

France and Britain: a double liberal tradition

In *The Explanation of Ideology*, anthropologist Emmanuel Todd (1985) looks at the emergence of contemporary ideologies. He hypothesises that the anthropological background of societies – identified in the way families and marriages are organised – contributes to unconsciously determining the value system from which ideologies are built. Hence, in the English and French societies, the family system that had prevailed before those countries embarked on the Industrial Revolution was that of the nuclear family. In this type of family, children acquire autonomy from their parents at a very early age, which leads them to leave the family home as soon as they reach adulthood. Most households therefore consist of an adult couple and their children, and families with more than two generations living together are rare. Before the modern era, this family model was also uncommon in the rest of the world. In most cultures, much more complex family systems prevailed. The stem family, for instance, is characterised by the domination of a patriarch who makes his eldest son his successor and sole heir. The latter may marry but must remain in the parental home, which implies that three generations cohabit. For Todd, this type of family structure is based on both authoritarian attitudes (family members must obey the patriarch) and unequal relationships (only one child benefits from the entire inheritance).

Traditional anthropological structures evolve very slowly. Generation after generation, family tends to reproduce itself identically while imbuing society with specific value systems. After the Industrial Revolution, when urbanisation and the end of the peasant world profoundly transform family models, the values conveyed by traditional family systems persist and tend to favour certain ideologies over others. The stem family, for example, tends to favour ideologies based on authoritarian and inegalitarian values such as fascism (Todd 1985).

According to Todd, liberalism, like other ideologies, is the product of a specific way of life embedded in anthropology before being the product of abstract ideas produced by philosophers. "The nuclear family is liberal in its intergenerational relations, irrespective of the appearance of any Lockean or Rousseauist political philosophy," writes Todd. "When the peasants of the regions concerned about learning to read and write, they become politically active and adhere as if 'naturally' to the ideal of freedom, even though this is predetermined" (Todd 2019, Introduction).

England and France, which were dominated by the nuclear family model, are culturally liberal societies. Nevertheless, they have their own particularities. France is anthropologically less homogeneous than England. For Todd, its liberalism is tempered by the complexity of a cultural geography shaped by the tension between a liberal centre and authoritarian peripheries. The difference between the two countries from which liberalism originated gave rise to two ways of considering the liberal ideal. This dual origin deeply permeated the theoretical approaches that developed it in the 18th and 19th centuries.

What is, in essence, liberalism? It is the system of values that justifies that young adults in their twenties should be able to leave the family home, marry the person of their choice, and adopt the profession they desire. The liberal ideal is based on the recognition of individuals as autonomously thinking beings who possess their own values and who are independent of their family origins or social status. To be liberal is to acknowledge that individuals are fulfilled by emancipating themselves from parental guardianship and, by extension, from any social guardianship that may be imposed upon them from the outside. "Human nature is not a machine to be built after a model, and set to do exactly the work prescribed for it, but a tree, which requires to grow and develop itself on all sides, according to the tendency of the inward forces which make it a living thing", wrote John Stuart Mill (1859, p. 135). "If society lets any considerable number of its members grow up mere children, incapable of being acted on by rational consideration of distant motives, society has itself to blame for the consequences" (*ibid.*, p. 146).

These quotations illustrate the complexity of the ideal of emancipation that liberalism intends to bring about. On the one hand, emancipation means that individuals are not constrained by a superior authority. Like the tree described by Mill, they must be able to give free rein to their "inner forces" and "develop itself on all sides". But on the other hand, for this to happen, individuals must break free from "mere children". Society, like family, while not hindering the free development of its children, has a responsibility to accompany them in their emancipation, to teach them freedom and the principles of responsibility that go with it. Without this, emancipation is just an empty word, a fake promise without substance.

The English perspective of liberalism tends to emphasise the first aspect of the ideal of emancipation – the removal of barriers; the French perspective tends to emphasise the importance of establishing an environment favourable to the development of individuals. To simplify matters, it can be said that the English approach is subtractive: it aims primarily at the removal of shackles, whereas the French approach is additive as it tends to add the social structures that are necessary for individuals' emancipation.

At the foundation of English liberalism is John Locke's theory of natural rights. Individuals have inalienable rights granted to them by nature. The exercise of these rights derives from a form of property. Humans are owners of themselves because the person "is a thinking and intelligent being endowed with reason and thought, and who can regard himself as the same thinking thing in different times and places; and he does so only by feeling his own actions, which is inseparable from thinking. ... For since consciousness always accompanies thinking, and it is that which makes every one to be what he calls self, and thereby distinguishes himself from all other thinking things" (Locke 1689, Book II, chap. 27, §9).

To say that individuals possess themselves is to admit that they are subjects in their own right. They have a subjectivity, an awareness of themselves. A deeply rational and conscious being like human cannot be alienated by others without at the same time losing what characterises them as thinking persons.

From Locke's theory many consequences can be derived. The first is that by possessing themselves, individuals also possess rights over their actions. The conscious and intentional act produced by human being implies a responsibility for the consequences. If I own myself, I become the owner of what I do. Any infringement of this ownership, any hindrance to one's responsibility, amounts to a denial of the thinking and conscious character of human being. It follows that society's action upon individuals must be limited and must aim at the preservation of their fundamental rights. The state must therefore restrict its action by preserving the subjective and conscious sphere of thinking individuals.

But how can the state's action and its ability to attack fundamental rights be restricted? First and foremost, by law. The *Magna Carta* granted by King John the Landless to the English barons in 1215 is often regarded as one of the foundations of the English rule of law. Its philosophy is, however, subtractive: it circumscribes the action of the king, that is to say of the state. Liberalism, writes Foucault, is in essence "self-limitation of governmental reason" (Foucault 2008, p. 20). It is this principle of self-limitation that is at the origin of the modern constitutions that appeared at the end of the 18th century. Another way of limiting the infringement of the individuals' natural rights presupposes the organisation of separation of powers. This great principle defended by Montesquieu (1758) inspired the drafting of the United States Constitution. By distinguishing between the legislative, executive, and judicial powers and by entrusting them to separate institutions, a balance of power that avoids arbitrariness is established.

The French tradition of liberalism was born in a different context. Until the revolution of 1789, the king reigned as an absolute monarch and concentrated all powers. The *États généraux*, the kingdom's only parliamentary assembly, had not been convened since 1615. The country was also severely affected by the Wars of Religion during the 16th century. The 1685 revocation of the civil rights formerly granted to Protestants caused hundreds of thousands of Huguenots to flee the country. This context explains why, in addition to criticising absolutism, French liberalism aimed to combat religious obscurantism and promote a society based on reason. The 18th century was marked by the first collapse of religious practice in France as literacy expanded. Subversive novels appeared, particularly libertine texts that testify to a first form of sexual emancipation. Women acquired new freedoms. From the 17th century onwards, women of letters made their way into the literary world and became acknowledged authors. In bourgeois and aristocratic circles, it was not uncommon for them to hold salons where intellectuals and artists met (Mason 1891).

In this context of profound social transformation, French liberalism did not intend to limit its criticism to the power of the state alone. It was also concerned with a deeper reflection that was addressed to all institutions, especially the Church. Thus, the project of global emancipation couldn't be satisfied with the simple removal of the obstacles that political power imposed on individuals. It was a question of rebuilding all social relationships on new bases.

The liberalism proposed by Jean-Jacques Rousseau is characteristic of this approach. For Rousseau, the question of freedom cannot be reduced to an ideal of less state. Indeed, in the absence of a sovereign, in the state of nature, relations between people would be based on the right of the strongest and no true society could then exist. "The association would necessarily become inoperative or tyrannical" (Rousseau 1762, Book 1, chap. 6). For a society to exist, therefore, individuals must renounce their natural freedoms in favour of civil and political liberties. This is the nature of the "social contract" that individuals conclude with the collective in order to establish a society in which sovereignty belongs entirely and inalienably to an authority that guarantees the common interest. "In order then that the social compact may not be an empty formula, it tacitly includes the undertaking, which alone can give force to the rest, that whoever refuses to obey the general will shall be compelled to do so by the whole body. This means nothing less than that he will be forced to be free" (*ibid.* Book 1, chap. 7). The paradox is obvious. It means that for Rousseau, true individual freedom does not emanate from a state of nature but is brought about by social institutions. A collective commitment, based on reason, allows individuals to delegate the natural liberties they have to a sovereign entity emanating from the social body.

The English and French approaches to liberalism might seem contradictory. To some extent, they are. For example, France and the United Kingdom deal with the social integration of religious minorities in quite different ways. In March 2004, the French government passed a law prohibiting high school students from wearing "ostentatious religious symbols" while at school. This law followed much controversy over whether or not Muslim teenage girls could attend a secular school while wearing an Islamic headscarf. Under the English conception of liberalism, the state has no place in determining a dress code for individuals. This view accepts that cultural or religious communities can freely govern themselves as long as they do not undermine public order. The government must therefore be self-limiting and refrain from instilling majority values in minority groups. In the French approach, the question was seen from a different angle. Since the high school students in question are minors, allowing them to wear the hijab encourages them to value the idea that women should adopt a different dress standard from men, which opens the way for community-based systems of oppression. In this secular or "republican" conception of liberalism, it is considered necessary to "force them to be free". The role of the state is thus to protect the freedom of young girls from the hold they may suffer from their religious community.

The French law has caused much incomprehension in the Anglo-Saxon world and has been called an attack on religious freedom. It should be noted, however, that it does not concern higher education because students in universities and vocational training programs are of age and deemed capable of freely consensual religious behaviour. Nor does it concern the public domain outside schools. It is based on an educational principle that is in no way incompatible with liberalism. From this point of view, the French and the English approaches are equally legitimate conceptions of liberalism. They both carry an ideal of emancipation. If they differ, it is on the means of how they achieve this ideal and on the relationship between the state and civil communities. Locke's inherited approach places greater emphasis on the importance of avoiding too great an influence of political power in the affairs of individuals or civil communities. Rousseau's approach focuses on avoiding the tyrannical functioning of the state of nature where the law of the strongest rules, and thus places the onus on the state to protect the most vulnerable members who are deemed likely to come under the excessive influence of others. Moreover, the French liberalism is tinged with anti-religious conceptions inherited from the 18th century, a time when religion was used as a way to support a tyrannical state, whereas in the Anglo-Saxon countries, religious belief is seen as a fundamental individual right that should be outside the realm of governmental decisions.

From "classical" liberalism...

In "Individualism: True and False", and later in *The Constitution of Liberty*, Friedrich Hayek also identifies two liberal schools. The first, which he considers to be the British tradition, is that of Locke, espoused by the Scottish Enlightenment authors David Hume, Adam Smith, and Adam Ferguson, and is ingrained "on a tradition rooted in the jurisprudence of the common law" (Hayek 1960, p. 110). The second, the French tradition, is "deeply imbued with Cartesian rationalism: the Encyclopedists and Rousseau, the Physiocrats and Condorcet, are their best-known representatives" (*ibid.*). Hayek believes that only the British approach is based on true individualism. Indeed, because of its "rationalism", the French tradition "always tends to develop into the opposite of individualism, namely, socialism or collectivism. It is because only the first type of individualism is consistent that I claim for it the name of true individualism, while the second kind must probably be regarded as a source of modern socialism as important as the properly collectivist theories" (Hayek 1945, p. 4).

Hayek's thesis is that French and British liberalism are incompatible. Only a subtractive approach based on limiting the state's influence in civil society would be consistent with the liberal ideal. The French tradition, from Rousseau to Saint-Simon, would lead directly to Marx and Lenin, embarking resolutely on the "road of serfdom".

But for those interested in the texts of liberal authors, Hayek's systematic opposition between these two approaches is indefensible. Every significant liberal, even the most representative British authors of classical liberalism such as Adam Smith, is led to reflect on the contributory role of the state and social structures in the establishment of free society, and thus borrows at least a little from Rousseau.

Smith's thinking is very often summed up in his well-known metaphor of the "invisible hand". Undergraduate textbooks in economics often present this expression as evidence of the author's confidence in the spontaneous functioning of markets. The world's most widely distributed textbook on economics, by Harvard economics professor Gregory Mankiw, explains, among other things, that:

> In his 1776 book *An Inquiry into the Nature and Causes of the Wealth of Nations*, economist Adam Smith made the most famous observation in all

of economics: Households and firms interacting in markets act as if they are guided by an "invisible hand" that leads them to desirable market outcomes. ... Smith's great insight was that prices adjust to guide these individual buyers and sellers to reach outcomes that, in many cases, maximize the well-being of society as a whole.

Smith's insight has an important corollary: When a government prevents prices from adjusting naturally to supply and demand, it impedes the invisible hand's ability to coordinate the decisions of the households and firms that make up an economy. This corollary explains why taxes adversely affect the allocation of resources: They distort prices and thus the decisions of households and firms. It also explains the great harm caused by policies that directly control prices, such as rent control. And it explains the failure of communism.

(Mankiw 2017, p. 10)

Mankiw's interpretation of the Smithian metaphor is highly questionable. The author of *The Wealth of Nations* never mentioned the invisible hand in the context of price formation. As a proponent of labour value theory, Smith believed that market only affected prices in a short-term manner. As for deducting from this metaphor the inefficiency of taxes on the allocation of resources or the bankruptcy of communist societies, it is an anachronistic fantasy.[8]

The distortion of the Smithian metaphor under the pretext of pedagogy often annoys scholars with an expertise in Smith's thought.[9] Indeed, the *Wealth of Nations* is far from asserting that only competing markets spontaneously lead to efficiency. As such, it should be noted that the book opens with a praise of the division of labour in a pin factory. Yet there was nothing spontaneous about the way labourers work and collaborate. The division of labour in the factory was not the result of blind market forces but of a conscious organisational effort.

Similarly, it cannot be said that Smith had an idyllic vision of how markets worked. His analysis of how wages were negotiated showed that he was not fooled by the unequal power relations between workers and employers.

What are the common wages of labour, depends everywhere upon the contract usually made between those two parties, whose interests are by no means the same. The workmen desire to get as much, the masters to give as little as possible. The former are disposed to combine in order to raise, the latter in order to lower the wages of labour.

It is not, however, difficult to foresee which of the two parties must, upon all ordinary occasions, have the advantage in the dispute, and force the other into a compliance with their terms. The masters, being fewer in number, can combine much more easily; and the law, besides, authorizes, or at least does not prohibit their combinations, while it prohibits those of the workmen.

(Smith 1776, p. 56)

In this chapter, Smith writes that employers have three structural advantages. First, they are fewer in number than the workers, which makes it easier for them to form a coalition; second, they have the law on their side, and often the police; and third, in the event of a labour dispute, employers have more wealth and can therefore hold a strike longer than workers can. "In the long run the workman may be as necessary to his master as his master is to him; but the necessity is not so immediate", he notes (*ibid.* p. 57).

In such a situation it would be futile to pretend that letting the market run its course is enough to establish the conditions for fair and equitable distribution. On the contrary, to restore the balance, government intervention is essential, and Smith argues that: "Whenever the legislature attempts to regulate the differences between masters and their workmen, its counsellors are always the masters. When the regulation, therefore, is in favour of the workmen, it is always just and equitable" (*ibid.*, p. 115).

Smith is well aware that the labour market does not bring equal individuals together. Economists Jean Dellemotte and Benoît Walraevens argue that Smith's analysis of the relationship between employers and workers is based on a relationship of subordination and not on a simple market exchange. They also show that, unlike in the other parts of his work, where Smith most often takes the point of view of an outside observer, he actually takes a side in this analysis. "One of the most astonishing aspects of this chapter is the way he ostensibly leads his reader to side with the workers and to disapprove of capital owners. [...] Wealthy people and capitalists are thus both characterised by Smith on several occasions as idle individuals" (Dellemotte and Walraevens 2013, p. 693 and 702). This impression is shared by economist Paul McNulty, for whom it is a Smith specificity: "His frankly sympathetic attitude toward the labouring classes stands in sharp contrast, not only with the harsh attitudes toward the workers which had previously been expressed by most of the Mercantilist writers, but also the guarded positions of his successors in English classical political economy" (McNulty 1973, pp. 345–6).

McNulty also believes that the idea that the forces of supply and demand tend towards a single equilibrium wage is not found in Smith's work. Wages, in Smith's thinking, are essentially determined by the social and political environment, by the balance of power, and by the advantage that wealth confers. Labour mobility, both sectoral and geographical, is low. All this implies that non-market forces weigh heavily on the level of wages and that there is nothing fatal about the fact that workers' incomes cannot grow above the level just sufficient to sustain the labour force. "Adam Smith was a strong advocate of high wages for both economic and ethical reasons", McNulty points out (McNulty 1973, p. 358).

The Wealth of Nations' vision of the economic world is thus far from a society driven only by the "invisible hand". As long as the market is compatible with the ideal of individual emancipation, Smith argues that state intervention is useless, if not harmful. This is the case when regulations are proposed by the merchant and manufacturing classes, whose interest is to "deceive and oppress the public", he warns in the conclusion of Book I[10]. But when market relations are unequal and unbalanced, as is clearly the case in the labour market, Smith is very much in favour of interventions that could improve the situation of workers. In general, he argues that the interest of the working classes is linked to the interest of society as a whole. Thus, the objective of political economy cannot be limited to the mere protection of the market order. Book IV opens with the following definition:

> Political economy, considered as a branch of the science of a statesman or legislator, proposes two distinct objects: first, to provide a plentiful revenue or subsistence for the people, or more properly to enable them to provide such a revenue or subsistence for themselves; and secondly, to supply the state or commonwealth with a revenue sufficient for the public services. It proposes to enrich both the people and the sovereign.
>
> *(Smith 1776, p. 328)*

Here lies another key element for understanding Smithian thought: the importance of "public service", which must be understood as the set of collective goods for which the whole society is responsible, especially in the regal domain. But Smith does not limit the responsibility of the state to the field of security. In Book V, which is devoted to the role of public institutions, he explicitly supports two other types of public interventions. The first concerns the financing and maintenance of certain infrastructures and collective services whose costs cannot be borne by users (e.g. street lighting). But it also puts forward another essential social expenditure, that is on education.

> The man whose whole life is spent in performing a few simple operations, of which the effects are perhaps always the same, or very nearly the same, has no occasion to exert his understanding or to exercise his invention in finding out expedients for removing difficulties which never occur. He naturally loses, therefore, the habit of such exertion, and generally becomes as stupid and ignorant as it is possible for a human creature to become. The torpor of his mind renders him not only incapable of relishing or bearing a part in any rational conversation, but of conceiving any generous, noble, or tender sentiment, and consequently of forming any just judgment concerning many even of the ordinary duties of private life. ... But in every improved and civilised society this is the state into which the labouring poor, that is, the great body of the people, must necessarily fall, unless government takes some pains to prevent it.
>
> *(ibid., p. 603)*

Another major author of classical liberalism, the philosopher and economist John Stuart Mill, also strongly advocates the principle of compulsory education and the indispensable role of the state in this regard:

> The State, while it respects the liberty of each in what specially regards himself, is bound to maintain a vigilant control over his exercise of any

power which it allows him to possess over others. ... Hardly any one indeed will deny that it is one of the most sacred duties of the parents (or, as law and usage now stand, the father), after summoning a human being into the world, to give to that being an education fitting him to perform his part well in life towards others and towards himself. But while this is unanimously declared to be the father's duty, scarcely anybody, in this country, will bear to hear of obliging him to perform it.

(Mill 1859, pp. 165–6)

It is worth noting that, although Mill differs from Rousseau and does not intend to adopt the notion of a "social contract",[11] to propose that education should become compulsory is indeed Rousseauist attitude since it can be called a matter of "forcing" the individual to be free.

In his essay *On Liberty*, Mill sets out to develop the broad principles that should underlie the relationship between the state and society. These principles are unquestionably liberal. He proposes as a cardinal principle that the freedom of individuals to act should be restricted only so that they cannot harm others. Based on this principle, Mill believes that the trade of alcohol, drugs, and other potentially dangerous substances should not be prohibited among well-informed adults. He is also a strong proponent of gender equality, non-interference in foreign policy, and a decentralised and weakly bureaucratic state. Yet, on economic and free trade issues, he does not believe that liberal principles can stand in the way of all forms of interventionism.

Again, trade is a social act. Whoever undertakes to sell any description of goods to the public, does what affects the interest of other persons, and of society in general; and thus his conduct, in principle, comes within the jurisdiction of society ... . Restrictions on trade, or on production for purposes of trade, are indeed restraints; and all restraint, *quâ* restraint, is an evil: but the restraints in question affect only that part of conduct which society is competent to restrain, and are wrong solely because they do not really produce the results which it is desired to produce by them. As the principle of individual liberty is not involved in the doctrine of Free Trade, so neither is it in most of the questions which arise respecting the limits of that doctrine: as for example, what amount of public control is admissible for the prevention of fraud by adulteration; how far sanitary precautions, or arrangements to protect workpeople employed in dangerous occupations, should be enforced on employers.

(ibid., p. 157)

In his *Principles of Political Economy*, first published in 1848, Mill, though a liberal, did not challenge the right of the state to intervene in revenue distribution. He even proposes to consider a society without growth where equality would be achieved through progressive taxation and a large inheritance tax.

It is only in the backward countries of the world that increased production is still an important object; in those most advanced, what is economically needed is a better distribution, of which one indispensable means is a stricter restraint on population. On the other hand, we may suppose this better distribution of property attained, by the joint effect of the prudence and frugality of individuals, and of a system of legislation favoring equality of fortunes, so far as is consistent with the just claim of the individual to the fruits, whether great or small, of his or her own industry. We may suppose, for instance (according to the suggestion thrown out in a former chapter), a limitation of the sum which any one person may acquire by gift or inheritance, to the amount sufficient to constitute a moderate independence. Under this twofold influence, society would exhibit these leading features: a well-paid and affluent body of laborers; no enormous fortunes, except what were earned and accumulated during a single lifetime; but a much larger body of persons than at present, not only exempt from the coarser toils, but with sufficient leisure, both physical and mental, from mechanical details, to cultivate freely the graces of life, and afford examples of them to the classes less favorably circumstanced for their growth. This condition of society, so greatly preferable to the present, is not only perfectly compatible with the stationary state, but, it would seem, more naturally allied with that state than with any other.

(Mill 1848, pp. 593–4)

This immersion in the texts of Smith and Mill demonstrates that classical liberalism is far from the caricature that is often made of it, especially among students. The two approaches to liberalism, the British approach stemming from Locke and the French approach stemming from Rousseau, appear not only compatible with each other, but profoundly complementary. A genuine emancipation project cannot be limited to proposing the withdrawal of the state alone. What Smith and Mill understood is that, even if it is essential to leave space for civil society and commercial exchanges to flourish, public action cannot be reduced to laissez-faire, even by virtue of the liberal ideal.

However, it is precisely this laissez-faire principle, which stems from a conservative conception of liberalism, that exerted its influence upon public policy during the 19th century. It is worth explaining how.

...to Manchester liberalism

Liberalism, as the French philosopher Marcel Gauchet points out, often generates a great deal of confusion. Its principles can be applied to many areas: politics, economics, and ethics. However, it constitutes the fundamental matrix in which most Western societies have evolved since the 19th century. This matrix is what Gauchet calls the "liberal fact", which "consists essentially in the separation of civil society from the state, that is to say, in the individual freedom of private individuals (and therefore their freedom to form a society among themselves) and in the correlative limitation of public power … However, it is not the only doctrine, the only prevailing ideology. It is here that we must dissociate the liberal fact from liberalism as an ideology. Not only does the liberal fact not provide all the answers, but it raises as many questions as it solves. It raises gigantic problems of organisation in the societies it enters, starting with the problem of its acceptability" (Gauchet 2004, pp. 88–9). In other words, if the liberal fact describes the way in which society and political institutions co-evolve, liberal ideology, for its part, is a theoretical conception based on the principles of laissez-faire and laissez-passer. It is a particular political project, one of many ways of organising government action and articulating the often contradictory dimensions of liberalism.

The thesis proposed by Gauchet is attractive but seems too restrictive concerning his conception of the liberal fact. While it can be accepted that liberalism aims to give primacy to civil relations over legal and political institutions, in other words to put the state at the service of society, it seems less relevant to assert that this must necessarily involve the strict separation of the two spheres. After all, when liberal authors argue for the organisation of a system of compulsory public education, they intend to intervene in the civil sphere. Similarly, when Smith wants to put the state on the side of the worker in wage bargaining, or when Mill designs a tax system that allows for a strong redistribution of income and wealth, they both propose that the state should interfere in the way social relations are conducted. Moreover, it should be stressed that the development of public education and the creation and strengthening of labour law are indeed products of liberal societies.

No doubt Gauchet understands the liberal fact as a great structuring principle that admits variations and exceptions. But in this case, what must be understood is that the separation principle never exists in a pure form in the minds of classical liberals. What does exist, however, and structures their thinking, is *the ideal of emancipation*. And in the realisation of this ideal, the state appears as one of the tools that can, under certain conditions, contribute to it. The liberal question is therefore not that of the rejection of all interventionism, but that of knowing which interventionism is compatible with this emancipatory project and which prevents it.

Another aspect that should be clarified is the idea that political or philosophical liberalism attached to human rights must be distinguished from liberalism which is only attached to economic freedoms. But the freedoms to own and dispose of property, choose what to buy, and what profession to pursue are undeniably part of political freedoms in the same way as freedom of expression, the ability to associate, to marry, and to move about. There are no "bad" economic freedoms on the one hand and "good" political freedoms on the other. There are good and bad uses of freedom. When the expression of freedom harms others, restrictions are legitimate. For example, the right of movement cannot be absolute since it is limited by the right of property. But the latter cannot be absolute insofar as it conflicts with other fundamental rights necessary for social life. In other words, liberalism is undoubtedly a global reflection on the articulation of the different rights and freedoms of each individual. This articulation is inevitably the product of complex arbitration. As has already been pointed out, it is in the name of liberal values that France prohibits the wearing of the hijab by students in schools and it is in the name of these same values that it is authorised in the United Kingdom.

The emancipation ideal that liberalism pretends to achieve can imply many kinds of policies. But some of them are only partially oriented towards the goal of real emancipation. Other political considerations can interfere. Indeed, the liberal policies that were initiated and defended politically in the United Kingdom during the 19th century owe less to the careful reading of the texts of Adam Smith and John Stuart Mill than to the political balances of power at that time. Back then, politics were marked by the increasing social tensions from which the socialist movements emerged. Socialism was also a child of liberalism, in that it took up the ideal of emancipation. Among socialists, as well as liberals, the state had an ambiguous role; it was sometimes seen as an oppressive agent and other times as a tool of deliverance. But what united the different socialist tendencies was that they did not hesitate to challenge some economic freedoms and question the principle of property.

The political debate in the 19th century pitted three main currents of ideas against each other: the liberals, who wanted to protect economic freedoms, the socialists, who wanted to restrict them in one way or another in the name of the primacy of social and political freedoms, and the conservatives, who wanted to preserve traditional balances and who had an authoritarian conception of the state.

Deprived of real institutional opportunities through census suffrage, socialist workers' movements could only engage politically in social struggles that occasionally took on an insurgent character. Thus, institutional political power was mostly the privilege of conservative and liberal parties, which, despite their frequent disagreements, found common ground in the defence of order and property. This political configuration explains why, in practice, 19th-century liberalism is largely tinged with conservatism and turns away from certain principles promoted by classical authors. This is particularly true for some liberal economists.

Smith's main contribution, compared to his predecessors, is that he found a theoretical basis for the idea of growth. Wealth, that is "all the necessaries and conveniences to life" (Smith 1776, p. 4) is the product of labour, he stated, and labour can grow in efficiency as the market grows in size, mechanisation advances, and the division of labour deepens. Taken seriously, the idea of growth is revolutionary. In a growing world, you can give more to some without taking from others. Consequently, any situation of material misery becomes unbearable. But confronted with the concerns raised by the French Revolution and the insurrectionary movements, liberal economists came to challenge this progressive vision. In his *An Essay on the Principle of Population*, which was first published in 1798, the English economist Thomas Malthus responded to the theories of his compatriot William Godwin (1793) and the Frenchman Nicolas de Condorcet (1795). These two authors believed that economic progress could be transformed into human progress. At a time when the average standard of living of workers was falling, those considerations appeared to be profoundly subversive.

In his book, Malthus argues that any attempt to improve the lot of workers is illusory. Rising wages and incomes, he argues, would lead to a more than proportional increase in the population, reducing the share of each and plunging society into chaos. Malthus was convinced that all civilisations throughout history had faced the problem of overpopulation and those that couldn't prevent their population growth ended up collapsing. Improving the incomes of the working classes means encouraging them to procreate and thus accelerating the risks of societal collapse. Malthus concluded that a social insurance system − a proposition put forward by Godwin − must not be set up. On the contrary, all the limits imposed by nature should be applied. This idea is illustrated by this famous passage from the second edition of the *Essay*.

> A man who is born into a world already possessed, if he cannot get subsistence from his parents on whom he has a just demand, and if the society do not want his labour, has no claim of right to the smallest portion of food, and, in fact, has no business to be where he is. At nature's mighty feast there is no vacant cover for him. She tells him to be gone, and will quickly execute her own orders, if he does not work upon the compassion of some of her guests.
>
> *(Malthus 1803, Book IV, chap. 6)*[12]

The economist and banker David Ricardo supports a similar vision, even though he justifies it using different lines of reasoning. Inspired by *The Wealth of Nations*, Ricardo does not criticise the idea of growth head-on. However, he believes that economic growth is only possible as long as the rate of profit is high. But since increases in wages mechanically lower profit, they lead to a decrease in investment and, consequently, in growth. In other words, economic progress and social progress are antagonistic. Convinced that assistance to the destitute is harmful, he joined Malthus in his criticism of the Poor Law.[13] But, unlike the latter, Ricardo supports free trade and the regulation of economic activity by free markets alone. This applies especially to the labour market: "Like all other contracts, wages should be left to the fair and free competition of the market, and should never be controlled by the interference of the legislature", he writes (Ricardo 1817, chap. V).

Based on Ricardo's work, another liberal approach flourished that was latter called *Manchesterism*. In the late 1830s, Manchester manufacturer Richard Cobden and liberal activist John Bright joined forces to form the Anti-Corn Law League, an organisation that advocated free trade in general and the repeal of the Corn Laws in particular. The Corn Laws were the main protectionist laws in Britain at the time. They imposed restrictions on cereal imports if their price fell below a certain threshold. In doing so, they protected agricultural income, in particular those of English lords who owned most of the agricultural land. It was vigorously opposed by manufacturers because it was keeping food prices up, and therefore workers' wages.

After a large and extensive campaign, the league won its main political battle in 1846, when the United Kingdom adopted free trade. This launched an era of liberal economic governance. Not only were trade restrictions and tariffs abolished but, more importantly, the government, following Ricardo's principles, opted for a laissez-faire economic policy.

During the 19th century, British social laws were limited to a strict minimum. A timid regulation of women and child labour,[14] legalisation of trade unions in 1871, and the implementation of some minimum safety rules in coal mines were the only important social measures.

By appropriating the French expression "laissez-faire", which dates from the mid-18th century, Manchester liberalism demonstrated a conservative conception of political action. Indeed, the idea of "laissez-faire" (lit. 'let do', the principle of non-intervention) and "laissez-passer" (lit. 'let pass', the principle of free trade) finds its source not in Smith's thinking but in that of the Physiocrats, the school of French economists at the end of the *Ancien Régime*. The economic conception of the Physiocrats was not at all that of Smith. The term "physiocracy" (the Greek for "government of nature") refers to the main thesis of this movement, which sees the economic system as an emanation of a natural order, a transcendent and divine situation that should be disturbed as little as possible. Physiocrats believed that the source of all wealth is agriculture, which benefits from a free gift of nature (the natural growth of plants); trade and industrial activities merely transport and transform this wealth. From this, they deduced that the role of a government is not to facilitate production or work (since wealth is exogenous input) but to make this wealth circulate as effectively as possible. In short, Manchester liberalism is a synthesis between the classical economic precepts of Ricardo and Smith and certain conservative principles taken from the Physiocrats and from Malthusianism.

Like the Physiocrats, Manchester liberals naturalise the economic sphere and intend to detach it from the social sphere by protecting it from any political interference. But this doctrinal principle of non-intrusion was about to be confronted with an increasingly complex economic and political reality at the beginning of the 20th century, in the face of which laissez-faire policies would no longer be possible.

The disorder of the liberal mechanics and the end of the laissez-faire doctrine

In *The Great Transformation*, published in the midst of World War II, Polanyi states that a great "utopia" was driving the 19th century, an attempted to organise society as a whole on the basis of self-regulating markets. The problem with this utopia, he believed, was that it required not only to create fully functional markets for goods but also to transform the factors of production – labour, land, and money – into merchandises. Yet managing labour or nature as commodities was extremely problematic and socially destructive. "[T]he idea of a self-adjusting market implied a stark utopia", writes Polanyi.

> Such an institution could not exist for any length of time without annihilating the human and natural substance of society; it would have physically destroyed man and transformed his surroundings into a wilderness. Inevitably, society took measures to protect itself, but whatever measures it took impaired the self-regulation of the market, disorganized industrial life, and thus endangered society in yet another way.
>
> *(K. Polanyi 1944, pp. 3–4)*

The self-regulation of markets, the laissez-faire dogma of the Manchester school, was incompatible with social life. To implement it, the traditional relationship between markets and society had to be reversed. Instead of markets being embedded in social life, they had to become autonomous, which meant putting society at the service of markets; in other words, embedding social relations in the market sphere. This reverse order was not tenable, Polanyi explained. Popular discontent, environmental destruction, colonial expansion, and diplomatic conflicts could not be managed within this framework. The result was the emergence of fascism, a severe economic crisis, and two world wars. The utopia had failed.

This utopia drew its strength from a few simple ideas. Through competition, it was said, economic power could not be concentrated in the hands of one person for long. Thanks to consumer demand, supply would be forced to adapt and meet social needs. Thanks to the gold standard, the stability of money would be assured and inflation would be eradicated. However, from the late 19th century, it became increasingly difficult to trust those self-regulatory mechanisms. Confronted with growing economic disorders, the state could no longer just "let things happen" and had, as a matter of urgency, to invent new interventionist doctrines.

Four major economic and social problems had to be managed.

First, the growth of extremely powerful multinational firms made it necessary to admit that economic power was also becoming concentrated and that this process of concentration, if none was careful, could lead to the disappearance of competition itself. In 1911, after a long legal battle, the United States Supreme Court ordered the dismantling of the oil empire of John Rockefeller, which then controlled more than 90% of oil production, transformation, and distribution in the United States, and of the American Tobacco Company, which controlled more than 80% of tobacco production and distribution. These decisions were based on the Sherman Act of 1890, which was designed to limit the monopolistic power of "trusts".[15] The Sherman Act was consolidated in 1914 by the Clayton Anti-trust Act. But the adoption of those texts couldn't solve all problems because their implementation was difficult and complex, and the case law had to constantly arbitrate between contradictory objectives, as economist Allyn Young noted in 1915:

> There seems to have been a very general impression that the decisions in the Oil and Tobacco cases declared a new judicial policy in the application of the Anti-trust act; that "good trusts" were to be distinguished from "bad trusts"; that combinations might restrain trade providing they did not "unduly" restrain it; that possibly even price agreements were permissible, if the prices agreed upon were "reasonable".
>
> *(Young 1915, p. 204)*

When dealing with competition issues, the liberal economic doctrine faces an inextricable problem. Besides the fact that the mechanism of competition that is supposed to ensure the self-regulation of markets is fragile and can get out of control and disappear, it must be constantly monitored by the state; a monitoring implies interventionist and arbitrary dimensions of the judicial authorities who are led to distinguish between "good" and "bad" trusts. The phenomenon of private monopolies thus doubly invalidates the laissez-faire. On the one hand, it appears that markets cannot regulate themselves, and on the other hand, it is impossible to isolate the economy from the influence of the state if the latter is led to regulate competition.

The second challenge to which liberal thinking must respond is that of consumer power. At the beginning of the 20th century, many intellectuals questioned the influence of advertising and propaganda on the behaviour of the masses. The work of Edward Bernays (1923, 1928) and Walter Lippmann (1922, 1925) showed that public opinion is largely produced by the mass media and hence it is possible to "manufacture consent", to use Lippmann's expression. The two authors draw on the experience of the creation of the Committee on Public Information in the United States in April 1917. Officially established to avoid misinformation and create "confidence" and "enthusiasm"[16] for the American war efforts, the Committee had a considerable influence on the public support for the war itself. Later, Nazi Germany would confirm the extreme effectiveness of propaganda in manipulating the masses and its dangers when used in the service of aggressive and totalitarian powers.

At a purely economic level, what raises questions is the effect of propaganda on the market, namely advertising, which also developed massively during the inter-war period, taking advantage of the boom in new media such as radio and cinema. In the liberal economic approach, the idea that supply and demand are jointly involved in the price formation presupposes that they are autonomous and independent from each other. However, what advertising shows is that the suppliers determine demand to a large extent, which breaks the principles of symmetry and independence. Advertising not only generates demand but also helps to direct it towards a particular firm to the detriment of its competitors, thereby distorting the mechanisms that regulate competition by strengthening the wealthiest and most established companies. Finally, advertising produces artificial differences between goods for the sole reason that those are of different brands, although economic theory considers them to be homogeneous. In short, the economic power of firms is exercised not only through the monopoly but also through the disturbance it causes in the competitive game which can no longer be regarded as independent of the influence of individual players. This problem raises the question of whether or not government should act as an agent regulating advertising because it would imply a break with the doctrine of laissez-faire, or whether it should refrain from any intervention at the risk of letting the competitive game of the market being distorted.

The third economic issue of the 1920s and 1930s, a disruption of trade and monetary policies, was taken even more seriously than the previous ones by the economists of the time. In the 19th century, the monetary system of capitalist economies was based on the principle of the metallic standard (gold or silver). The convertibility of currencies was guaranteed by the issuing institutions, a guarantee that allowed price stability and maintained confidence in money. The shock of the Great War shattered this system. Once peace returned, many states found themselves heavily indebted, particularly towards the United States, while Germany had to face the payment of large sums of money to the victors as war reparations. International debts were owed in gold, a metal that at the same time formed the basis of most of the economies' monetary system. Therefore, in order to honour its debts, Germany was expected to pay in gold, which would result in the disappearance of its monetary base, while other countries, that were likely to accumulate gold, would be forced to sterilise part of their stock to avoid inflation. Another option for Germany was, as Keynes (1919) notes, to become an exporter structurally, which would mean that other European countries would have to agree to import German goods on a massive scale. But creating major trade imbalances could just as easily disrupt world trade on a permanent basis.

Indeed, that is what happened. In the 1930s, international trade was affected both by protectionist measures between the former warring parties and by the economic crisis. In order to recover and get out of the slump, countries were forced to emerge one after the other from the regime of the metal standard. But if the metal standard (in practice the gold standard) was no longer sustainable, what would replace it? More fundamentally, how could the stability of currencies, whose value was indispensable for the orderly adjustment of market prices, be guaranteed? The German experience of hyperinflation in 1922–1923 showed that money could suddenly lose its value and the disappearance of trust in money could cause real economic chaos in any advanced economy.

Most pro laissez-faire economists, such as the Austrian Ludwig von Mises or the Frenchman Jacques Rueff, advocated for a return to the metal standard. However, to make this possible, stocks of gold and silver should be evenly distributed. This was far from being the case. A rebalancing of the holdings of precious metals would require countries with surplus stocks to put them back on the market by abandoning sterilisation measures.[17] Otherwise, only an active trade surplus policy could enable countries without gold to rebuild their monetary bases. But such a strategy would imply protectionist policies, which was in contradiction with liberal principles. On monetary and trade issues, the ideal of self-regulating market was deadlocked.

The fourth challenge facing the laissez-faire doctrine was political. The social measures taken by Otto von Bismarck starting in the 1880s in Germany showed that, contrary to Ricardo's reasoning, meeting certain workers' expectations was not necessarily incompatible with economic prosperity. Moreover, the Great War reinforced social and political contestation. The Spartakist movement that shook Germany in 1918–1919, but above all the victory of the Bolsheviks in Russia in 1917, made many political leaders realise that preserving the economic order required some social adjustments.

One of the great fears of liberals was that the extension of universal suffrage and the growing industrialisation of society would increase the political influence of the working class as it grew in numbers. If those who had nothing became the majority, wouldn't democracy turn against capitalism? Conversely, questioning democracy and re-establishing an authoritarian form of government would have run counter to the most basic liberal principles.

Another question that plagued economists was whether or not socialism could succeed and whether or not the planned economy system proposed by the Soviet Union was viable. If liberal capitalism was to be defended, it was imperative to be able to assert the relevance of the market in assuring the proper functioning of the economy. However, some twenty years after the outbreak of the October Revolution, the Soviet Union appeared to be demonstrating a high degree of political stability while dispensing with a system of free markets. As unemployment exploded in capitalist countries, it appeared to be spared from the crisis of the 1930s. Of course, one could rightly be wary of Soviet statistics. But even if some foreign observers came back horrified by the totalitarian nature of the regime (Gide 1936), most agreed that the Soviet economy had not collapsed, contrary to the prognosis made by Mises as early as 1922 (Mises 1922).

This paradox between the prognosis of theory and the reality of the facts was cause for an intense debate among economists on the possibility of economic calculation in a socialist regime. On the liberal side, Austrian economists Ludwig von Mises and Friedrich Hayek insisted on the impossibility of establishing an efficient economic system through planning and centralisation; on the socialist side, many economists such as the German Cläre Tisch, the Pole Oskar Lange, and the British Henry Dickinson, to name a few, tried to show the conditions of feasibility for a planned economic system (Hayek 1940). This technical and complex debate, with multiple dimensions, gave rise to new approaches in economics, including a renewed interest in the general equilibrium model of Léon

Walras and Vilfredo Pareto (on the side of economists who defended planning) and the original theory of information (on the side of the Austrians).

The inter-war period was an era of intense ideological struggles. The principles of Manchester liberalism became inoperative and the question arose as to which doctrine to follow in order to organise the economic system. Socialism appeared to be one of the possible answers, and not only in workers' and trade union circles but also among many intellectuals. The main argument in favour of socialism was that it seemed to be validated by events. According to Marxist theory, the capitalist economy, based on a dynamic of accumulation of private capital, tends to devour the social structure on which it is founded by intensifying class conflicts. In order to overcome these conflicts, it would be necessary to make the working class the motor of the profound social transformation capable of reorienting the productive machine and responding to high-priority social needs. Socialists propose, in short, to rationally manage the factors of production that are capital and labour in order to put them at the service of the common will. In so doing, socialism aims to give birth to a society of abundance whose economy would be under democratic control.

In a context of unemployment, deflation, trade wars, and monetary instability, the idea that organisation was better than competition and that independence was preferable to trade wars found undeniable support. But from the point of view of the upper classes, the threat to private property implied by socialism was obviously problematic. So those who rejected both socialism and liberalism were quick to favour a third way, namely the path of fascism. Fascism in fact carries a specific project, that of national unity and independence. Its economic doctrine is based on corporatism, which proposes to suspend competition between large companies and to force them to organise themselves in large industrial sectors, under the auspices of the state. While remaining privately owned, companies must therefore submit first and foremost to the national interest. The fascist project also assumes that the economy can function in an autarkic way, which raises the question of access to raw materials and implies a policy of territorial expansion. Generally speaking, all social institutions are required to fade away from the state. The conflicting nature of social classes is denied. As a result, the democratic game, precisely because it is based on these class conflicts, is considered dangerous and subversive. The entire will of the people must be embodied in a single party with a totalitarian vocation. "Everything within the State, nothing against the State, nothing outside the State", Benito Mussolini urged in the Chamber of Deputies in 1927.

The Lippmann Colloquium, an extension to *The Good Society*

In this very particular context of the late 1930s, when the war was threatening and liberal ideas had shown their powerlessness to respond to the economic slump, at the time when liberal doctrines were being threatened by competing ideologies carried with much exaltation, a colloquium organised by the French philosopher Louis Rougier opened in Paris in 1938, which was to mark the history of 20th-century liberalism.

For many contemporary intellectuals, including Michel Foucault and those inspired by him, the Lippmann Colloquium embodied the founding act of neo-liberalism. And it indeed concludes with the idea of "neo-liberalism", calling so the set of principles adopted during the last morning session. However, as Serge Audier points out, this colloquium should not be seen as the laboratory from which the neoliberal ideology was manufactured and then implemented throughout the world in the 1980s. What came out of it was far too ambiguous on the doctrinal aspect and not innovative enough on the theoretical level to make it the starting point for a specific ideology. In reality, if this colloquium was important, it was mainly because it synthesised and brought together the major fundamental questions that arose continuously in the second half of the 20th century. And because it constituted the matrix from which will emerge the cluster of theories that we now call "neoliberalism".

The other interesting aspect of this colloquium, and what makes it so special, is the names of those who participated in it, many of whom left their imprint on post-war intellectual history. Among the twenty-six participants, let us note Austrian economists Friedrich Hayek and Ludwig von Mises; French economists Louis Baudin, Robert Marjolin, Étienne Mantoux, and Jacques Rueff; French philosophers Raymond Aron and Louis Rougier; German economists Wilhelm Röpke and Alexander Rüstow; Hungarian scientist and epistemologist Michael Polanyi (who was also Karl Polanyi's brother); Spanish jurist José Castillejo; New Zealand economist John Bell Condliffe; French industrialists Auguste Detœuf and Louis Marlio; and, of course, American columnist Walter Lippmann, who was the headliner.[18]

It is worth noting the relative diversity of the participants. Even if they were the majority, economists mingled with a few non-economists. On the political level, the whole spectrum of liberalism was represented. That ranged from social liberals rather favourable to Keynes (Condliffe, Polanyi, and Lippmann himself) to doctrinaire liberals such as Mises, Hayek, Rueff, and Mantoux, to conservative liberals such as Röpke, Rüstow, and Baudin. This diversity explains why the five days of the conference only led to the superficial consensus. But the final statement was not the main objective. Rougier's invitation was primarily aimed at creating an international association, the *Centre international d'études pour la rénovation du libéralisme* (International Centre for the Study of the Renovation of Liberalism), whose goal was precisely to engage a more in-depth reflection on the issues of liberalism and ways of responding to them. The outbreak of war the following year put an end to this initiative. It should nevertheless be noted that the idea was taken up by Hayek when the Mont Pelerin Society was founded almost ten years later. He admitted, very late,[19] that he had been inspired by the Lippmann Colloquium to initiate his own project.

Rougier most likely decided to organise the meeting because he was convinced that a profound renewal of liberalism should be undertaken. The philosopher believed that intellectual debate was hampered by a certain number of certainties that he called "mystiques".

> "A doctrine becomes a mystique", he writes, "when it is removed from the control of experience and the test of discussion and treated as an intangible dogma, or when it is founded on a basis that makes no empirical or rational sense and expresses only passionate conviction."
>
> *(Rougier 1929 p. 13)*

An iconoclastic thinker, anti-Christian and sceptical about the functioning of democracy, Rougier was deeply hostile to state intervention, not only to Soviet socialism but also to Bismarckian social interventionism, which he accused of provoking the cartelisation of the German economy, protectionism, and ultimately World War I. However, he believed that the laissez-faire principles dear to the Manchesterians had become a "mystique" and had to be replaced by what he called "constructive liberalism", which implied a certain amount of state interventionism (Rougier 1938).[20]

While writing his book *Les Mystiques économiques*, the first edition of which was published in 1938, Rougier read and seemed to have been very inspired by Walter Lippmann's *The Good Society*, which was released the previous year and which he described as an "indispensable complement" to his own theses. It was therefore quite natural that he decided to organise this conference a few months later with the American journalist.

By the end of the 1930s, Lippmann was already a well-known and respected figure in the American intellectual landscape. In 1914, he co-founded the left-wing magazine *The New Republic*. After World War I, he advised President Wilson and participated in the negotiations for the Treaty of Versailles. He left *The New Republic* in the 1920s and became a columnist for the more conservative *New York Herald Tribune*, which did not prevent him from supporting Franklin Roosevelt's candidacy in 1932, even though he was critical of how the New Deal was implemented. Being a friend of Keynes, to whom he pays tribute in the acknowledgements of *The Good Society* and whom he says "has done so much to demonstrate to the free peoples that the modern economy can be regulated without dictatorship", he also thanks Mises and Hayek, saying that they have enabled him to understand "the whole problem of collectivism" (Lippmann 1937, pp. vii-viii). In short, Lippmann is a difficult character to classify, very influential not only as a journalist and columnist but also as an intellectual. The organisation of the conference in France around his work should thus not be seen as a complete surprise.

The title of Lippmann's book is a direct reference to the work of the British psychologist and sociologist Graham Wallas, whose book *The Great Society* was published twenty-three years before. In this book (referred to in the previous chapter), Wallas examines the psychological and social consequences for humanity of the emergence of the world governed by global economy based on international division of labour.

Inspired by evolutionary theories, Lippmann attempted to answer a similar question. Philosopher Barbara Stiegler sums it up as follows: "How can the human species be readapted to an unstable, constantly changing and completely open environment when its entire evolutionary history has adapted it to a stable and relatively closed environment, from the rural community to the city-state theorised by the Greeks?" (Stiegler 2019, p. 14). Lippmann believed, as did Wallas, that the emergence of industrial capitalism generated an anthropological shock, as it confronted the natural needs of human communities for stability with the economic reality of accelerated flows and erased borders. This maladjustment of peoples to the reality of capitalism can explain their tendency to reject liberalism and opt for ideologies based on a form of closure to the world.

The second problem Lippmann intends to address is that of the limits of democracy. In *Public Opinion* (1922), Lippmann had already noted the difficulties encountered by the society in understanding the world and deduced from this the inability of democracy to function without a body of experts capable of enlightening the masses and pushing social evolution in an assertive direction.

> I argue that representative government, either in what is ordinary called politics, or in industry, cannot be worked successfully, no matter what the basis of election, unless there is an independent, expert organization for making the unseen facts intelligible to those who have to make decisions.
>
> *(Lippmann 1922, p. 31)*

Confronted with these two problems – of adaptation and democracy – Lippmann considered that the solutions proposed by both collectivists and liberals were at best illusory, at worst dangerous.

On the collectivist side, the columnist intended to respond to what he called the "dogma of the age", namely planning. "We planned in times of war, why not in times of peace?" is what one heard at the time in certain Roosevelt circles. But for Lippmann, the idea "that government with its instruments of coercion must, by commanding the people how they shall live, direct the course of civilization and fix the shape of things to come" is not only dangerous in terms of civil liberties but also profoundly mistaken from a scientific standpoint (Lippmann 1937, p. 4).

> The authority would have to calculate these shifting demands correctly in order to do away with the chaos and waste of competitive individualism. It would require some mighty arithmetic. As a matter of fact a regiment of Einsteins could not make the calculation because the problem is inherently incalculable. For even if we make the fantastic hypothesis that the planning authority could draw up reliable estimates of what the demand would be in all combinations of prices, for all the thousands of articles that Americans

buy, there is still no way of deciding which schedule would fit the people's conception of the most abundant life.

(ibid., pp. 100–1)

Lippmann is no less harsh with laissez-faire solutions. Contrary to the theories of Herbert Spencer, who promotes doctrinaire liberalism hoping for social adaptation in accordance with the principles of Social Darwinism, Lippmann asserts that laissez-faire is neither socially sustainable nor scientifically justified. In particular, he rejects the idea that the economic sphere should be isolated from public action.

> The preoccupation of the latter-day liberals with the problem of laissez-faire is a case of the frustration of science by a false problem. It is not an uncommon occurrence. It is something like the persistent effort of astronomers to explain the motions of the solar system by treating the earth as the fixed centre of it; the progress of astronomical science was arrested until it had been observed that the earth was not the fixed centre of the solar system. Now the progress of liberalism was, I am convinced, halted by the wholly false assumption that there was a realm of freedom in which the exchange economy operated and, apart from it, a realm of law where the state had jurisdiction.
>
>
>
> *(ibid., p. 191)*
>
>

As if that was not enough, he also accuses liberal economists of insensitivity to social suffering and mocks the way they call "friction" and "disturbances" the consequences of the misery generated by the market society.

> It was idle to tell the victims that on the whole, in the abstract, and in the long run, all was for the best in the best of all possible worlds. It was foolish to tell the victims that no relief or reform could be given and that none was needed; that the system was just even though it seemed unjust to them. The maladjustments, which the economists called frictions and disturbances, which the victims called injustice and misery, were too numerous to be dismissed by the teaching of resignation to the masses.
>
>
>
> *(ibid., pp. 208–9)*
>
>

Hence, while Lippmann believes that the liberalism of Adam Smith and Jeremy Bentham sought to take social issues into account, he states that liberals of the mid-19th century were merely apologists for the status quo. By abandoning all reflection on how to enable society to adapt to the needs of the industrial economy, they opened the way for criticism and solutions proposed by authoritarian regimes.

Finally, Lippmann criticises a certain propensity to abstract economic thinking that is far from considering the complexity of the real world. "We come next to the fact that the actual markets in which the economy is regulated are very far from being the ideal markets which the classical economics assumes", he writes (*ibid.* p. 220). Lippmann is particularly interested in the effects of the economic concentration permitted by legal innovations such as holding companies. These tend to lead to private planning systems that effectively abolish both the laws of the market and government planification by making the directors of limited corporations responsible for investing wherever they choose, thus deviating from the principles of market logic.[21]

Lippmann argues that the only real alternative to planification is the principle of economic regulation based on prices determined by a system of free competing markets. However, this theoretically functional system is undermined by realities that are not well considered by the theory. In addition to the problem of competition, there is also the question of common goods such as educational and environmental preservation.

> Values created by the schools in educating the next generation, by public works to preserve the fertility of the soil, do not have a market price and would, therefore, not be undertaken by ordinary private enterprise. This is the realm of investment by public authority which does not have to pay its way and show returns measured in money within a short span of time. For the most farsighted private investment cannot look much beyond one generation; only the exceptionally prudent plant trees for their children.
>
> *(ibid. p. 228)*

How can we deal with these problems? How can we guarantee the proper functioning of the market price mechanism while adapting society to the consequences of the globalised economy in a state of imperfect democracy? Lippmann argues that the answer necessarily requires strong public intervention. Except that this is not the kind of intervention that planning theorists conceive of. The state must create the conditions for markets to function well by establishing a framework that allows individuals to be free and markets to fulfil their regulatory roles. "Thus in a free society the state does not administer the affairs of men. It administers justice among men who conduct their own affairs", Lippman writes succinctly (*ibid.* p. 267).

In short, the state must allow markets to function properly, but it must avoid taking discretionary measures, that is to say, measures that could result in the deterioration of the regulatory mechanisms naturally produced by competing markets. Three main areas of public intervention are nevertheless necessary.

The first one concerns monitoring of competition and improvement of markets. Monopolies and parasitic behaviour must be tackled. We can also, under certain conditions, implement corrective mechanisms to remedy the social imperfections that economists ignore. For example, since individuals are territorially anchored, it must be admitted that work will never be perfectly mobile. However, to allow for some form of economic adjustment, it is possible to create greater mobility of capital, and, through investment in education, "to make most men versatile and adaptable in the place where they were born" (*ibid.* p. 214). The state must also protect markets from fraudsters, which implies that "it is the function of government to see that weights and measures are honest", especially since commodities become more complex as technology advances, making the buyer less and less able to judge their quality (*ibid.* p. 221).

In the same spirit, public authorities must maintain and conserve the quality of soils and natural resources to prevent the short-term logic linked to the end of human life from altering the heritage of future generations. Also, major public infrastructures must be maintained and financed by the government.

The second field that requires monitoring, if not a form of public intervention, is that of money. Destabilising episodes of inflation and deflation must be avoided by all means, says Lippmann, since "exchanges could not be made by direct barter: they are possible only because all goods and services are reducible to a common denominator. They are valued, not in relation to each other, say a bushel of wheat against a music lesson, but in relation to money. They have a price, and in so far as money is not neutral, prices will be unjust and all economic calculation impaired" (*ibid.* p. 220). When it comes to monetary regulation, Lippmann is much less confident than some liberals are in the supposed virtues of the gold standard. He therefore calls for the design of a new monetary system that guarantees the neutrality of money without developing its nature.

Finally, the state must intervene in the social field. True to his concerns about social adaptation and his method based on the government of experts, Lippmann believes that the public authorities must accompany populations in their necessary adaptation to the "great society" of globalised capitalism.

The implementation of this project involves moving in two directions. First, a social insurance system must be established to protect workers from economic cycles, but also, to a certain extent, companies themselves[22]. Ideally, this should be based on a taxation system that can distinguish between income derived from rents and income actually earned, or else it should be possible to separate income spent on private consumption from income earmarked for reinvestment. But as this is technically very difficult to do, Lippmann proposes that "[i]n the practical present a cruder policy is unavoidable: one which redistributes large incomes by drastic inheritance and steeply graduated income taxes" (*ibid.* p. 227). According to him, progressive taxation would be an effective way of taxing more income from rents and monopoly power.

The second direction that should be taken to protect the social order and facilitate the people adaptation would be to educate and even genetically improve the humankind.

> There is the whole unresolved task of educating great populations, of equipping men for a life in which they must specialize, yet be capable of changing their specialty. The economy of the division of labor requires,

and the classical economics assumes, a population in which these eugenic and educational problems are effectively dealt with. But they are not yet dealt with. Nor do they settle themselves, as the dogma of laissez-faire supposes. And so they must take their place upon the agenda of liberal policy.

The economy requires not only that the quality of the human stock, the equipment of men for life, shall be maintained at some minimum of efficiency, but that the quality should be progressively improved. To live successfully in a world of the increasing interdependence of specialized work requires a continual increase of adaptability, intelligence, and of enlightened understanding of the reciprocal rights and duties, benefits and opportunities, of such a way of life.

(ibid., pp. 212–13)

These remarks on eugenics must be understood in the context of the time when Nazi barbarism had not yet shown all its consequences. They were no less surprising considering that Lippmann had never ceased to fight against Spencer's eugenicist vision, even going so far as to criticise the relevance of IQ tests.[23] Still, such an idea illustrates all the ambiguity of Lippmann's views, whose liberalism implies a form of human conditioning. Moreover, while he denounces the lack of social consideration from the partisans of laissez-faire, he does propose an elitist conception of society. In addition, at no time is the question of the emancipation of individuals raised. For what is at the heart of this analysis is to make human societies compatible with economic necessities. This is one of the essential characteristics of the neoliberal system. If the latter differs from Manchester's conservative liberalism, it is not in terms of ends but in terms of means. Neoliberals intend to achieve the same project that Polanyi denounced, namely the embedding of society in a system of markets. But they wish to do so in a more harmonious way, negotiating some social compromises and relying, if necessary, on public power to maintain and preserve the social order.

The debates and proposals of the *Colloque Walter Lippmann*

Lippmann's book should not obscure the diversity of points of view that coexist in the neoliberal nebula. *The Good Society* is a singular book, a reflection of a singular author who, moreover, finds himself on the margins of academic debate. However, the influence this book has had should not be underestimated. It is symptomatic that *The Good Society* is cited in Hayek's three major works.[24] Moreover, even if it is clear that Hayek does not share Lippmann's point of view on the progressiveness of taxation or on the idea of making the state a social insurer against economic cycles, the two authors share a certain conception of the law. Indeed, in the last part of his book, Lippmann praises the principle of self-limitation of the ruling power: "There is such a thing as lawless legality", he writes, "and it is to be found where men deny that in making or interpreting laws they are bound by the spirit of law" (Lippmann 1937, pp. 331–2). But this idea is a "cardinal heresy", he continues, and it entrusts arbitrary power to the absolute discretion of an individual, which is contrary to the principles of any civilised society. Hayek developed a conception very close to this one and he never ceased to insist on the importance of the rule of law as a means of avoiding the dictatorship of the majority in his later works.

The influence of Lippmann's book can be measured by another anecdote. In his opening address to the symposium, Louis Rougier spoke of the philosophy that, in his view, should be that of a liberal:

> To be a liberal is not, like the "Manchesterian", to allow cars to circulate in all directions, as they please, which would result in incessant congestion and accidents; it is not, like the "planner", to fix to each car its exit time and its itinerary; it is to impose a traffic code, while admitting that it is not necessarily the same at the time of fast transport as it is at the time of stagecoaches.
>
> *(Audier 2012a, p. 415)*[25]

The metaphor of the traffic code, which Rougier was particularly fond of and which he often used, is borrowed from Lippmann's work[26] and met great success. Indeed, following Lippmann and Rougier, at least two other authors used it: Hayek (1982, pp. 138-9), in *Law, Legislation and Liberty* (explicitly quoting Lippmann) and Wilhelm Röpke in *The Social Crisis of Our Time*, which also cites *The Good Society* on numerous occasions (Röpke 1942, pp. 185–6). Thus, although Lippmann's personal convictions were complex and difficult to categorise, his book undeniably nourished the neoliberal system.[27]

The influence that the participants in the Lippmann Colloquium had on each other should not be minimised either. Many of them found themselves in the post-war period in the Mont Pelerin Society. These reciprocal influences do not imply identity of views. If the themes they approach and certain major principles are common, the answers can, however, vary greatly. The thesis defended by Audier, according to whom there is not one but a diversity of "neo-liberalisms", is therefore perfectly accurate. The way in which the debates at the Paris meeting were conducted is an excellent illustration of this.

Overall, the themes discussed at the Lippmann Colloquium are indeed those that preoccupied the liberals of the time. In his inaugural speech, Rougier denounces the confusion that makes either socialism a bulwark to protect democracy or fascism the ultimate refuge of capitalism. He considers that the two ideologies are "two varieties of the same species" (Audier 2012a, p. 413) and states that attempts to organise partial or total planning of the economy would inevitably lead to "a blind, arbitrary and tyrannical economy, leading to great waste" (*ibid.*). Similarly, Rougier considers it impossible to preserve political freedoms while at the same time constraining economic freedoms and takes offence at "the blindness of left-wing men who dream of political democracy and economic planning, without understanding that planning implies the totalitarian state and that liberal socialism is a contradiction in terms" (*ibid.* p. 414).

Nevertheless, faithful to his undertaking to renew liberalism, Rougier also denounces the "mystique" of those who believe that the liberal regime is based on natural order, whereas it is also "the result of a legal order that presupposes legal interventionism by the state" (*ibid.*, p. 415). In his opinion, the Manchester liberals committed the sin of excessive optimism, which led them to neglect sociological balances and underestimate the importance of the national factor at the time when populations remained divided into nations. He also stresses the importance of adopting a multidisciplinary approach in order to meet the challenges of liberalism and break with abstract and disembodied economic models.

Finally, Rougier unfolds the program of the conference and evokes the importance of proposing an "agenda of liberalism" (according to Lippmann's formula) in order to answer certain key issues, in particular to know "which forms of [economic] intervention are compatible with the price mechanism, which forms are incompatible with the laws of the market" (*ibid.* p. 416), to understand whether or not the causes of the decline of liberalism are endogenous in nature and to evaluate the capacity of economic liberalism to meet the social demands of populations.

The agenda was broad and the questions raised were ambitious. It is therefore not surprising that the relative heterogeneity of the participants led to a relative heterogeneity of responses. Two points, in particular, were debated: the preservation of competition and the social question.

Does capitalism naturally engender harmful economic concentration that merits state intervention? German economists Wilhelm Röpke and Alexander Rüstow clearly answer yes to this question. For Röpke, classical liberalism is based on the idea of a market structured by a multitude of small producers. However, technological progress has made this vision obsolete since it tends to favour large productive units. Röpke believes that the economy has solidified into compact and economically powerful blocs, and that this has led to downstream regulation by the state and to an exaggerated importance of the state, to the point of establishing a form of "stateisation" of the economy.

Rüstow agrees that "a monopolising, neo-feudal, predatory tendency" that takes advantage of "the intellectual and moral weakness of the state, which at first ignores and neglects its duties as a policeman of the market and allows competition to degenerate", must be avoided by all means (*ibid.*, p. 438). Instead, the market economy needs a "strong and independent state", explains Rüstow, which would guarantee the institutional conditions necessary for markets to function. "The coincidence of the selfish special interest and the general interest, which liberalism has discovered and enthusiastically proclaimed as the system of the market economy, is only valid within the limits of free competition in services, and therefore only to the extent that the government, which is responsible for policing the market, ensures that economic agents observe exactly these limits", he claims (*ibid.* p. 470).

Austrian economists are far from sharing the German viewpoint. For Mises, "the capitalist system does not constitute a favourable field for the natural development of monopolies" (*ibid.* p. 435). He points out that technology has much more ambiguous effects than Röpke argues, and that its progress does not systematically favour concentration, but can, on the contrary, create new opportunities for competition. In the rail sector, for example, the development of road and air transport has undermined monopoly situations. Moreover, the problem is less the monopoly itself than monopoly prices. Even a company in a monopoly situation cannot afford to charge exorbitant prices and limit its output, creating an artificial scarcity, because it would risk losing its advantage by attracting competitors.

In short, for the Austrians, it is not the "negligence" of the state that explains the phenomena of concentration but its excessive interventionism. Either the state directly favours cartels by imposing regulations which hinder the competitive dynamic or it favours them indirectly by restricting international trade. Indeed, protectionism fragments the economic system into a multitude of small markets where it is much easier for a firm to acquire market power.

Not surprisingly, the second major issue – the social issue – is also hotly contested. The dividing line lies between the advocates of the Austrian school, who stand for uncompromising liberalism, and those of the German school, who support amended liberalism and consider it essential to preserve a social order that is independent and partly protected from economic dynamics. Rüstow's lengthy presentation defending the second viewpoint is quite astonishing.

> Man does not live on bread alone", he says. Thus, "it appears that the most important economic-social task is to shape the economy in such a way that it provides as many men as possible not with the highest possible income but with a vital situation that is as satisfactory as possible.
>
> *(ibid. p. 468)*

Rüstow expressed his concern about the social and spiritual dissolution and the abandonment of traditional hierarchies that capitalism has engendered. He believes the rural peasants feel freer and more fulfilled than urban workers, because they remain in control of their economic environment, even if they work more without necessarily earning more. An isolated individual no longer manages to integrate socially and loses this "vital spirit" indispensable to his or her development. "The market has become an area of atomisation, from which there is no vital integration", Rüstow explains (*ibid.* p. 470). It is therefore this question that must be addressed as a priority because the multiple crises of the 1930s were, in his opinion, only the consequences of a much deeper illness of the social body.

Rüstow's views were severely criticised by Mises who sees them as a form of backwards-looking romanticism. According to the Austrian Mises, the social levelling which the German economist deplores is a result of the abandonment of old-fashioned privileges that are, in any case, incompatible with individualistic principles. Moreover, if Rüstow were right in his comparison between farmers and workers, why then were so many peasants attracted to the city and agreeing to be employed in factories?

The Frenchman Jacques Rueff also defended uncompromising liberalism by attacking interventionism, which he accused of disrupting market mechanisms. In particular, Rueff criticised state intervention in the labour market where the temptation to introduce a minimum wage or create an unemployment insurance system was strong. He argued that these interventions are dangerous and unnecessary, even from the point of view of workers. "As long as the price mechanism has worked, we have seen wages follow price movements. ... As soon as the state intervened to maintain the wage rate, unemployment increased. ... All state intervention in the economy has impoverished workers" (ibid. p. 460–1). Asked by Lippmann whether it would still be possible to remedy the suffering produced by the market, Rueff finally conceded that a balanced budget unemployment insurance system would be sustainable, but maintained that interventions in wage levels could only lead to disaster.

Other debaters came to nuance Rueff's uncompromising views. The industrialist Louis Marlio, for example, believed that the price mechanism was functioning less and less because of the growing size of economic units. As for economist John Condliffe, he pointed out that in Great Britain, it was less the existence of unemployment insurance that prevented the labour market from being balanced than the excessively high gold parity of the sterling pound decided in 1925.

The comments made by both parties, as recorded in the acts of the Lippmann conference, make it possible to measure the differences, sometimes considerable, between the speakers. Nevertheless, these differences did not prevent the meeting from ending with the unanimous approval of a summary text presented by Walter Lippmann himself. This "agenda of liberalism" gives a glimpse of the main points of agreement and shows that these are far from being anecdotal.

The first point is clearly the most important. It states:

> Economic liberalism admits as a fundamental postulate that only the price mechanism operating in free markets makes it possible to obtain an organisation of production capable of making the best use of the means of production and leading to the maximum satisfaction of human desires as they are actually experienced by men and not as a central authority claims to establish them on their behalf.
>
> *(ibid. p. 485)*

The second and third points propose the principles of state intervention. It is specified that the state's main task is to establish a legal regime that allows the free development of economic activities and that all its interventions must be based on a system of previously established norms. The fourth point stresses the importance of deciding upon social goals in a democratic procedure, and the fifth affirms that public goods such as national security, education, or social insurance can be financed through taxation. Finally, the last point summarises the precedents by stressing that market prices must be affected by the system of ownership and contracts, that society can set itself objectives that are not necessarily those of the maximum utility, and that the community can assume certain sacrifices, provided that the transfer operations are carried out transparently. "Intervention in such cases must address the causes of the situation to be corrected and not give the state the means to arbitrarily modify individual situations", the declaration reports (*ibid.* p. 486).

This concludes Louis Rougier's attempt to renew liberalism with the organisation of the *Colloque Walter Lippmann* in Paris in 1938. But World War II, which broke out the following year, brutally put an end to the hopes of the partisans of a liberal renovation.

1944: The liberal defeat and *The Road to Serfdom*

In 1944, it seemed clear that fascist and liberal ideologies were condemned. The dismissal of Mussolini, the armistice signed with the Kingdom of Italy in September 1943, and the capture of Rome in June 1944 sounded the death knell of Italian fascism. The advance of Russian troops to the east and the Allied landing on the Normandy beaches sealed the fate of its German counterpart.

But liberalism, too, was defeated, not militarily but institutionally, politically, and even scientifically. "Can capitalism survive? No. I don't think it can", wrote Joseph Schumpeter, president of the American Economic Association in 1942 (Schumpeter 1942, p. 61). In the preface to *Capitalism, Socialism and Democracy*, perhaps his best-known work, he explains: "a socialist form of society will inevitably emerge from an equally inevitable decomposition of capitalist society" (*ibid.* p. 410). A former entrepreneur and great defender of liberalism, Schumpeter does not see the advent of socialism as progress. He believed that the capitalist dynamic based on entrepreneurship was no longer possible in the era of multinationals that weakened the creative impulse by transforming the relationship to the property of capital: "The capitalist process, by substituting a mere parcel of shares for the walls of and the machines in a factory, takes the life out of the idea of property", he lamented (*ibid.* p. 142).

To support the war effort, the US and the UK had undergone a major transformation of their economies and organised the planning of part of industrial production, including strict price controls. In Britain, the 1942 Beveridge Report, drafted by Liberal economist William Beveridge, called for the expansion and unification of the British pension insurance system and the creation of a public health care system. Although its implementation was postponed to the post-war period, the project for establishing a social state broke for good with earlier Manchestarian principles and disappointed many of the liberals who were presented at the Lippmann Colloquium. For Hayek in particular, the Beveridge

Plan illustrated the slippery slope upon which the United Kingdom found itself and its inevitable march towards collectivism and dictatorship.

Undoubtedly, the Bretton Woods agreements, the outcome of negotiations between (mostly) London and Washington which were signed in July 1944 by the forty-four Allied countries (including the USSR, which however then failed to ratify it), were the best proof of the decline of liberal principles.

It has been noted above that the monetary and trade disorders of the 1930s seemed inextricable from a laissez-faire point of view. The Second World War and the new loans the Allies had to take out from the United States made any prospect of re-establishing a gold standard illusory for the foreseeable future since most of the world's gold was held by a single country at that time.

The restoration of an international monetary system and the resumption of trade between nations required an entirely new architecture. This is what the Bretton Woods conference participants worked on. The resulting agreements were based on three main ideas. The first idea was a new international monetary system indirectly based on gold. The dollar de facto became the only currency convertible into gold on the one hand, and the currencies of the other signatory countries had to maintain a fixed exchange rate against the dollar (and therefore against each other), on the other. The aim was to ban the currency wars and unilateral devaluations that had profoundly destabilised the world economy during the 1930s. However, the agreements did not formally prohibit a country from devaluing but imposed a collective agreement for any devaluation of more than 10%. A new international organisation – the IMF – was created to provide a forum for discussion and help for states looking to preserve the convertibility of their currencies. By removing the international monetary system from market forces, the Bretton Woods system required administrative control of capital flows. Indeed, foreign exchange transactions could not be left entirely free because it would have compromised the ability of governments to support their currencies.

The second idea arising from these agreements was to better organise trade flows by avoiding tariff wars. An international trade organisation responsible to establish the rules of a harmonious trade system based on the principles of multilateralism was supposed to be created and to be integrated into the United Nations. The objective of promoting employment and social progress alongside trade was in its founding Havana Charter of 1948. This text allowed states to take protective measures and grant public aid to industrial and agricultural sectors in difficulty, it sought to ensure respect for a balanced trade situation, and aimed at preventing mercantilist and trade war practices. Overall, the philosophy of the Havana Charter was much more compatible with the principles of moderate protectionism than with those of free trade. It should be noted, however, that the Havana Charter was not ratified by the US Congress, which preferred to maintain the GATT agreement based on a philosophy much more favourable to free trade.

The third idea that emerged from the Bretton Woods agreements is that of reconstruction. Participants were well aware that Europe was going to emerge ruined from the war and that massive sources of funding would need to be found in order to rebuild housing and infrastructure. As a response, the International Bank for Reconstruction and Development was created, which is now part of the World Bank.

Bretton Woods marked a profound break with the principles of liberalism. The role envisaged for the state was no longer simply to create a framework in which competing markets can flourish freely but to intervene within the markets themselves by organising reconstruction, supporting certain economic sectors, strictly regulating currency rates, and, most importantly, partially isolating national economies from the global environment. These arrangements did not preclude the establishment of a liberal system within each economy. But, by controlling their financial and trade borders, governments had a great deal of room for interventionist policies. In short, Bretton Woods' capitalism was a fourth way, so to speak. It was neither standard liberalism nor communism nor fascism; it opened a middle way to regulated capitalism, a domesticated and national competition regime, moderate protectionism, compatible with both private property and a strong public sector.

For the liberals of the Lippmann Colloquium, the idea that it is possible to partially control capitalism through regulatory interventionism without profoundly altering its nature would be heresy. Any public intervention generates sectoral imbalance and, since markets are linked to each other, sectoral imbalance inevitably turns into general imbalance. These imbalances must then be compensated for by new interventions that accentuate the initial imbalances and set in motion an interventionist process that can only accelerate until the economy is fully planned. A very enlightening metaphor by Röpke illustrates this fear perfectly:

> The welfare state is the favorite playground of a cheap sort of moralism that only thoughtlessness shields from exposure. But what is equally bad is that to turn back on this path is as difficult as to turn a car on a narrow, steep Alpine road. This is what we realize to our consternation once it is beyond doubt that the road leads to the abyss. We have a warning example in Lord Beveridge, who rightly sounds the alarm today when faced with the consequences of the British welfare state, but who, we can only hope, must have enough self-criticism to remember the outstanding part he himself played in the creation of that welfare state as an advocate of inflationary "overfull employment".
>
> Now we can see the problem quite clearly. If the welfare state can be compared to a powerful machine that has neither brakes nor reverse gear, but a vigorous forward movement, and if, at the same time, there can be no question of destroying that machine, the problem arises of how to control its power. If the welfare state has no built-in self-limiting capacity, then the necessary limits must be drawn from outside, lest it outgrow us and ultimately become the ruin of a free and prosperous society, not to speak of depriving man of the dignity of being responsible for himself.
>
> *(Röpke 1958, pp. 204–5)*

The most famous book devoted to the question of the interventionist runaway and its dangers is undoubtedly *The Road to Serfdom* written by Hayek between 1940 and 1943 and first published in March 1944.

Like Rougier a few years earlier, Hayek asserted that socialism and fascism are the two rival factions of collectivism, which endangered the freedom of the United Kingdom. For him, the fight against Germany was as much an ideological battle as it was a military one. Regarding the outcome of this battle, unlike Rougier, Hayek was pessimistic. He believed that English liberalism had gradually allowed itself to be contaminated by German ideology, which he judged to be imbued with socialism, to the point where planners would end up dominating British politics. "We have progressively abandoned that freedom in economic affairs without which personal and political freedom has never existed in the past", Hayek laments in the first chapter. "Although we had been warned by some of the greatest political thinkers of the nineteenth century, by de Tocqueville and Lord Acton, that socialism means slavery, we have steadily moved in the direction of socialism" (Hakek 1944, p. 13).

The whole point of Hayek is to demonstrate that there are two antinomic and incompatible models. The liberal model which is based on private initiative and organised within the framework of competitive markets and the model which, through central direction and organisation, intends to direct all economic activities by planning "according to some consciously constructed 'blueprint'" (*ibid.*, p. 37). However, despite the socialists' belief that the second model could improve the social situation and allow for a more just and efficient economy, Hayek intends to demonstrate that any economic system based on partial or total planning of the economy inevitably leads to tyranny.

First of all, such a planning process, because of the complexity of its implementation, would not be democratically manageable or controllable by an elected assembly: "it would become inevitable to delegate the task to the experts", Hayek writes (*ibid.*, p. 68). But "[t]he delegation of particular technical tasks to separate bodies, while a regular feature, is yet only the first step in the process whereby a democracy which embarks on planning progressively relinquishes its powers" (*ibid.*, p. 70). Moreover, such a governing authority, by controlling all economic resources, will inevitably come to control their use, which will undermine not only economic freedoms but also all political freedoms. "Economic control is not merely control of a sector of human life which can be separated from the rest; it is the control of the means for all our ends" (*ibid.*, p. 95).

Beyond the political question, there is also the problem of the efficiency of an economic system based on planning. Hayek believes that the competitive market is an indispensable and irreplaceable tool because it makes it possible to coordinate a multitude of individual plans. Indeed, it is

> the only method by which our activities can be adjusted to each other without the coercive or arbitrary intervention of authority. ... Any attempt to control prices or quantities of particular commodities deprives competition

of its power of bringing about effective co-ordination of individual efforts because price changes then cease to register all the relevant changes in circumstances and no longer provide a reliable guide for the individual's actions.

(ibid., pp. 37–8)

In other words, the mechanism by which all available information is conveyed to individual decision-makers is the price system. It is the price system that allows entrepreneurs to adjust their activities and adapt to the changes occurring in their environment. There is no need, therefore, for an overarching organisation that would coordinate everyone's actions. All that is needed is for everyone to follow their own interests. By adopting behaviour centred on their needs and knowledge, producers and consumers help transmit relevant information to the markets since changes in supply and demand are reflected in prices. These prices, in turn, trigger new economic behaviour and allow the economy to function smoothly. "The more complicated the whole, the more dependent we become on that division of knowledge between individuals whose separate efforts are co-ordinated by the impersonal mechanism for transmitting the relevant information known by us as the price system" *(ibid.,* p. 52).

This mechanism described by Hayek is, however, only a principle which presupposes a certain amount of state intervention in order to function. It is the responsibility of the state to "create the conditions in which competition will be as effective as possible", or "to supplement it where it cannot be made effective" *(ibid.* p. 40). The state may also provide certain public services, prohibit the use of toxic substances, limit working hours, or prescribe certain sanitary rules. Finally, it can provide a minimum monetary income for everyone and encourage the creation of a broad system of social services "so long as the organisation of these services is not designed in such a way as to make competition ineffective over wide fields", Hayek adds *(ibid.,* p. 39). What is important is that "government in all its actions is bound by rules fixed and announced beforehand – rules which make it possible to foresee with fair certainty how the authority will use its coercive powers in given circumstances, and to plan one's individual affairs on the basis of this knowledge" *(ibid.,* pp. 75–6). It is this principle of the "Rule of Law" that Hayek forcefully prescribes. For the law, he believes, can in no way alter the balances achieved in a system of competitive markets and, through discretionary intervention, benefit one to the detriment of the other. It is up to the public authorities to set "the rules of the game", but above all they must avoid intervening ex post, preventing individuals from sovereignly exploiting their own resources or from enjoying the fruit of their efforts.

It is in this sense that Hayek vigorously rejects a certain "dogmatic *laissez-faire*" that he holds partly responsible for the political decline of liberal ideas:

It is important not to confuse opposition against this kind of planning with a dogmatic laissez-faire attitude. The liberal argument is in favour of making the best possible use of the forces of competition as a means of co-ordinating human efforts, not an argument for leaving things just as they are. It is based on the conviction that where effective competition can be created, it is a better way of guiding individual efforts than any other. It does not deny, but even emphasises, that, in order that competition should work beneficially, a carefully thought-out legal framework is required, and that neither the existing nor the past legal rules are free from grave defects.

(ibid., p. 37)

In short, while it is important for the state to provide a framework for the proper functioning of economic activity, it is essential to avoid that such a framework could interfere in private affairs and distort the game through which markets spontaneously organise the coordination of economic behaviour. For Hayek, the real danger comes from the hubris of leaders who believe that it is possible to organise and direct the collective behaviour of a society according to their own values. In contrast to Lippmann, Hayek is wary of the power of experts and their ability to lead, direct, or even understand social change. Thus, he does not hesitate to guard against any attempt to create or transform the economic order that results from the action of the market:

It was men's submission to the impersonal forces of the market that in the past has made possible the growth of a civilisation which without this could not have developed; it is by thus submitting that we are every day helping to build something that is greater than anyone of us can fully comprehend. It does not matter whether men in the past did submit from beliefs which some now regard as superstitious: from a religious spirit of humility, or an exaggerated respect for the crude teachings of the early economists. The crucial point is that it is infinitely more difficult rationally to comprehend the necessity of submitting to forces whose operation we cannot follow in detail, than to do so out of the humble awe which religion, or even the respect for the doctrines of economics, did inspire.

(ibid., p. 210)

German ordoliberalism vs. American neoliberalism?

Hayek's book was intended as a tribute to freedom; it concludes with a curious ode to "submission". This paradox is, in a way, symmetrical to that of Jean-Jacques Rousseau who, as previously noted, intended to "force" individuals to be free. In Rousseau's view, the state must positively contribute to the freedom of individuals. For Hayek, on the contrary, individuals must deprive themselves of their ability to collectively run the economy. This position makes it possible to measure the philosophical gap between Hayek's vision and that of Adam Smith or John Stuart Mill. Hayek's concern is not the emancipation of individuals but the removal of government barriers to the free market system. Indeed, he would later continue to reinforce this line to the point of accusing some liberals of playing into the hands of socialism and even going back on some of the interventionist proposals he defended in *The Road to Serfdom*.[28]

Thus, rather than renewed liberalism, the Hayekian vision is more akin to a neo-Manchesterism. The main difference with the Manchester school is that Hayek does not believe in the existence of a transcendent natural order in the manner of physiocrats. Hayek's economic order is artificial and immanent in the sense that it emanates from the combination of individual interactions and behaviours brought about by the price system. This order is only possible within the framework of a fragile institutional equilibrium, which is the result of a legal system that needs to be adapted to technological transformations and possible social changes. The state must, therefore, be as a neutral protector as possible of this framework in which market interactions flourish, to be a referee rather than a passive and distant spectator.

This Hayekian vision is shared by all neoliberal authors. Indeed, neoliberalism tends to articulate the study of law and economics to achieve the political objective of instituting a free market society.

On this issue, it is worth mentioning the considerable influence of another school of thought which largely contributed to the legal thinking that made possible the establishment of a neoliberal order, namely the Freiburg school. Regrettably, the intellectuals developing this approach could not participate in the Lippmann Colloquium, even though they had their rightful place there. Two fierce opponents of the Hitler regime, the Germans Walter Eucken and Franz Böhm, were the two great figures of the University of Freiburg. However, they did not go into exile like Röpke and Rüstow. As a result, political circumstances prevented them from taking part in the conference held in France on the subject of liberalism. Nevertheless, this absence from the conference that was supposed to be the founding moment of neoliberalism is sometimes the pretext for trivial disputes about the differences between the ordoliberalism of the Freiburg school and the neoliberalism that emerged from the Lippmann Colloquium and the Mont Pelerin Society. This opposition appears all the more meaningless as Eucken, along with Hayek, Röpke, and Friedman, participated in the 1947 meeting that founded the Mont Pelerin Society. As for Franz Böhm, he too became actively involved in the work of the Society from 1949 onwards.

The fact that the Freiburg School was officially founded in 1936, two years before the Lippmann Colloquium, is also not a sufficient reason to justify an ordoliberal singularity. As stated above, the Paris event is by no means a founding moment. Rather, it was the receptacle for a thought that had already been widespread among many intellectuals and economists, including in Germany. Another specificity of the Freiburg school is that it is part of an academic debate that is essentially German since it aims to respond to the theses of German historicism, a philosophical current that defends the principle of a historical and contextualised construction of values and major social theories. "Romanticism and the school of historicism have destroyed the belief in a natural system in both law and political economy", the authors of the 1936 manifesto state (Böhm *et al.* 1936, p. 16). Historicist theory, they wrote, had propagated "relativism" and "fatalism", and to counter that doctrine, they intended to re-found the legal and economic sciences from scratch.

Among the crucial questions that the Freiburg school intends to answer is that of cartels and monopolies. The authors of the Ordo Manifesto were concerned about the growth in number and influence of monopolistic firms in Germany since the end of the 19th century and the fact that this tendency to monopolise the economy had never been seriously taken into account. Yet "the overall system of the economy is destroyed by the formation of monopolies", they believe (*ibid.* p. 21). To respond to these challenges, the authors wish to show that it is possible to elaborate a theoretical framework based on historical experience that combines creativity and reason: "we wish to bring scientific reasoning as displayed in jurisprudence and political economy, into effect for the purpose of constructing and reorganising the economic system" (*ibid.*, p. 23). In particular, they suggest that the economic system should be seen as a whole in which each individual unit participates and that the way political power influences and structures it should be treated more seriously. To carry out this task, the authors suggest that research on the functioning of markets and competition should be undertaken and that collaboration between the legal and economic disciplines should be pursued.

The 1936 Manifesto appears both as a research programme aimed at a better understanding of economic dynamics and, very clearly, as a normative project proposing a general restructuring of the German economy. With peace restored and Nazism defeated, Freiburg academics gained considerable influence and actively participated in the establishment of a new liberal economic order. This influence led them to broaden their approach significantly. In 1948, the academic journal ORDO was founded. It brought together the bulk of their work. In the preface to the inaugural issue, Walter Eucken explains the principles on which ordoliberalism is based:

> More or less government activity? The question misses the point. We are not dealing with a problem of quantity, but of quality. The state should neither try to control the economic process nor leave the economy to itself: state governance of institutional forms – Yes; government planning and steering of economic processes – No.
>
> To recognize the difference between form and process and to act accordingly is essential. This is the only way to achieve the goal that not a tiny minority, but all citizens can shape the economy through the price mechanism. The only economic order in which this is possible is that of "complete competition".
>
> It can only be achieved if all market participants are denied the opportunity to change the rules of the market. The state must, through an

appropriate legal framework, shape the market – this means to specify the rules of the game in which business is conducted.

(Eucken 1948a)

In the article he writes in the same journal issue, he returns to the nature of the control that the state must exercise. "Control of the economic system is vital" (Eucken 1948b, p. 37), he argues and criticises the naive vision of 19th-century classical economists who were inclined to let things happen, reducing the economy to a "'natural' order in which competitive prices automatically control the whole process" (*ibid.*, p. 38). This view, Eucken argues, was based on overconfidence in economic processes.

His colleague, the economist and lawyer, Franz Böhm, also acknowledges the important role of the state in structuring markets. Not only must the state take "the measures of a legislative or administrative nature which aim at influencing the market form, that is, creating favourable conditions for the emergence of effective competition", but it also must ensure "the provision for a stable currency, which is indeed of central importance because price stability determines the aptitude of market prices to guide the production process in an economically correct way and to secure prices against speculative disturbances" (Böhm 1966, p. 56).

The maintenance of a competitive regime and that of price stability appear to be the two great obsessions of German ordoliberals. But they are far from being the only ones to insist on these points. This is, in fact, the case for all neoliberal schools, including American neoliberalism.

The neoliberalism of the Chicago school has sometimes been contrasted with that of the German school.[29] And, indeed, they often differ in the economic policy measures they advocate and in some of their conceptions. However, to insist on these differences is to forget that neoliberalism is not a theory but a set of major principles and values relating to the functioning and regulation of the market economy. They may unite different schools of thought. In fact, there are a number of elements that make it possible to establish proximity between the Chicago and Freiburg schools.

The book *Capitalism and Freedom* published in 1962 by Milton Friedman synthesises quite well the main ideas defended by the Chicago school. Although published nearly twenty years after *The Road to Serfdom*, Friedman borrowed many of Hayek's ideas and cited him on numerous occasions. Like Hayek, he believed that planification and the market economy were fundamentally incompatible and that even simple technical measures such as exchange controls could transform the US economy into a system of planned economics.[30] Friedman, as well as Hayek, praised economic freedom as the indispensable condition for political freedoms.[31]

Like other neoliberal schools, Friedman puts the question of competition at the heart of his concerns, to the point of writing in the introduction that the main theme of his book is "the role of competitive capitalism ... as a system of economic freedom and a necessary condition for political freedom" (Friedman 1962, p. 4). Similarly, he argues that such competition requires a legal framework and state intervention, the role of which he defines as follows: "to preserve law and order, to enforce private contracts, to foster competitive markets" (*ibid.*, p. 2). In addition to this major function, government sometimes helps to do collectively what is difficult or costly to do separately. It is also the state's responsibility to manage "neighbourhood effects" such as pollution when it affects the well-being of others. For this reason,

> [t]he existence of a free market does not of course eliminate the need for government. On the contrary, government is essential both as a forum for determining the "rules of the game" and as an umpire to interpret and enforce the rules decided on.
>
> *(ibid., p. 15)*

Thus, as he explicitly states: "The consistent liberal is not an anarchist" (*ibid.*, p. 34).

Although it undoubtedly belongs to the vast field of neoliberal doctrines, the economic approach of the Chicago school is marked by some specificities that set it apart. The first one is that, unlike other schools, it appears much less sensitive to the question of disciplinary openness. Chicago economists are first and foremost economists and when they take an interest in other disciplines, such as sociology in the case of Gary Becker, they do so on the basis of the concepts and methods of the neoclassical approach, the theory that has dominated economics since the 1950s. This specificity explains the great influence the Chicago school had in the academic field compared to that acquired by other neoliberal approaches.

Another specificity of the Chicago School is to assume a methodology based on the principle of unrealistic hypotheses. In a 1953 book devoted to the scientific method applied to economics, Friedman asserts that economic modelling does not have to be based on realistic hypotheses but on hypotheses and models that are reasonably simple and relevant enough to produce fruitful results (Friedman 1953). In doing so, he intended to reaffirm the principle of perfect competition in response to proponents of imperfect competition theories, such as British economist Joan Robinson who criticised the standard model's lack of realism (Robinson 1933). Friedman considered this criticism unfounded since no model can, by definition, strictly represent the complexity of reality.

In the same spirit, the Chicago School is attached to a simplified model of human behaviour, the *homo œconomicus* model, which considers economic agents to be strictly calculators and optimisers. It is understood by these economists that this model represents a fiction, not a reality. Nevertheless, this fiction is necessary for the abstract and model-based approach of this school.

These methodological divergences between the different neoliberal approaches are obviously crucial from an academic point of view. But for the question that concerns this chapter, namely the definition of neoliberalism, it is relatively secondary. Indeed, in our analysis, neoliberalism is not an economic theory but a political doctrine. Political struggles can be shared without adopting the same scientific approach. Moreover, there is no overlap between neoclassical economic theory (which will be discussed in the next chapter) and the neoliberal system. While the former can feed the latter by contributing arguments to it, it is also possible to develop a scientific approach based on neoclassical theory while fighting neoliberalism. Similarly, the Austrian school fights the neoclassical school scientifically but joins the economists of the Chicago school in most of their political struggles.

Elements of the neoliberal system

In his series of lectures on biopolitics given at the Collège de France in early 1979, Michel Foucault attempted to define the essence of neoliberalism as follows:

> [H]ow was the market defined in eighteenth century liberalism, or rather on what basis was it described? ... The model and principle of the market was exchange, and the freedom of the market, the non-intervention of a third party, of any authority whatsoever, and a fortiori of state authority, was of course applied so that the market was valid and equivalence really was equivalence. The most that was asked of the state was that it supervise the smooth running of the market, that is to say, that it ensure respect for the freedom of those involved in exchange. ... Now for the neo-liberals, the most important thing about the market is not exchange ... it is competition ... that is to say, not equivalence but on the contrary inequality. ...
>
> This is where the ordoliberals break with the tradition of eighteenth and nineteenth century liberalism. They say: ... when you deduce the principle of laissez-faire from the market economy, basically you are still in the grip of what could be called a "naive naturalism". ... Competition is an essence ...; it has its own structure. Its effects are only produced if this logic is respected. It is, as it were, a formal game between inequalities; it is not a natural game between individuals and behaviors. ... It can only be the result of lengthy efforts and, in truth, pure competition is never attained. Pure competition must and can only be an objective, an objective thus presupposing an indefinitely active policy. Competition is therefore an historical objective of governmental art and not a natural given that must be respected.
>
> *(Foucault 2008, pp. 118–20)*

Reading and listening to Foucault, the vision of the market in economic thinking had gradually been transformed. Initially a place of exchange for Adam Smith, it became a theatre of competition at the end of the 19th century. This changeover was the occasion of rupture that only the neoliberals were able to take into account, namely the idea that competition was a matter of social structure and not of individual behaviour. In this sense, it requires vigorous state action not only to protect it but also to strengthen it and activate its fundamental characteristics. This vision profoundly changes the economic role of the state. It no longer has to simply govern alongside the market but must now "govern for the market" (*ibid.* p. 121).

The emphasis on the principle of competition to the detriment of the principle of exchange also changes how public action is represented. Laissez-faire means tolerance: in other words, we are not concerned with the result but only with the method. Laissez-faire means allowing the economic society to organise itself according to its own logic. By contrast, if the aim is to implement a system of competition, then the question of efficiency necessarily arises. This is the problem that most neoliberal authors address: to answer the question of how to regulate competition in such a way that it leads to the most efficient behaviour possible.

Thus, by taking responsibility for establishing a competitive system, the law itself becomes an economic object. This is what marks, according to jurist Alain Supiot, the transition from government to governance. Governance does not seek to establish the right law according to transcendent or moral criteria which are external to the economy. Instead, it tries to "program" individuals to behave in an economic and thus efficient way, following the incentives produced by the market price system. In moving from government to governance, Supiot argues, we pursue a "cybernetic imaginary" based no longer on the calculations of the ideal state but on perpetual and continuous social adaptation: "People are no longer expected to act freely within the limits laid down by the law, but to react in real time to the multiple signals they receive, in order to meet the targets they are assigned" (Supiot 2017, p. 10).

Foucault's analysis of neoliberalism, however, is incomplete. It lacks the most important difference between liberalism and neoliberalism which is that the market, for neoliberals, is not only a place for individual performance stimulated by competition but also, and above all, *the place where prices are created*. It is the mechanism of prices that constitutes the real ordering of collective behaviour because it is understood that, programmed by competition and driven by the search for their own interest, economic agents will systematically respond to price signals to build a new economic equilibrium. Competition is therefore not simply a desirable state in itself; it is also a means of establishing fair prices that will coordinate the actions of all.

In contrast, among classical economists, the market is not the place where prices are determined, since value find its source in labour, that is to say in the cost of production. From the end of the 19th century, economists modified their theory of value in favour of more subjective value which would be the product of emerging market forces. The problem is that flaws in competition mean that some markets are, in fact, under the control of a few producers, distorting the price creation mechanism. It is therefore crucial to re-establish and enforce competition, to not only generate individual performance but most of all to guarantee the performance of the price system and hence of the economy as a whole.

It is therefore difficult to totally agree with Foucault when he states that the neoliberal approach seeks "not a society subject to the commodity-effect, but a society subject to the dynamic of competition. Not a supermarket society, but an enterprise society. The *homo oeconomicus* sought after is not the man of exchange or man the consumer; he is the man of enterprise and production" (Foucault 2008, p. 147).

It is true that the concept of "human capital", as Foucault rightly points out, does exist within the Chicago school. The idea of the "corporate-man" is also developed very far by Friedman. He proposes (based on the work of Gary Becker) that, in order to finance students' higher education and solve the problem of "underinvestment" in their education, they could, like limited companies, issue and sell shares that would be worth to their beneficiaries some of the income resulting from the additional earnings obtained during their working life. But while he sees no legal impediment to the establishment of such contracts, Friedman notes that they would be extremely difficult to implement and admits they would be the equivalent to a form of "partial slavery" (Friedman 1962, p. 103).

In sum, even if one may find the idea amusing, the corporate-man is only a marginal element of a specific approach and not a fundamental characteristic by which neoliberal thought can be defined. Moreover, it would be hard to find such a conception of human beings in the texts of Röpke, Eucken or Böhm, or even Lippmann and Rougier. Lastly, neoliberalism is worth less in theory than in implementation. And as far as public policies are concerned, the idea of valuing and supporting the entrepreneurial dynamic of the individual within oneself remains marginal, although it can obviously exist in a fringe of the population.[37]

To sum up, what are the main principles underlying the neoliberal system as a doctrine of public action?

In the first place, neoliberalism assumes that the economic performance of society is based on the establishment of *an efficient price system*. Indeed, it is this price system that makes it possible to create adequate incentives by which economic agents coordinate themselves. It is the markets that create prices. That is why it is absolutely essential that markets are kept efficient. Unlike classical liberals, neoliberals do not believe that this performance can emerge spontaneously from a state of nature. The government must therefore intervene to create the right social environment for market performance.

This adequate environment rests on four pillars.

First, there are the external pillars of trade policy and money. Trade policy must be based on the principle of *free trade*. By expanding the size of the market, free trade is an indispensable tool to prevent the concentration of economic (and political) power of large companies and of the state. Moreover, as Hayek (1939) points out, regional or global economic integration limits the powers of individual states by allowing agents to compete with domestic standards and regulations.[33] The free movement of people, goods, and capital is the best defence against excessive taxation or intrusive regulations.

Money is the second pillar required for the performance of markets in their price-creating function. Not only is stable currency (i.e. without inflation or deflation) essential to enable prices to induce appropriate behaviour, but it is also indispensable for external trade. There can be no foreign trade or capital flows if a country's currency does not inspire confidence in its potential partners. While all neoliberal authors adhere to this objective of *monetary stability*, they differ on how to achieve it. On the ordoliberal side, monetary stability must be achieved through the existence of a central bank independent from political power and focused on its monetary mission. For Friedman, monetary stability must be achieved through a clear and pre-established rule on the growth of the money supply. According to Hayek, money must be kept out of the control of any public authority and its creation must be entrusted entirely to the private banking system. Finally, other neoliberals believe that only the restoration of a true gold standard would guarantee monetary stability. As we can see, while the objective is the same, the means of achieving it are different.

These two external pillars must be complemented by two internal market pillars. The first of these is the establishment of an *efficient competition regime*. This is probably one of the most sensitive issues, and, not surprisingly, the solutions put forward vary greatly. The ordoliberals favour the establishment of an independent authority to ensure competitive equilibrium, an idea rejected by the Austrians and the economists of the Chicago school. For Friedman, most natural monopolies can be left to the private sector and unregulated. As a general rule, technological developments and fear of the entry of a competitor are sufficient either to limit the duration of the monopoly or limit the amount of rent the monopolist is likely to obtain. However, Friedman and Hayek do not oppose the legal prohibition of monopolistic practices that could seriously hamper the proper functioning of markets. Similarly, the state can induce the creation of competitive markets that would increase the performance of a service. This is the idea defended by Friedman and Hayek when they propose to fully privatise the education system and provide families with education vouchers that give them the right to choose the school (Larcheret 2020).

The second domestic pillar of state action is that of *social order*. For neoliberals, the maintenance of social order is not simply a matter of security. It is not just a question of guaranteeing property rights and protecting the nation from external dangers. It is also, and especially, about maintaining social peace. This may involve certain social concessions, the recognition of the right to organise, or any other measure that makes it possible to avoid the profound disruption of the economic order. This is what the deliberately ambiguous term "social market economy", used by ordoliberals, attempts to define. What is meant by this phrase is that the economic order must be concerned with the social order and that social concessions are allowed only if they do not disrupt the proper functioning of markets. If social rights make it possible to improve the social dialogue in companies and avoid strikes, then it is probably worth implementing them. If, however, they distort the price system too deeply and, for example, no longer allow wages to be adjusted to the situation on the labour market, then they should be banned. To preserve social order, Friedman and Hayek offer the solution to allocate a monetary income to the poorest households that does not disrupt their incentives to work. This is the principle of the negative income tax. Other authors are now advocating the idea of a universal basic income. From a neoliberal point of view, the advantage of paying income in money rather than as a public service is that it is perfectly compatible with the market order and implies minimal state intervention (Friedman and Friedman (1980), chap. 4).

Thus, for markets to succeed in bringing about a relevant price system that is likely to guide individual behaviour effectively, they must rest on those four pillars; an efficient competition regime, a preserved social order, a stable currency, and a trade policy based on free trade, the free movement of capital, and, if possible, the free movement of persons and workers.

The problem is that these four pillars may sometimes require public intervention in one way or another. A neoliberal theory of the state is therefore needed. This theory assumes that public action takes place at two levels: a fundamental level and a superficial level. The fundamental level is part of the legal architecture. It must be based on the principle of the *rule of law* which presupposes that the limits of the law are very precisely determined. Similarly, the executive and legislative powers must be governed by an independent justice system in the case of the former, and by a constitutional text, or even international treaties, in the case of the latter. Many neoliberal authors, including Milton Friedman, also believe that the current systems of protection of the market economy are insufficient and that the constitutional texts should be enriched with norms and principles to protect the market economy. In the final part of their book *Free to Choose*, Friedman and his wife Rose argue for a series of amendments to the US Constitution, including the addition or modification of a number of amendments to impose free trade, prohibit price controls, ensure proportionality of taxation, and preserve the value of money. Other authors, including James M. Buchanan,[34] have defended the principle of a constitutional ban on public deficits (Buchanan 1997).

Beyond the question of the legal system and the rule of law, there is also the problem of concrete action by governments and public administrations. The central issue is that such action must be predictable and, as far as possible, determined by a set of rules decided upon beforehand. In other words, the state must *avoid any discretionary intervention* that would likely disrupt the plans of economic agents and thus market balances. Taxation should be as neutral as possible and ideally avoid both multiple exemptions and progressivity.[35] In the same spirit, the state should have a balanced budget to prevent disrupting the function of financial markets and raising the cost of capital for private agents. However, according to the same logic, it is possible to play the role of the insurer in the event of an external shock. Thus, from a neoliberal point of view, it is not illogical that states came to the rescue of household and corporate incomes at the time of the COVID-19 pandemic. In doing so, they did more to save the market order than to destabilise it.[36]

Figure 2.1 illustrates the main principles on which the neoliberal system is based. It can be represented as a temple dedicated to the great economists who collectively built this inspiring work.

Before concluding this chapter, the question raised in the introduction should be answered. Do we find, in the functioning of the European Union, the four pillars and the base of the temple illustrated below. We can only answer in the affirmative. The principles of monetary stability, free trade, free competition, and even the social market economy are indeed parts of the architecture of the European treaties. The restrictions on public deficits and the principles of the rule of law are also included. Finally, the neoliberal order has even been extended recently since the European Budget Pact of 2012 requires member states to enshrine the "golden rule" (which forbids structural public deficits) in their constitutional law (Adams et al. 2014). Similarly, in terms of social policy, the European Union clearly favours measures that are least disruptive to the markets. For example, European recommendations on employment policy are most often based on the principle of flexicurity. This involves providing generous unemployment benefits to those who lose their jobs, such as effective training and reintegration schemes (often provided by the private sector) while allowing for greater flexibility in

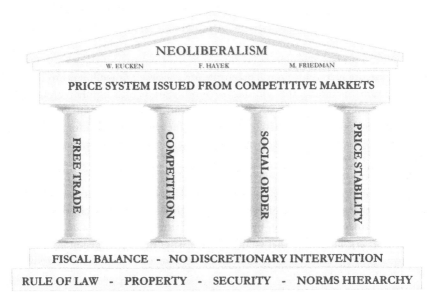

FIGURE 2.1 The temple of neoliberalism.

employment contracts. The state, in short, financially insures the risk of unemployment in exchange for greater contractual flexibility for employers.

Notes

1 The influence of the Mont Pelerin Society and the Chicago School can be measured by the number of Nobel Prizes in economics that have been awarded to their members. At the height of this influence, between 1974 and 1995, seven members of the Mont Pelerin Society and eight economists from the University of Chicago were awarded the Nobel Prize. Four Laureates belong to both institutions: Milton Friedman, George Stigler, Ronald Coase, and Gary Becker. A total of 39 percent of the Nobel Prizes in economics awarded during this period were given to members of one or the other of these institutions. It should be noted that from the mid-1990s onwards, their influence declined. Between 1996 and 2020, only one member of the Mont Pelerin Society was awarded the Nobel Prize in Economics and five members of the Department of Economics at the University of Chicago received it, representing 12.5% of the total number of awards.
2 David Stuckler and Sanjay Basu (2013) estimate that in addition to the economic disaster caused by austerity, the shock therapy of the transition period resulted in the death (by suicide, alcoholism, heart attack, etc.) of about 10 million people in Russia.
3 To ensure that the behaviour of the government will be as expected, it has often been decided to open up the capital of competing public companies to a few private shareholders so that their demand for profitability and the evolution of the share price on markets will induce the public authority to seek the maximum return.
4 Article 206 of the Treaty on the Functioning of the European Union (TFEU) states: "By establishing a customs union in accordance with Articles 28 to 32, the Union shall contribute, in the common interest, to the harmonious development of world trade, the progressive abolition of restrictions on international trade and on foreign direct investment, and the lowering of customs and other barriers." Similarly, according to Article 63, section 1: "Within the framework of the provisions set out in this Chapter, all restrictions on the movement of capital between Member States and between Member States and third countries shall be prohibited."
5 Joseph Schumpeter (1954), *History of Economic Analysis*, New York: Oxford University Press, p. 394.
6 At the beginning of the 1960s, the Mont Pelerin Society experienced a deep crisis between the Swiss and German branch on the one hand, which was in favour of "neo-liberalism", and the Austrian and American branch on the other, which wanted to revive the tradition of 19th-century liberalism. In reality, as will be shown later on, the two schools do not differ on the main principles (Audier 2012b, pp. 199–411).
7 "A government which maintained law and order, defined property rights, served as a means whereby we could modify property rights and other rules of the economic game, adjudicated disputes about the interpretation of the rules, enforced contracts, promoted competition, provided a monetary framework, engaged in activities to counter technical monopolies and to overcome neighborhood effects widely regarded as sufficiently important to justify government intervention, and which supplemented private charity and the private family in protecting the irresponsible, whether madman or child – such a government would clearly have important functions to perform. The consistent liberal is not an anarchist" (Friedman 1962, p. 34).
8 Symptomatically, Mankiw puts in the mouth of the Scottish economist a conception of economics similar to that of Hayek and Friedman, as we shall see later.
9 "Such interpretations usually treat the metaphor as a symbol for either the supposed harmonious operation of 'the market', or the spontaneous convergence of private interests, and most often both at once. They regularly appear in economic journalism, textbooks, high school and university teaching, and even in academic

papers, without anyone bothering to go back to the original text. Actually reading Smith's writings no longer seems to be considered necessary." (Dellemotte 2009, pp. 28–29).

10 Book I of the Wealth of Nations concludes with this strong warning: "The interest of the dealers, however, in any particular branch of trade or manufactures, is always in some respects different from, and even opposite to, that of the public. ... The proposal of any new law or regulation of commerce which comes from this order ought always to be listened to with great precaution, and ought never to be adopted till after having been long and carefully examined, not only with the most scrupulous, but with the most suspicious attention. It comes from an order of men whose interest is never exactly the same with that of the public, who have generally an interest to deceive and even to oppress the public, and who accordingly have, upon many occasions, both deceived and oppressed it" (Smith 1776, p. 200).

11 In the opening lines of Chapter 4, Mill writes: "Though society is not founded on a contract, and though no good purpose is answered by inventing a contract in order to deduce social obligations from it, every one who receives the protection of society owes a return for the benefit, and the fact of living in society renders it indispensable that each should be bound to observe a certain line of conduct towards the rest" (*ibid.*, p. 139).

12 It is worth noting that this passage was removed in subsequent editions.

13 Malthus and Ricardo are particularly critical of the English Poor Law. Established in 1601 during the reign of Elizabeth the First, this law obliged parishes to assist the poor. It provided for an obligation to work, but in reality this counterpart was rarely demanded. The criticisms of Malthus and Ricardo led to the 1834 reform, which prohibited the principle of domestic assistance. In order to benefit from such assistance, the indigent had to leave their homes and settle in a "workhouse" in which discipline was extremely strict, and living and working conditions abysmal. The workhouse system lasted de jure until 1930 and de facto a few more years after the World War II.

14 The Factory Act of 1833 is considered to be the first social welfare law. It prohibited children under 9 years of age from working in factories and imposed a maximum working week of 48 hours (six 8-hour days) for those between the age of 9 and 13. Children under 13 must have received a basic education of at least two hours a day. The 1844 Act imposed a maximum working day of 12 hours for women and adolescents aged 13–18. The work of children under 11 was not prohibited until 1893.

15 Trust are associations of companies created to generate a monopolistic situation in specific industries by getting around states' legislations.

16 *Official U. S. Bulletin*, 10 mai 1917, vol. 1. p. 4.

17 The issue of gold sterilisation was raised by Jacques Rueff during the Lippmann Colloquium of 1938. Rueff deplored monetary interventionism and, in particular, the gold sterilisation measures taken by France to remove part of its gold stock from monetary quantification to avoid losing it because of trade imbalances (Audier 2012a p. 460).

18 For a detailed analysis of the personalities presented at the colloquium, see Audier (2012a, pp. 139–260).

19 Hayek denied this influence for a while, but there's no doubt about it, according to Audier, who claims that "for a long, very long time, Hayek overlooked the importance of the Lippmann Colloquium and the contribution of Rougier and Lippmann. ... There is something very astonishing and, to say the least, abnormal in this incomplete reconstruction of the past. This is evidenced by the fact that Hayek himself insisted, but only in a second, later version of his article, on mentioning the Colloquium in a note, not without having made his *mea culpa*." Audier (2012a), *op. cit.*, pp. 378–9.

20 For a deeper analysis of this book and its 1949 second edition, see Nadeau (2007).

21 "No one who really believes in the principle of a free market as the regulator of the economy can, I think, fail to see that the limited liability corporation must be

deprived of the right to retain profits and invest them, not according to the judgment of the market but at the discretion of the managers. For the retention of the profits immobilizes capital, whereas the economy of the division of labor requires that capital shall move readily to the places and to the men who make the highest bids for it" (Lippmann 1937, p. 226).

22 Lippmann is rather evasive on how companies should be supported. He writes: "It is not only the industrial workers, however, who suffer from industrial progress. All producers are subject in some degree to the same risk when new processes are invented, when more efficient competitors arise, or when tastes change. To be sure, they cannot all be insured and indemnified out of the public treasury. But their losses can be reduced. How that is to be done is a problem of great complexity which I would not pretend to be able to solve" (Lippmann 1937, p. 224).

23 On this subject, see: Stiegler 2019, pp. 76–77.

24 The Road to Serfdom (1944), *op. cit.*, p. 28; *The Constitution of Liberty* (2011) [1960], *op. cit.*, pp. 182-183 (note); *Law, Legislation and Liberty*, Routledge, (1982), p. 179 (note) and p. 182 (header of book II).

25 It is worth noting that an English edition of the act of the Lippmann Colloquium has been recently released (Reinhoudt and Audier 2018). All quotations beyond, however, refer to the original French edition and has been translated from French by the author.

26 "Officials can, for example, regulate the traffic on the roads: they can see to it that the ruthless and the reckless do not interfere with the other drivers. ... But if, instead of defining the rights of all the drivers, the officials seek to prescribe the destination of each driver, telling him when he must start, by what route he must go, and when he must arrive, some few, those who have the ear of the authorities, will undoubtedly go just where they want to go, more swiftly, more pleasantly, than under a free system of equal rights. But the rest will be going where they do not wish to go, and it must become their ambition to oust the existing traffic officers and install officers who will direct the traffic to their advantage" (Lippmann 1937, p. 283).

27 It is notable that Milton Friedman also quotes *The Good Society* in *Free to Choose*, (Friedman and Friedman 1980, chap. 6).

28 In the preface to the 1976 edition, Hayek writes: "When I wrote the book, ... I rather under-stressed the significance of the experience of communism in Russia ... I had not wholly freed myself from all the current interventionist superstitions, and in consequence still made various concessions which I now think unwarranted."

29 Serge Audier looks in detail at the opposition between the Swiss and German schools, on the one hand, and the Austrian and American schools, on the other. It structured the debates of the Mont Pelerin Society and led to the schism of 1962 when about twenty members, including its president Wilhelm Röpke and its secretary Albert Hunold, left the organisation with a bang (Audier 2012b, pp. 336–41).

30 "Interferences with international trade appear innocuous; they can get the support of people who are otherwise apprehensive of interference by government into economic affairs; many a business man even regards them as part of the "American Way of Life"; yet there are few interferences which are capable of spreading so far and ultimately being so destructive of free enterprise. There is much experience to suggest that the most effective way to convert a market economy into an authoritarian economic society is to start by imposing direct controls on foreign exchange" (Friedman 1962, p. 57).

31 In the 2002 preface he writes: "in accordance with the theme of this book, increases in economic freedom have gone hand in hand with increases in political and civil freedom and have led to increased prosperity; competitive capitalism and freedom have been inseparable" (Friedman 1962, preface).

32 The idea of some ultra-liberal thinkers to consider themselves as productive capital, or even the way some people monetarily value their influence on social networks, may well be a form of realisation of the concept of the corporate-man. But it should

be stressed that these initiatives are not the result of a public policy conceived as such.

33 See Chapter 1 for an in-depth analysis.

34 Although Buchanan defended his thesis at the University of Chicago and is heavily influenced by that school (as well as the Austrian school), he is not considered to be a member of the Chicago school but the founder of public choice theory and the Virginia School of Political Economy.

35 It should be noted that this issue is a matter of debate since Walter Lippmann, as we have seen, defends a highly progressive tax system. Similarly, some neoliberals, such as Alexander Rüstow, are in favour of a high inheritance tax in the name of equal opportunities.

36 Interestingly, in 2000, Friedman was positive about the stimulus policies of the New Deal: "You have to distinguish between two classes of New Deal policies. One class of New Deal policies was reform: wage and price control, the Blue Eagle, the national industrial recovery movement. I did not support those. The other part of the new deal policy was relief and recovery... providing relief for the unemployed, providing jobs for the unemployed, and motivating the economy to expand... an expansive monetary policy. Those parts of the New Deal I did support. [INTERVIEWER: But why did you support those?] Because it was a very exceptional circumstance. We'd gotten into an extraordinarily difficult situation, unprecedented in the nation's history. You had millions of people out of work. Something had to be done; it was intolerable." The full interview on public television PBS is available on: https://www.pbs.org/wgbh/commandingheigh ts/shared/minitext/int_miltonfriedman.html.

References

Adams, Maurice, Federico Fabbrini and Pierre Larouche (2014), *The Constitutionalization of European Budgetary Constraints*, London: Bloomsbury Publishing.

Audier, Serge (2012a), *Le colloque Lippmann : Aux origines du 'néo-libéralisme', précédé de Penser le 'néo-libéralisme'*, Lormont: Le Bord de l'eau.

Audier, Serge (2012b), *Néo-liberalisme(s). Une archéologie intellectuelle*, Paris: Grasset, coll. 'Mondes vécus'.

Bernays, Edward L. (1923), *Crystallizing Public Opinion*, New York: Liveright Publishing Corporation.

Bernays, Edward L. (1928), *Propaganda*, New York: Liveright Publishing Corporation.

Böhm, Franz (1966), "Rule of law in a market economy", in A. Peacock and H. Willgerodt (eds.), (1989), *Germany's Social Market Economy: Origins and Evolution*, London: Palgrave Macmillan.

Böhm, Franz, Walter Eucken and Hans Grossmann-Doerth (1936), "The Ordo Manifesto of 1936", in A. Peacock and H. Willgerodt (eds.), (1989), *Germany's Social Market Economy: Origins and Evolution*, London: Palgrave Macmillan.

Buchanan, James M. (1997), "The balanced budget amendment: Clarifying the arguments", *Public Choice*, 90: 117–138. doi:10.1023/A:1004969320944.

Condorcet, Nicolas de (1795) [1796], *Sketch for a Historical Picture of the Progress of the Human Mind*, Philadelphia: M. Carey.

Dellemotte, Jean (2009), "Adam Smith's 'Invisible Hand': Refuting the conventional wisdom", *L'Économie politique*, 44(4): 28–41. doi:10.3917/leco.044.0028.

Dellemotte, Jean and Benoît Walraevens (2013), "Adam Smith on the subordination of wage-earners in the commercial society", *The European Journal of the History of Economic Thought*, 22(4): 692–727. doi:10.1080/09672567.2013.792375.

Eucken, Walter (1948a), preface to the first issue of the ORDO revue.

Eucken, Walter (1948b), "What Kind of Economic and Social System?", in A. Peacock and H. Willgerodt (eds.), (1989), *Germany's Social Market Economy: Origins and Evolution*, London: Palgrave Macmillan.

Foucault, Michel (2008), *The Birth of Biopolitics: lectures at the Collège de France*, London: Palgrave Malmillan.

Friedman, Milton (1953) [1966], *Essays in Positive Economics*, Chicago, IL: The University of Chicago Press.

Friedman, Milton (1962) [2002], *Capitalism and Freedom*, Chicago, IL: The University of Chicago Press.

Friedman, Milton and Rose Friedman (1980) [1990], *Free to Choose, A Personal Statement*, Sans Diego: Harcourt.

Gauchet, Marcel (2004), "Le socialisme en redefinition", *Le Débat, Gallimard*, 131(4): 87–94. doi:10.3917/deba.131.0087.

Gide, André (1936) [2011], *Return from the U.S.S.R.*, Redditch, UK: Read Books Ltd .

Godwin, William (1793) [2009], *Enquiry Concerning Political Justice, and its Influence on General Virtue and Happiness*, Moscow: Dodo Press.

Hayek, Frierich (1939), "The Economic Conditions of Interstate Federalism", *New Commonwealth Quarterly*, 5(2): 131–149.

Hayek, Friedrich (1940), "Socialist Calculation: The Competitive 'Solution", *Economica, New Series*, 7(26): 125–149.

Hayek, Friedrich (1944) [2001], *The Road to Serfdom*, London: Routledge.

Hayek, Friedrich (1948) [1996], "Individualism: *True and False*", in Hayek, Friedrich (ed.), *Individualism and Economic Order*, Chicago, IL: The University of Chicago Press.

Hayek, Friedrich (1960) [2011], *The Constitution of Liberty, The Definitive Edition*, Chicago, IL: The University of Chicago Press.

Hayek, Friedrich (1982), *Law, Legislation and Liberty*, London: Routledge.

Keynes, John M. (1919), *The Economic Consequences of the Peace*, London: Macmillan & Co., Limited.

Krugman, Paul (2007), *The Conscience of a Liberal*, New York: W. W. Norton & Company.

Lacheret, Arnaud (2020), "The spreading of vouchers among French Local Governments: when private companies reshape the meaning of a tool", *International Review of Public Policies*, 2(2): forthcoming.

Lippmann, Walter (1922) [1991], *Public Opinion*, New Brunswick, NJ: Transaction Publishers

Lippmann, Walter (1925) [1993], *The Phantom Public*, New Brunswick, NJ: Transaction Publishers.

Lippmann, Walter (1937), *The Good Society*, Boston, MA: Little, Brown and Company.

Locke, John (1689) [1997], *An Essay Concerning Human Understanding*, London: Penguin Classics.

Malthus, Thomas (1803), *Essay on the Principle of Population, Second Edition*, London: J. Johnson.

Mankiw, Gregory (2017), *Principles of Economics, Eighth Edition*, Boston, MA: Cengage Learning.

Mason, Amelia Gere (1891) [2010], *The Women of the French Salons*, Charleston, SC: Nabu Press.

McNulty, Paul J. (1973) "Adam Smith's Concept of Labor", *Journal of the History of Ideas*, 34(3): 345–366. doi:10.2307/2708957.

Mill, John Stuart (1848) [1885], *Principles Of Political Economy*, Project Gutenberg Edition, pp. 593–594.

Mill, John Stuart (1859) [2003], *On Liberty*, New Haven, CT: Yale University Press.

Mises, Ludwig von (1922) [1951], *Socialism: An Economic and Sociological Analysis*, New Haven, CT: Yale University Press.

Montesquieu, Charles de (1758) [1989], *The Spirit of the Laws*, Cambridge: Cambridge University Press.

Nadeau, Robert (2007), "Le conflit des libéralismes : Rougier versus Hayek", *Philosophia Scientiæ*, CS 7: 135–159. doi:10.4000/philosophiascientiae.437.

OECD (1994), *Jobs Study: Facts, Analysis, Strategies*, https://www.oecd.org/els/emp /1941679.pdf

Polanyi, Karl (1944) [2001], *The Great Transformation: The Political and Economic Origins of Our Time*, Boston, MA: Beacon Press.

Reinhoudt, Jurgen and Serge Audier (2018), *The Walter Lippmann Colloquium: The Birth of Neo-Liberalism*, London: Palgrave Macmillan.

Ricardo, David (1817) [2004], *On the Principles of Political Economy and Taxation*, Mineola, NY: Dover Publications.

Robinson, Joan (1933) [1969], *The Econmics of Imperfect Competition*, London: Palgrave Macmillan.

Röpke, Wilhelm (1942) [1950], *The Social Crisis of Our Time*, Chicago, IL: The University of Chicago Press.

Röpke, Wilhelm (1958) [1969], "Robbing Peter to Pay Paul: On the Nature of the Welfare State", in Röpke, Wilhelm (ed.), *Against the Tide*, Auburn, AL: Ludwig von Mises Institute.

Rougier, Louis (1929), *La Mystique démocratique ; ses origines, ses illusions*, Paris: Flammarion.

Rougier, Louis (1938), *Les Mystiques économiques ; comment l'on passe des démocraties libérales aux États totalitaires*, Paris: Librairie de Médicis.

Rousseau, Jean-Jacques (1762) [1998], *The Social Contract*, London: Penguin.

Schumpeter, Joseph A. (1942) [2003], *Capitalisme, Socialism and Democracy*, London: Routledge.

Schumpeter, Joseph A. (1954), *History of Economic Analysis*, New York: Oxford University Press.

Smith, Adam (1776) [2007], *An Inquiry into the Nature and Causes of the Wealth of Nations*, Amsterdam: Metalibri Digital Edition.

Stiegler, Barbara (2019) *'Il faut s'adapter'. Sur un nouvel impératif politique*, Paris: Gallimard.

Stiglitz, Joseph A. (2002), *Globalization and its Discontents*, New York: W. W. Norton & Company.

Stiglitz, Joseph E. (2019) *People, Power, and Profits: Progressive Capitalism for an Age of Discontent*, New York: W. W. Norton & Company.

Stuckler, David and Sanjay Basu (2013), *The Body Economic, Why Austerity Kills*, New York: Basic Books.

Supiot, Alain (2017), *Governance by Numbers: The Making of a Legal Model of Allegiance*, London: Hart Publishing.

Todd, Emmanuel (1985), *The Explanation of Ideology: Family Structure & Social Systems*, translated by David Garrioch, Hoboken, NJ: Blackwell Publishers.

Todd, Emmanuel (2019), *Lineages of Modernity: A History of Humanity from the Stone Age to Homo Americanus*, Cambridge, UK: Polity Press.

Williamson, John (2008), "A short history of the Washington consensus", in N. Serra and J.E. Stiglitz (eds.), *The Washington Consensus Reconsidered: Towards a New Global Governance*, Oxford, UK: Oxford University Press, pp. 14–30.

Young, Allyn A. (1915) "The Sherman Act and the New Anti-Trust Legislation: I", *Journal of Political Economy*, 23(3): 201–220.

3

NEOLIBERALISM

Repair it or leave it?

As we have seen in the previous chapter, Milton Friedman did not describe himself as neoliberal and barely used the term at all. For him, as well as for Hayek, the real dividing line was between liberals (free-market advocates) and collectivists or socialists who do not believe in markets. Moreover, in 1962, at the time *Capitalism and Freedom* was released, the Mont Pelerin Society was going through a major crisis that opposed the German and Swiss members – who were often called "neo-liberals" – to the majority headed by Hayek and accused of being "paleo-liberals" for their supposedly strong attachment to the 19th-century laissez-faire doctrine (Audier 2012a, pp. 336–341).

This conflict opposing the "neo-liberals" to the "paleo-liberals" eventually resulted in the resignation of about 20 members, among them major figures of the Society such as its secretary and editor of *The Mont Pèlerin Quarterly* Albert Hunold and renowned German economists Wilhelm Röpke and Alexander Rüstow.

The Mont Pelerin Society situation explains easily why Friedman could not call himself "neoliberal" in the beginning of the 1960s: it would have been interpreted as a show of support for the side he was opposing. But this fact does not mean Friedman was not well aware of neoliberalism; neither does it mean that he was not supporting such a vision. A few years before, he was even writing that "neo-liberalism offers a real hope of a better future, a hope that is already a strong cross-current of opinion and that is capable of capturing the enthusiasm of men of good-will everywhere, and thereby becoming the major current of opinion" (Friedman 1951).

The "neo-liberalism" that Friedman was referring to is very close to the one defined in the previous chapter. Here is how he was defining the main principles neoliberalism should rest on:

> Neo-liberalism would accept the nineteenth century liberal emphasis on the fundamental importance of the individual, but it would substitute for

the nineteenth century goal of laissez-faire as a means to this end, the goal of the competitive order. It would seek to use competition among producers to protect consumers from exploitation, competition among employers to protect workers and owners of property, and competition among consumers to protect the enterprises themselves. The state would police the system, establish conditions favorable to competition and prevent monopoly, provide a stable monetary framework, and relieve acute misery and distress. The citizens would be protected against the state by the existence of a free private market; and against one another by the preservation of competition.

(ibid.)

According to Friedman, a neoliberal state must thus focus on the preservation of the competitive order and a stable monetary system, implement social interventions to maintain the social order by helping disadvantaged people, and of course – although it is not written in the above quote – follow a free trade policy. *Capitalism and Freedom* follows the same track and, if we believe Friedman's definition, must be taken as a neoliberal manifesto.

Neoliberalism has clear and specific principles that can be found easily in the discourse of all its supporters, Friedman included. However, although it constituted the main framework of most economic policies since the late 1970s, the neoliberal attempt to reshape the world did not reach its proponents' expectations. Instead of stability and prosperity, it generated financial instability, wealth inequality, and popular discontent. As the COVID-19 crisis spread all over the world, the neoliberal doctrine appeared without its imperial clothes, its failure to create a better world evident. In 2020, the Chinese system and the Trump policies seemed to be the leading opposing political models. But these models cannot be called neoliberal; neither can they be viewed as liberal in the classical meaning. Faced with its failure, the whole neoliberal doctrine stands in dire need of an overhaul. What went wrong, and what needs to be done to fix it? Is the liberal goal of achieving individual emancipation still possible in such a context?

A social emergency

In an opinion column published on 19 March 2020 in the American magazine *Foreign Affairs*, at a time when billions of people around the world were confined at home to avoid spreading the COVID-19 pandemic, the former chief economist of the World Bank, the Serbian-American Branko Milanović, explained the dramatic consequences the health crisis could raise. The consequences would not only be economic or medical, he warned, but could profoundly affect the functioning of our civilisation. If the epidemic crisis was short and containment measures lasted only a few months, return to normal could be possible; but if they lasted a year or more, if new epidemic waves resurfaced and forced governments to restrict travel, then it is likely that the pandemic would have irreversible effects on the global economy. Countries could return to a form of self-sufficiency and "globalization could unravel". Such a breakdown of the world economy would be similar to that experienced by the Roman Empire between the fourth and sixth centuries, Milanović argued, breaking up trade channels and reducing economic spaces to the national and regional scales.

Beyond the trade issue, Milanović emphasised that the profound transformation of our economic system could have grave social consequences. "[T]he human toll of the disease will be the most important cost and the one that could lead to societal disintegration. Those who are left hopeless, jobless, and without assets could easily turn against those who are better off", he alerted (Milanović 2020). The increase in riots among the most vulnerable populations could not be ruled out. According to Milanović, if governments were then tempted to respond with military and paramilitary action, this pandemic could eventually lead to the disintegration of our societies. This is what we must avoid at all costs, he concluded.

He was certainly not aware of the prophetic significance of his statement. About two months later, the death of George Floyd, choked by a Minneapolis police officer while the events were being filmed, triggered days of riots in major American cities. This murder, as the prosecutor would eventually call it, is a testament to the racial tensions that have always been present in the United States. But it was also a sign of the dramatic social situation Black Americans faced. They were undoubtedly the main victims of the pandemic. The peaceful demonstrations launched under the slogan "Black Lives Matter", where people from all communities gathered, sometimes degenerated into riots and looting. But thefts rarely involved luxury goods. Regular food was stolen most of the time. Some families, whose members were deprived of employment and resources, had only this extreme solution to survive. As of May 30, at a time when protests were growing in strength, nearly a quarter of the US labour force, or 42.6 million people, had claimed their rights for unemployment benefits in the past few weeks. Some were able to find another work, but the unemployment rate was still 13.3% of the labour force.[1] Floyd himself had just lost his job as a security guard a few days before he was arrested, due to the lockdown measures ordered by the state governor.

In the face of this social explosion, President Donald Trump overplayed the defence of his White, conservative electorate to the point of going, unusually for him, to a small church in Washington, D.C., where he brandished the Bible in the company of his chief of staff and ministers of justice and defence. He promised the restoration of "law and order" and threatened to call in the National Guard "to dominate the streets". He then returned to the White House, surrounded by thousands of protesters wearing face masks.

Fortunately, the escalation so feared by Milanović did not happen. The arrest and indictment of the four policemen involved in Floyd's death, the Pentagon's reluctance to use the army and, more generally, the strong public support for the protests helped ease social tension. The disintegration programme of the American society was postponed.

Milanović's warning should not be ignored. Even if we suppose the health crisis will last less than some epidemiologists fear, it has already hit an American society that the economic and social developments of recent decades had greatly weakened.

In order to better understand the root of the problem, we must look at the research work of Branko Milanović. In his book published in 2016, he attempted to understand the social consequences of the process of accelerating globalisation that began in the late 1980s. The originality of his approach lies in the fact that he measured the evolution of income directly at a global level. Placed in this context, the data show that globalisation has been associated with two contradictory logics. On the one hand, there has been an increase in inequalities within countries; on the other hand, there has been an overall reduction in inequalities between one country and another. Thus, if this dynamic is to continue, the future may well resemble the situation that prevailed before the industrial revolution: little inequality between countries and high inequality within each country.

We are not quite there yet. In the meantime, the dynamics of inequality are evolving in a complex way. How can we apprehend them and what are their social consequences? In a graph that has become famous and is now known as the "Elephant Chart", Milanović shows that the world population is far from being uniformly affected by the consequences of globalisation (Milanović 2016, p. 11). Between 1988 and 2008, income growth in the least developed countries – those with the poorest populations, accounting for a tenth of the world's population – was lower than average. These areas, being far from commercial channels and often mired in conflict or in serious economic difficulties, have been unable to take advantage of the opportunities offered by the expansion of trade. Above this category in the income scale are the world's "middle classes", which accounts for about 60% of the human population, including the vast majority of the inhabitants of densely populated Asian countries, such as India, China, and Indonesia. The years of trade intensification have contributed to increasing their real incomes by more than 50%. Then, there are the middle and working classes of rich countries, people who are among the richest 30% but who do not belong to the small class of the richest 1%. These populations have seen their real incomes increase much less than those of people in developing countries. Some of them, those around the 80th percentile, have experienced almost no gain in purchasing power. Finally, the upper classes of the rich countries and the very wealthy elite of the developing countries, the famous 1%, are among those whose real incomes have risen the most over the last 20 years.

The Elephant Chart makes it possible to understand that important disparities lie behind the process of convergence of nations. While globalisation benefited the middle class in developing countries (which still accounts for more than half of the world's population) and the super-rich (who make up only a tiny fraction

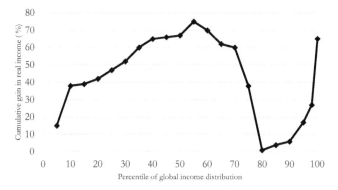

FIGURE 3.1 Changes in real household incomes worldwide (1988–2008). Source: Milanović (2016).

of it), it has also led to a form of economic downgrading for a large quarter of the world's population, especially the working classes in the richest economies. These people may have felt that they were being left behind by the rich in their own countries on the one hand and caught up by the poor inhabitants of faraway countries on the other. This feeling may have fuelled a deep moral turmoil, captured by populists.

The mechanism that explains this economic dynamic is linked to the profound industrial reorganisation of the world economy, and thus is connected to globalisation. Taking advantage of low transport costs and the almost disappearance of tariffs, companies have reorganised their value chains by producing manufactured goods at low cost in some developing countries. This flow of capital to Asia has contributed to increasing manufacturing employment, labour productivity and, ultimately, wages. Within a few decades, South-East Asia has become the productive centre of the world. In contrast, industrial production has stagnated or declined in most rich countries. The United States was the first to be affected as manufacturing employment fell from 15.8% of the labour force in 1990 to 9.6% in 2019.[2]

Figure 3.2 shows the changes in industrial employment in China and the United States during the phase when the globalisation process accelerated (1990–2008) and then when the world trade growth slowed (2008–2018). Although these figures are not of the same order of magnitude and the scope of industry is broader than that of manufacturing alone, they nevertheless provide a good measure of the shift caused by the reorganisation of global industrial production towards Asia.

The chart shows the same phenomenon of division of labour and industrial polarisation that we saw in the first chapter, but on a global scale. South-East Asia has benefited from agglomeration effects, the dynamics of which have been accentuated by its low labour costs, whereas most developed countries have

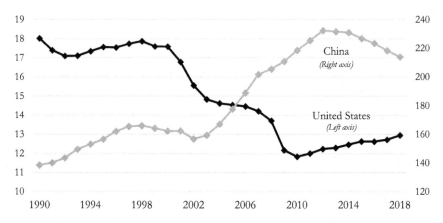

FIGURE 3.2 Comparative change in industrial employment in China and manufacturing employment in the United States between 1990 and 2018 (in millions). Source: Bureau of Labor Statistics, www.bls.gov (for American statistics), and CEIC Data, www.ceicdata.com (for Chinese statistics). Consulted on June 5, 2020.

maintained only part of their manufactural production within their territory. This production concentrated in the most dynamic regions of the United States, fleeing almost entirely from the Midwestern states and the Great Lakes region, which were once the heart of the American automotive industry.[3]

The loss of manufactural employment has been compensated for by the creation of other jobs in the service sector. But these jobs were often less productive and less paid. This explains why the real income of the American middle class has hardly risen at all. The sectoral transformation of economic activity towards services also contributed to a change in mentalities. The US economy has been closing its factories, creating thousands of Uber drivers, security guards, delivery drivers, personal assistants, computer service salespeople, smartphone repairers, telephone platform operators, etc., in their place. These occupations are more individualistic than manufactured work: they do not facilitate collective organising or unionisation. Service sector employees are more isolated than factory workers; they do not know the solidarity of the workshop; they often work alone in front of customers, with number objectives that lead them towards developing a competitive spirit rather than a team spirit.

This transformation of employment has changed the United States and pushed workers to focus on more narrow and personal objectives. It fuelled a competitive spirit and a feeling of downgrading in the American middle class that led to a greater withdrawal into oneself and one's community. The loss of interest in politics or social investment was reinforced by the explosion of the income of a very small segment of the population, those who can afford family apartments in Manhattan or a house overlooking the San Francisco Bay Area.

As we saw in the first chapter, populism is facilitated by this kind of social contexts which give rise to the widespread development of distrust.

However, it was not White Americans and members of the declassed middle classes who were revolting in the United States at the end of May 2020. It was Black Americans, who mostly fall into an even less advantaged social category. This population, like the former, is also a victim of deindustrialisation but they do not necessarily feel they downgraded because they have never felt that America belongs to them. Their social situation has always been that of the lower class. Globalisation has also contributed to making their lives difficult by increasing tax competition and drying up the sources of public revenue. The abandonment of the social programmes during the Reagan decade, the "make work pay"[4] policy of the 1990s, and the ultra-security measures that led to a completely new rate of imprisonment for Blacks,[5] have undoubtedly increased the social pressure on them.

By deciding to hold up a Bible in front of a Washington church, Trump showed that he had chosen his side, that of the decommissioned Whites, over another side, that of poor Black Americans. He thus fed a conflict between two major categories of losers. Those who want to "regain control" after losing their well-paid industrial jobs, and those who just want to survive despite struggling in the social situations which keep them in a dominated condition.

Branko Milanović is right. There is an urgent need to avoid a social and societal collapse in the United States. But if it does happen, such a collapse will not be caused by the pandemic alone. The American social fracture is the result of a long process of disintegration that also affects, to varying degrees, most Western societies. These social tensions are expressed today through populism but may take on more violent forms in the future. Repairing society is therefore essential, not only to find an answer to populist leaders who, like Trump, do not hesitate to stir up community wars and pose a serious threat to democracy, but also to avoid a civilisational breakdown and the return of violence that has long been maintained at historically low levels in the light of human history (Pinker 2011).

How can society be repaired? How can a lasting response be found to this situation that is stirring up social disorder in large parts of the world? The first chapter of this book concluded with the idea that populism was not simply a consequence of rising economic inequality but the product of a deeper feeling, that of living in a degraded democracy in which most elected officials had lost all power to act. For Yascha Mounk (2018), this political powerlessness is itself the result of liberal institutions which, by separating powers, tend to limit the action of elected leaders. Western societies would thus be faced with a dilemma between the anti-democratic liberalism of the European Union and the anti-liberal democracy of populist regimes. But the question of populism cannot be reduced to such a dichotomy. Indeed, contrary to Mounk's assertion, Western societies are not only "liberal", in the sense that they accept the principles of the rule of law and the separation of powers; they are also "neoliberal", in the sense that they seek to defend a specific institutional order that aims to preserve the proper functioning of the competitive economy from any public disturbance. This neoliberal construction, not the simple principles of classical liberalism, is what undermines democracy. By placing the state at the service of the market, neoliberalism has greatly reduced the room for political action and has contributed to weakening the social basis on which economic activity is founded.

Two conclusions can be drawn from this observation. The first, which is defended by most progressive economists, is that the social pillar of the neoliberal architecture should be strengthened to limit the adverse effects of excessive international competition on societies. Proponents of this approach do not intend to question the world economic integration process. They are in favour of free trade, free competition, and relative monetary stability. They all believe in the virtues of market mechanisms and their ability to establish prices, and in collective behaviours that make optimal use of available resources on the influence of prices.

The recognition of the profound social imbalances pushed progressive economists to propose a set of reforms. Thus, in the name of preserving social order, they advocate a more inclusive and egalitarian economic system (Naidu et al. 2019). In the United States, the COVID-19 pandemic has prompted the defence of a universal health system such as the ones that exist in Europe. Some are advocating regulation of drug prices, aware that the pharmaceutical industry's economic model, which is based on intellectual property rights, is anyway incompatible with the principle of free competition. They support better regulation of financial markets to avoid moral hazard, a more progressive tax system, new international institutions, and more heterodox monetary policies to avoid deflation. Some suggest more radical measures, such as the introduction of a substantial universal basic income, or defend the principle of guaranteed employment, making government the "employer of last resort" for all those left out of the labour market. For the rest, they generally consider that it would be neither useful nor healthy for political power to regulate prices (except for wages), destabilise world trade, or nationalise a large part of the productive system. They argue that market self-regulation mechanisms should be maintained wherever possible, that government action should interfere with market exchanges as little as possible and avoid discretionary interventions that could affect the allocation of resources. They believe that globalisation has generally been a good thing, even if it has resulted in some excesses that should be addressed.

But the depth of the current turmoil could give rise to further reflections. After all, if neoliberalism is the cause of social depression experienced by most developed economies, would it be impossible to challenge the policy and fundamentally change the architecture behind it? This would mean calling into question not its basis, the principle of the rule of law, which is a contribution of classical liberalism, but its summit—the typically neoliberal certainty that any system of state planning would be inefficient and tyrannical, and that only a market system based on free competition would make it possible to establish a fair and efficient economic order. Where does this certainty about the presumed efficiency of market mechanisms come from? Is it certain that this is the best way of allocating resources to the uses that are most socially relevant?

This assertion, forcefully asserted by all neoliberal authors, has never been irrefutably demonstrated. The efficiency of markets is not a scientifically established fact. It is a presumption, and until it is demonstrated, it is a matter of belief. To be clear, no one is suggesting that markets would not have *any* efficiency or that market prices would not have *any* relevance. However, it is impossible to state, in the best of our current knowledge, that a system of perfectly competitive markets (if this is at all possible to establish) would mechanically generate an economic optimum. Because of this scientific uncertainty, and in the view of the harmful consequences of the policies pursued over the last few decades, the debate on the respective roles of the state and the market in the regulation of economic activities in general and in the process of globalisation in particular, should be reopened. As John Stuart Mill rightly pointed out, free trade is justified only as long as it contributes to collective well-being, and not because of superior principles.

So, the choice before us is relatively straightforward. Anyone dissatisfied with the existing order must either repair neoliberalism, presumably by strengthening its social pillar, or invent a new institutional model based on foundations other than the presupposed efficiency of competing markets.

In this last chapter, I intend to discuss the proposals made by some economists who are dissatisfied with the actual state of the world and who would like to reverse the trend of increasing inequality. Although they understand the economic dynamic generated by this social situation accurately, I believe the solutions they advocate fail to sufficiently question the neoliberal architecture. However, those questions must be raised, too. As an economist, I cannot be satisfied with the contemporary complacency with free markets and the insistence that the state cannot achieve any economic production without their help. For this reason, in the last part of this chapter, I will explain the reasons why the economic science has been unable to elaborate a satisficing model that proves the efficiency of free markets, and why I therefore believe it is necessary to invent a relationship between state and market that goes beyond the neoliberal principles.

Rediscovering inequalities

For decades, economists turned their backs on social issues. The steady post-war growth was broadly egalitarian in most developed countries. Although poverty and social problems did not, of course, disappear, those ills were seen as falling outside the realm of economics. The Keynesian economist John Kenneth Galbraith could thus write in 1958 that "few things are more evident in modern social history than the decline of interest in inequality as an economic issue" (Galbraith 1958, chap. 5).

As we saw in the previous chapter, the Bretton Woods economic order partially isolated national economies. Trade and financial imbalances were small, and most economies operated within a predominantly domestic production system, which did not prevent international trade from growing smoothly. Tariff barriers effectively limited the intensity of global competition, and controls on capital movements prevented tax havens from diverting wealth produced in other countries. This environment gave governments significant regulatory power.

The collapse of the Bretton Woods system in the early 1970s, the liberalisation of exchange rates, the reduction of tariffs and transport costs, and the progressive removal of all controls on financial flows brought about the emergence of the neoliberal order and greatly reduced the capacity of governments to regulate their economies. However, those transformations did not immediately increase inequalities. Inflation, which began to take off after 1975, led to a reduction in real interest rates and in the weight of the banking and financial sector. In Western countries, corporate margins were affected by rising oil prices and emerging competition from Asian countries. Trade unionism, which remained strong in a context where the developed economies were still highly industrialised, managed to keep wages at high levels, particularly in Europe. Overall, during the 1970s, income and wealth inequality declined in most countries of the world and increased only slightly in some Western countries (Galbraith 2016, p. 101).

The 1980s and 1990s marked a turning point. Under the influence of Milton Friedman's work, the war on inflation became the priority of economic policies. In the United States, interest rates rose sharply to curb money creation. Many countries that had borrowed in US dollars, particularly developing countries in Africa and Latin America, faced borrowing costs rising. This situation precipitated financial crises in countries that had no choice but to turn to the International Monetary Fund (IMF). In the industrialised countries of the West, very high-interest rates encouraged companies to reduce their debts by cutting back on investment, which in turn accelerated deindustrialisation, increased unemployment, and reduced the influence of trade unions. Finally, the fall of communism and the Asian crisis of 1997 spread neoliberal precepts to the rest of the world. During these two decades, inequalities increased sharply, as James Galbraith explains:

> [I]n the 1980s, ultra-high interest rates and rolling debt crises reversed the balance of financial power. This now unquestionably favored the rich and crushed the poor, first in Latin America and Africa, then in the communist states, and finally in Asia.
>
> From this pattern the power of global financial forces is evident. Only those countries that had avoided commercial international debt escaped the storm, and only for so long as they could or chose to maintain their independence. Their capacity to do that was very limited, in this era of globalization, neoliberalism, and what was called the "Washington consensus" for economic policy, namely to privatize, deregulate, open up to external competition, and cut public spending and taxes.
>
> *(ibid., pp. 101–2)*

In the early 2000s, the situation changed again. Financial crises multiplied in developed countries: first in 2000–2001, with the bursting of the Internet bubble and the September 11 attacks, then in 2007–2008 with the subprime mortgage crisis. Taking advantage of low inflation, governments pursued very accommodating monetary policies that sharply reduced interest rates and the cost of capital. This decrease favoured debtors and rebalanced the relationship between the finance sector and the agents of the real economy. According to Galbraith, inequalities within countries globally ceased to increase even though they remained at a high level. Despite monetary policies favourable to borrowing and investment, the stimulus effects for economic activity and purchasing power were weak. While rising interest rates succeeded in reducing inflation in the 1980s, their fall to levels close to zero did not increase prices. This situation, which bore close resemblance to a deflation, weighed on the indebted agents, first and foremost the states. Wages did not rise either and tax revenues stagnated; governments were forced to limit public spending, particularly in Europe; social dissatisfaction became widespread.

The issue of inequality, which had disappeared from the economists' agenda, gradually remerged as an issue worthy of study during the 2000 and 2010 decades. In 2004, laureate of the Nobel Prize for Economics Robert Lucas, a member of the Chicago School and a proponent of reduced public intervention, started a speech by saying: "We live in a world of staggering and unprecedented income inequality", and concluded it by declaring: "Of the tendencies that are harmful to sound economics, the most seductive, and in my opinion the most poisonous, is to focus on questions of distribution" (Lucas 2004).

For Lucas, the problem of inequality can never be addressed through a redistributive policy since the development lag of poor countries explains most of the inequality in the world. This gap is set to narrow in the long run, he believes, as long as companies in the lagging countries are allowed to grow freely by taking advantage of the market incentives and fabulous opportunities of world trade. "We just have to rely on the principles of classical economics and not on interventionism", Lucas says.

This thesis is based on the earlier argument that seeks to demonstrate that there is a trade-off between social justice and economic efficiency (Okun 1975). According to this theory, for growth to occur, incentives to produce and invest must be preserved. Moreover, if we believe in the law of supply,[6] the higher the remuneration for economic behaviour, the more it will be adopted on a massive scale. In other words, when redistribution takes place, we take from those who have been the most efficient to give to the ones who didn't contribute to the economy. By doing so, incentives for the most efficient behaviours are reduced and the outcome must thus be slower economic growth.

This reasoning is however problematic because it rarely fits the facts. The most prosperous economies are often more egalitarian than average. In addition, social consequences and political stability must also be considered. No economy can prosper in a climate of civil war. Poverty and inequality clearly generate political tensions that can lead to further social and economic deterioration.

Growth must be socially sustainable to last, which means that its fruits must be at least partially shared.

The outbreak of the subprime crisis in the United States in 2007 brought the issue of inequality back into the light. Subprime loans are real estate loans granted to poor households wishing to become homeowners. For years, successive American governments have sought to support access to homeownership for the working classes, which is supposed to improve their social integration and reduce crime rates. Taking advantage of rising property prices and government measures, the banking sector increased the availability of this type of credit. As subprime mortgages were risky, interest rates were high, resulting in many loans not being repaid. When that happened, the banks would take ownership of the homes and pay themselves out by selling the acquired properties. As long as real estate prices were rising, this type of operations was very profitable for banks. But when the real estate market collapsed, financial institutions that had engaged in subprime lending suddenly ran up losses since the value of their claims dropped to near zero. The crisis then spread around the world.

The magnitude of the crisis made economists realise that poverty and inequality could also be factors of economic and financial instability.

An extremely famous graph by economists Thomas Piketty and Emmanuel Saez contributed to this awareness. Published for the first time in 2003 and updated regularly thereafter, it shows, over a century, the share of US national income (before taxes and redistribution) that is captured by the richest 10% (Pikety and Saez 2003, p. 10). In 2009, the two economists updated their data; the curve that emerged was quite surprising. It showed two sharp peaks in 1928 and 2007 when the income share of the top decile reached almost 50% of national income. Between these two peaks, a U-shaped curve appeared. From 1951 onwards, the share of high incomes fell below 35%; it remained stable under this threshold until 1981 and then rose steadily until 2007. The effects of the financial crises (1929, 1987, 2001) were visible and systematically resulted in a fall in incomes of the upper classes, which can be explained by the fact that they were more affected than average by the health of the financial markets (Atkinson et al. 2011, p. 6).

This graph is striking because both peaks observed correspond to the years preceding the two largest US financial crises, that of 1929 and 2008. Thus, even if it was not presented in this way, the graph seemed to suggest that there was a maximum to the level of wealth that could be captured by the wealthiest, and, when a peak was reached, a major financial crisis would ensue. This graph contributed to the questioning of economists: what if the Great Recession was the consequence of an unbalanced economic growth that led to an unsustainable level of economic inequality?

The OECD warnings

It was around this time that the Organisation for Economic Co-operation and Development (OECD) started looking at inequality as well. Its first report devoted specifically to this topic appeared in 2008. The organisation's conclusions were clear. In most of the 30 OECD countries, income inequality had increased since the mid-1980s. But the report immediately nuances that finding: "the increase in inequality ... has not been as spectacular as most people probably think it has been" (OECD 2008, p. 15). More importantly, it notes that the cause of inequality is not unequivocal and cannot be attributed solely to the globalisation process.

In his foreword, the OECD Secretary-General, Ángel Gurría, explains the motivations behind the survey. Fears of rising inequality are being used by "those who argue that we should resist the increased integration of our economies and societies and that the larger cross-border flows of goods, services and people are putting at risk the living and working conditions of millions of people" (*ibid.*, p. 3). "I believe that these responses are wrong," he says; "but also that the anxieties from which they stem should be taken seriously. Globalisation offers opportunities to live fuller and better lives—but making the best of these requires correcting the asymmetries in the distribution of the benefits and costs of globalisation" (*ibid.*).

Unlike the work of Piketty and Saez, this OECD report does not address the issue of high incomes. In particular, it states that "for many OECD countries, the most immediate concern is poverty rather than inequality *per se*" (*ibid.*, p. 301). As a result, the proposed solutions put more emphasis on strategies for inclusion of working-age populations than on redistributive policies. For the OECD, social benefits should be targeted more towards poor households. The main objective in the fight against poverty must be to encourage people to return to work by ensuring that the assistance they receive (social aids, unemployment allocations, etc.) do not reduce work incentives, which is why the report proposes "tighter obligations on beneficiaries to accept suitable job offers; time limits on the periods when benefits can be drawn; and benefit sanctions in the case of non-compliance" (*ibid.*, p. 303). Finally, the OECD believes that if the effects of inequality on growth are not demonstrated, it is important to remain vigilant as it creates social tensions and increases "the risk that these inequalities will lead to the adoption of policies that are inimical to economic performances" while there is "a strong focus in current discussions on the role of 'globalisation' as a driver of greater inequalities" (*ibid.*, p. 284).

As can be seen, this 2008 report is far from breaking with neoliberalism. On the contrary, the measures it recommends are in line with those advocated in the 1990s, which sought to combat unemployment by increasing the flexibility of the labour market.

The next report, published in December 2011, was marked by the economic and social crisis. Its tone is very different from that of 2008. In the editorial titled "Mind the gap", Gurría points out that inequalities have increased sharply in almost all OECD countries, especially those with a more egalitarian historical pattern, such as Germany, Denmark, and Sweden. He is especially alarmed by the consequences of the crisis for young people and mentions the specific problem of high incomes and the "polarisation" of wages and salaries. Similarly, and this is a novelty, he worries about the social consequences of the labour market reforms that the organisation's previous reports have strongly defended.

> Labour markets have profoundly changed in OECD countries since the 1980s, marked by a series of reforms to increase their flexibility. The markets for goods and services have also been deregulated, and policies to increase competition have been pursued. These reforms have promoted productivity and economic growth and have brought more people into work. But on the "b-moll" side they have also contributed to widening earnings gaps: many of these jobs were part-time or low-paid.
>
> *(OECD 2011, p. 18)*

More broadly, Gurría calls for tax policy reform "to ensure that wealthier individuals contribute their fair share of the tax burden" (*ibid*.) and calls for the fight against tax evasion. He notes the importance of public services in reducing inequalities and calls for investment in human capital to promote access to employment for the most disadvantaged. Finally, while calling for public policies that could "make markets more efficient", he states that the study "dispels the assumption that the benefits of economic growth will automatically trickle down to the disadvantaged and that greater inequality fosters greater social mobility. Without a comprehensive strategy for inclusive growth, inequality will continue to rise", he concludes (*ibid.*, p. 19).

One may think when reading this editorial that the OECD Secretary-General is about to raise the socialist red flag. In reality, the content of the report is much more nuanced than the presentation text suggests. For example, while acknowledging the role of taxation and redistribution in combating inequality, the report also points out the limitations of these instruments by underlining their "disincentive" effects. It also notes that governments face serious budgetary constraints that lead them to reduce social spending (*ibid.*, pp. 40–1). Thus, its conclusion is not so much that redistributive policies should be strengthened but rather that access to skilled and better-paid jobs should be improved. To do so, the report argues, investment in human capital is needed most of all and can be achieved by increasing the level of education and qualifications of the workforce.

Why focus on the necessary financial contribution of the "wealthier individuals" and the importance of achieving "inclusive growth" in the editorial if the report concludes with proposals that are, after all, fairly conventional? Probably because the political situation was much more pressing, and touching people's minds and hearts was important. The year 2011, which was drawing to a close, was marked by the Arab revolutions, by the Indignados movement in Spain, and by the Occupy Wall Street protests in the United States. These demonstrations, whose favourite slogan was "we are the 99%", were openly hostile to inequalities and challenged globalisation. The report seems to express worries about that:

> Inequality also raises political challenges because it breeds social resentment and generates political instability. It can also fuel populist, protectionist, and anti-globalization sentiments. People will no longer support open trade and free markets if they feel that they are losing out while a small group of winners is getting richer and richer.
>
> *(OECD 2011, p. 40)*

To sum up, the more neoliberal globalisation is challenged, the more the OECD is concerned about economic inequality. Its reports sound like a warning to governments to act and respond to the challenge, guarantee social order, and protect globalisation and markets from possible political reversals.

After this report was released, very few social measures were effectively taken by OECD countries. The euro crisis reinforced the dynamics of inequality between and within European countries. From 2011 onwards, populist movements took root. Thus, the 2015 OECD report adopts an even more alarmist tone. In this study titled *In It Together: Why Less Inequality Benefits All*, the organisation demonstrates for the first time that, in contrast to the classical thesis, there is an inverse correlation between inequality and economic growth. The report stresses that the fight against inequality should not be a matter of social or political considerations alone but that it is an important economic issue.

> Some may consider that the social and political costs of high and rising inequality are in and of themselves sufficient to justify action. The central argument of this publication is different. It is that, beyond its serious impact on social cohesion, high and often growing inequality raises major *economic* concerns, not just for the low earners themselves but for the wider health and sustainability of our economies. Put simply: *rising inequality is bad for long-term growth.*
>
> *(OECD 2015, p. 22)*

The issue of high incomes is an important aspect of this new study. The OECD's priority is no longer just to fight poverty but also to tax corporations and the richest households. The global success of Thomas Piketty's book *Capital in the Twenty-First Century* forced the OECD to rethink its priorities. It argues that while measures to ensure the inclusion of the working classes (through employment) should be maintained, redistribution should not be neglected. The report's summary stresses that redistribution is "a powerful instrument to contribute to more equality and more growth" (*ibid.*, p. 17). It also quotes Piketty and states that better taxation of inheritances is necessary in order to promote inter-generational social mobility, and that high incomes and companies should not be able to escape fair taxation by taking advantage of different tax laws and the lack of cooperation and transparency shown by some countries (*ibid.*, p. 49).

By asserting that redistribution policies promote growth, the OECD is definitively turning its back on the thesis of Nobel Prize winner Robert Lucas and, more broadly, on the classic opposition between efficiency and justice. But its reasoning is purely empirical. It finds that within its members, there is a negative correlation between growth and inequality without explaining it theoretically. Yet, this result should challenge economists as it calls into question certain foundations of contemporary economic thinking; but only a few studies have been undertaken to explain this paradox theoretically.

We need to take note of a key fact: the lower growth in the most unequal countries is not due to external causes resulting from social unrest or political instability as OECD countries generally enjoy a high degree of political stability, but on internal economic dynamics. It is, therefore, necessary to find which mechanisms could explain this inverse relationship. There are three possible answers. The first is borrowed from the Keynesian thought. It suggests that the less unequal countries have a higher and more stable average propensity to consume than the more unequal countries. This is explained by the fact that the poorest households have a higher propensity to consume than the richest. Taking from the rich who consume less in proportion to redistribute to the poor who consume almost all their income should thus help to increase consumption and improve growth. The problem with this explanation is, as Keynes himself acknowledged, that increased consumption is only useful for growth in a cyclical context when the employment rate is low and there is unused production capacity. However, to increase growth in a sustainable manner, consumption should be reduced in favour of investment. Besides, it is difficult to find a statistical correlation between the level of inequality and the level of household consumption expenditure.

Another explanation is that inequality may affect the ability of the working classes to access health and minimal education, making a large part of the population unemployable. This explanation works fairly well in general, but it appears less relevant for OECD countries, most of which, even the most unequal, have satisfactory health and education systems, or at least sufficient to ensure the employability of the majority of the population.

A final explanation is that market inequality in democracies pushes voters to demand for more redistributive policies. However, such measures reduce incentives and thus growth. This explanation was taken seriously and studied in 2014 by IMF economists who looked at whether it was possible to find data evidence of a relationship between the level of inequality and redistributive policies, and what their respective effects were on economic growth. Their report challenged the theoretical result. First of all, they did find a negative relationship between inequality and growth. Second, they found that the level of market inequality creates, as supposed, a demand for more redistribution. But this redistribution policy does not harm growth, on the contrary: "redistribution appears generally benign in its impact on growth; only in extreme cases is there some evidence that it may have direct negative effects on growth" (Ostry et al. 2014, p. 4). Thus, the positive effect of fiscal redistribution on growth obtained by reducing the level of inequality must be greater than its negative effect on incentives.

This result is problematic because it means that the incentive effects may reach a limit and that above a certain threshold, income variation no longer succeeds in adjusting behaviour. In other words, the law of supply is partially invalidated, which also invalidates conventional representations of how markets work. The consequences are important but mostly ignored by economists.

From an economic policy perspective, if incentives tend to level off, this could mean that the many OECD recommendations on incentives to return to work, such as those found in its 2008 report, which call for "benefit sanctions in the case of non-compliance", may be counterproductive.

From a theoretical point of view, this result also poses a fundamental problem as to the relevance of neoliberal views. If prices and incomes no longer produce the behaviour expected by the theory, how can neoliberal policies that are supposed to make the market efficient be justified?

Why is inequality increasing?

Let's leave this issue for the moment and get back to inequality. There is now a consensus among economists that inequality has increased in most countries since the late 1970s. Recently, there has also been some consensus that, above a certain threshold, inequality is detrimental to growth, and not simply because of the political instability it creates but for economic reasons that classical theory and models find difficult to grasp.

It is therefore important to understand the causes of this inequality dynamic. Is it a natural phenomenon inherent to capitalism? Is it linked to globalisation, to neoliberal measures? Is it the product of technological change?

Many economists believe that the rise in inequality is, at least in part, the consequence of the computer revolution and the emergence of new information technologies. They would make skilled jobs more productive and low-skilled workers less useful. As a result, the labour market would become polarised between those who know how to use the new communication tools and those who do not. But this thesis is far from being proven. For example, James Galbraith points out that the use of new technologies does not require a high level of skill, which is confirmed by the massive adoption of smartphones and the widespread use of computers today. Moreover, it is also possible that computers, by eliminating many assistant jobs, have increased the workload of executives who now have to type their own texts, send their own email, and spend more of their time on parasitic tasks (Galbraith 2016, p. 73). Thus, the new information technologies may have paradoxically *reduced* the average productivity of executives, a decrease that has been offset by their increased number and by the disappearance of some assistant jobs. In short, according to standard theory, the new technologies should result in a relative decline in the salaries of executives and maintenance of the salaries of hairdressers or bus drivers, whose work has been very little affected by the arrival of computers. Obviously, that is not what happened. It is therefore doubtful whether the rise in inequality observed since the early 1980s has a purely technological cause.

Another explanation, more convincing, is that inequality has increased due to a change in economic policies from the 1980s and 1990s. As noted earlier, the Washington Consensus became the norm in most countries of the world. However, "structural adjustment policies" are not neutral with regard to the distribution of wealth, especially the part that aims to organise a strategy discreetly called "fiscal consolidation", another name for austerity programmes. The IMF acknowledges the impact of these measures on the growth of inequality. In a 2012 report it calculated that "a consolidation amounting to 1 percentage point of GDP was associated with an increase of about 0.6 per cent in inequality of disposable income (as measured by the Gini coefficient) in the following year", adding that when austerity was very strong, the effect on inequality was even more significant (IMF 2012, p. 53).

These findings are hardly surprising. Austerity policies often imply a reduction in social assistance or public employment which affects the poorest households more. In addition, such measures generally rely on raising consumption taxes which are easy to collect and high-yielding fiscal sources, but which diminish the purchasing power of the middle and working classes. Finally, opening up to foreign goods and capital tends to intensify competition and result in an asymmetry between those who are mobile and can benefit from openness and those for whom the disappearance of borders is mainly a threat to their employment.

Another effect of open borders is the change in economic policy logic it brings about. In a country relatively protected from international competition, the government must pursue autonomous policies and rely on its internal resources to boost its economy. In an open economy, the perspective is different. Resources may leak out or be captured from outside. Consequently, mobile resources and those attached to their territory must be treated differently. The former must be attracted or at least prevented from escaping; the latter are subject to government decisions and can be taxed easily.

In the way the global economy currently operates, capital and commodities are mobile. This mobility allows an investor wishing to satisfy internal demand to arbitrate between local production (producing and selling locally) and foreign production (producing in another country and importing for its local market). Under these conditions, the choice is made based on the return on capital. If the price of the commodity is given by the market, it is the total costs of production and transportation that will determine the profitability of capital and thus how this trade-off will be resolved. Labour, which in most cases does not have such mobility, has virtually no arbitrage capacity. Individuals cannot turn easily toward foreign employers if they seek better employment. Even where it is legally possible, for instance in the European Union, it creates major social problems for both emigration and immigration countries.[7] Any opening of borders (especially when it concerns only capital and goods) creates asymmetries between capital and labour for the benefit of the holders of capital who are also the richest people.

It should be noted that this situation has its own dynamics. The opening of borders, when it is generalised to the whole world, gives rise to cumulative effects that reinforce inequality. A simple thought experiment helps understand this mechanism. Consider a closed country in which the rate of return on capital is about 4–5%. Given the risk inherent in any entrepreneurial project, this rate of return is relatively low but sufficient to allow investment and job creation. Since savers have no choice but to invest locally, it can be estimated that they will have no difficulty in financing the country's activity. In such a context, increasing the profitability of capital by lowering taxes or reducing labour costs is likely to have little effect on growth because of the limits on incentive mechanisms (see the previous section).

Let us now apply free trade and the free movement of capital to this economy. Now, investors can choose between producing locally or producing abroad. But in the neighbouring country, it turns out that public policies are more favourable to capital and production costs (taxation, wages, etc.) are lower. By building a factory there, an entrepreneur can expect an average profitability of 6–7%. He thus no longer has any incentive to produce locally. The level of investment collapses in the first country and increases in its adjacent partner. Faced with such a situation, a government that refuses to see its domestic industry disappear – as productive capital ages and becomes obsolete from lack of new investment – has no choice but to increase the profitability of capital, which means lowering corporate taxation or labour costs. For example, reforms to make the labour market more "flexible" or to fight against trade unions have no other aim but to prevent wage increases and improve the competitiveness of the domestic industry. However, since tax resources must be found to finance public infrastructure and guarantee a pro-business environment, the government has an incentive to tax immobile factors: middle- and lower-income households, residential real estate, and everyday consumer goods.

In this open economy, if economic policies succeed in increasing the profitability of capital to a level higher than that of the neighbouring country, not only will this encourage its own industrialists to produce locally but it may also encourage neighbouring companies to invest, until the other country, in turn, responds with new attractiveness measures. The process is endless. It leads to increasingly pro-capital policies until the breakdown of the social order and the unsustainable rise in inequality push governments to act in the opposite direction. But this is where the impasse lies. How can the logic of economic policies be changed if circumstances do not? Of course, there can always be calls to move away from tax and social competition and cooperate internationally, as the OECD is doing; but this means forgetting that competitive logic is at the heart of how markets work and these calls are likely to fall flat if economic interests and structures make them inoperative.

One solution can be to act on these structures and envisage a gradual re-regulation of the movement of capital and goods. But on the one hand, this would imply going back on the most fundamental neoliberal principles, which is not currently envisaged by most leaders. On the other hand, decades of openness have led to a deep interweaving of economies. When the components of a commodity are produced abroad in many countries, an abrupt re-establishment of customs controls can profoundly destabilise economies, at least temporarily. Any attempt by an isolated country to challenge globalisation can therefore only be made in a prudent and organised manner.

What must be understood is that it is not the market alone that fosters inequality between capital and labour; it is also the dynamics that force governments to take measures to safeguard their manufactural industries in an uncooperative manner. Here we are confronted with a flagrant contradiction of the neoliberal doctrines presented in the previous chapter. Neoliberal authors differ from Manchester liberals in that they want to transform the "spectator" state into a "referee" state. They advocate interventions that should be limited to the preservation of the four "pillars of the temple" without interfering with the economic calculations of agents who are supposed to act freely in response to market incentives. But, in its reality, neoliberalism proposes to create a global competitive order that obliges the state to intervene *as an actor in its own right*. As we just saw, the logic of attractiveness policies pushes governments to alter the incentive systems produced by the market. If neoliberals were consistent in their doctrines, they would denounce these untimely interventions by policies in favour of capital because they are contrary to the principles they set out.

If they do not do so, it is because the basis of neoliberal reasoning is also problematic. Is it possible to define a "natural" rate of return on capital that does not depend on public policies, i.e. on tax levels, social institutions, and the rules that organise the labour market? – obviously not. In other words, trying to make the state a "referee" of the economic game that would protect the "natural" incentives of the market when there is absolutely nothing natural about the relationship between capital and labour can only lead to a political impasse. Unable to find the natural rate of return on capital, governments are led to implement policies to adjust companies' incentives in a discretionary manner and thus become fully engaged in a competitive dynamic with the rest of the world. This is how the referees compete with each other and participate fully in the "game" with the ultimate consequence of strengthening the advantages granted to agents with the most mobile factors of production to the detriment of workers and owners of immobile resources.

How markets and globalisation affect inequality

The competitive dynamics that governments engage in to attract productive capital is well-known to economists. In a recent book that conducts a historical survey of fiscal policy developments, economists Emmanuel Saez and Gabriel

Zucman showed how competition between countries ended up drying up the revenues that the United States collected from businesses. In the early 1950s, they argue, US corporate taxes represented about 6% of national income, almost as much as household income taxes. The latter had been increasing until the 1970s and then stabilised at about 10% of this income. On the business side, however, taxation was collapsing. Saez and Zucman calculated that corporate taxes fell to only 1% of the national income in 2018, their lowest level since the early 1930s (Saez and Zucman 2019, chap. 4).

Overall, the authors denounce the consequences of anti-tax ideologies rather than the effects of globalisation. However, their book perfectly describes the mechanisms that allow companies to optimise their taxes by using the services of specialised agencies that operate in the tax avoidance market. Admittedly, the free movement of goods and capital allows multinationals to play with different legislations to optimise their tax bills; but states have the means to counter this trend, the authors believe. They point out that the United States taxes its nationals who reside in foreign countries and manage to force Swiss banks to renounce tax secrecy. The main reason for this particular US ability is that the main banks operating in international markets cannot do without the American market, so the United States can force companies to pay a minimum amount of tax. There is no need, therefore, to reach an agreement with every country in the world. It is possible to make companies pay taxes that are not based on the accounting profit made locally – it is easily reduced artificially – but on their real economic activity as measured by the proportion of sales they make in a given country. Thus, even if it is not possible to negotiate a formal arrangement with Switzerland, the multinationals based there can still be taxed.

> If Nestlé makes 20% of its global sales in the United States, then – whatever the countries where Nestlé employs its workers or has its factories, wherever its headquarters are located, wherever it holds its patents – the United States can assert that 20% of the company's global profits have been made in America and are taxable there.
>
> *(ibid., chap. 6)*

What is valid for the United States, which has a huge market, can also work for European countries or any other state, provided that they join forces and have real leverage vis-à-vis multinational companies. This type of cooperation agreement between countries that suffer from tax evasion can work because it brings together countries that share the same interests, which is not the case with an agreement that has to be negotiated directly with tax havens. The OECD and the G20 are currently negotiating such agreements, which could lead to significant progress in the fight against tax evasion.[8] Nevertheless, so far since 2012 this strategy has not prevented the acceleration of tax dumping strategies between developed countries, as noted by Saez and Zucman. The solution is not that simple since contradictions remain between the goodwill displayed at the international level and national practices that are still based on fiscal attractiveness strategies.

A question, however, remains. Is the return of higher taxes on business and capital not likely to harm investment and growth? Saez and Zucman think it is highly unlikely: "Over the last hundred years, there is no observable correlation between capital taxation and capital accumulation", they write (Saez and Zucman 2019, chap. 5). Similarly, they find no link between the level of savings, which fluctuates around 10% in the United States and major European countries, and the taxation of capital, which has fluctuated between 5% and 50% in a few decades. Here we find a result that once again contradicts traditional representations in economics and shows the limits of incentive mechanisms. Everything works as if, in some cases, prices had only a limited influence on behaviour. Lower returns on capital do not necessarily divert economic agents from entrepreneurship, firms from investing, and households from saving. Agents behave as if the *absolute* level of return on capital was less important than its *relative* level when it is associated with the agent's free arbitrage. In other words, in a closed economy, an average return on capital of 5% may be quite sufficient to induce business investment, whereas in an open economy, 10% may not be enough if a neighbouring country is able to offer a higher return.

Saez and Zucman are certainly right to highlight the role of anti-tax ideology in growing inequality. Nevertheless, taxation can only be a mechanism for correcting inequality arising from the economic system itself. But where do this prior inequality comes from? Shouldn't we ask ourselves about the primary distribution of wealth and incomes before using the tax system to redistribute? The question is all the more serious as fiscal redistribution can be perceived as illegitimate or arbitrary, especially by those who believe that the market distributes profit based on objective and natural criteria that remunerate the real economic contribution of everyone.

Beyond anti-tax ideologies, it is, therefore, appropriate to question the pro-market ideology which considers market inequalities as natural and legitimate because of the presumed efficiency of market transactions. Such ideology is just as questionable. Moreover, it is precisely because it is doubtful that market-based monetary inequality is the product of an efficient distribution of wealth that it would be appropriate to carry out ex-post redistribution. This is where Saez and Zucman's analysis shows its limitations. Their book is in no way an indictment of the market: "Markets are the most powerful institution invented so far to satisfy the infinity of human desires; the most efficient way to supply diverse products that address the changing needs of billions of individuals", they write. However, they add that markets are tools "devoid of any concern for the common good" (*ibid.*, chap. 3). As a result, it would be legitimate for the state, which is responsible for the common good, to redistribute what the markets have distributed. This pro-market and pro-redistribution postulate nevertheless poses problems of internal consistency. Either markets are efficient tools, in which case altering the monetary distribution they make will result in less efficiency; or markets are not efficient tools, in which case rather than correcting their effects through taxation afterwards, it would be preferable to regulate them so that they do not generate a high inequality in the first place.

By refusing to look at the mechanisms of primary distribution (that of markets), Saez and Zucman refrain from asking a few essential questions, especially since there is a good reason to believe that the action of markets is not neutral with regard to the development of inequality. Bruce Boghosian, a mathematician from Tufts University in the United States, recently proposed a market model based on a multitude of bilateral transactions (Boghosian 2019). This model is extremely simple and assumes that with each trade occasion, agents have a 50–50 chance of winning or losing an amount equivalent to a fraction of the wealth of the poorest agent. Starting from a situation of equal distribution, the multiplication of transactions very quickly reaches a situation of extreme polarisation.

The idea that the market is a casino where everyone can win and lose is quite familiar to economists. Milton Friedman himself used this metaphor to evoke the functioning of a market economy.[9] Intuitively, we are led to think that if, as in a casino, the chances of winning are equal, then the effect of chance will tend to redistribute wealth randomly without changing the structure of the initial distribution. Conversely, if in the real world a few individuals become very rich, then it is because their chances of winning have been above average, implying that they have a particular talent or skill that make them perform better than average. In other words, the wealth of the rich is deserved. The Boghosian model illustrates the naivety of this intuitive representation since it shows that there are configurations where agents are equally skilled (the winner of each transaction is determined by chance alone) that nevertheless lead to unsustainable levels of inequality.

Can globalisation be tamed?

If inequality is a natural consequence of the functioning of the market, and if the gains of one person have nothing to do with one's own merits, then it should be concluded that, contrary to neoliberal precepts, the role of the state can also be to intervene in the internal mechanisms of markets.

This question cannot be debated according to the binary logic presented by the 1920s and 1930s debate on socialist calculus. It is not a question of opposing a system of centralised planning on the one hand and a perfectly free-market system on the other. Rather, it is about inventing a new role for the state: not organising and controlling the whole economy but mobilising resources to produce what society deems necessary to produce. It is also a question of admitting that the state has *already* become, by force of circumstances, a market player, and that it has largely moved away from its expected role as a referee. Everything in current economic policies contributes to modifying the arbitrages of agents. But instead of facing this situation and accepting to play a full role as strategists, most leaders indulge in the illusion that there is an exogenous economic order produced by markets. Thus, they leave it up to the market to decide which countries will host the industrial investments of tomorrow's economy ... but still hope to attract investors by offering them tax exemptions that often cost more than the cost of building a factory!

The idea that the state can directly influence economic structures is not new. For centuries, it was considered natural to pursue industrial policies based on public spending. The French multinational Saint-Gobain, the current leader in the glass industry, exists because Louis XIV decided to build the Château de Versailles and his minister Jean-Baptiste Colbert did not want to buy the glass and mirrors needed for its construction from Italian manufacturers. In the United States, military and NASA spending has been a tremendous vector for developing today's American technologies and major companies. But these policies are only possible if we refuse to play the game of free and undistorted world competition. If Colbert had organised an international call for tenders to build the *Galerie des Glaces*, as is done today under trade agreements, the construction of the Château de Versailles would undoubtedly have made the fortune of a Venetian glassmaker rather than create one of the finest French companies.

Moreover, international institutions rarely prevent states from intervening and cheating with the rules of globalisation. This form of neomercantilism often proves to be beneficial to the countries that adopt it, as economist Dani Rodrik acknowledges:

> The standard narrative about how trade has benefited developing economies omits a crucial feature of their experience. Countries that managed to leverage globalization, such as China and Vietnam, employed a mixed strategy of export promotion and a variety of policies that violate current trade rules. Subsidies, domestic-content requirements, investment regulations, and, yes, often import barriers were critical to the creation of new, higher-value industries. Countries that rely on free trade alone (Mexico comes immediately to mind) have languished.
>
> *(Rodrik 2018, p. 13)*

By contrast, when neoliberalism is supported by powerful supranational institutions, as in the European case, its effects on prosperity are inconclusive. According to Hayek's prognosis, the European architecture is quite effective in limiting the capacity of states to intervene in the economy without substituting a political authority that can do so at the federal level. The result is powerful asymmetric effects in the allocation of resources that reinforce populist dynamics (see Chapter 1). Worse, the only weapons available to states are taxation or social dumping which generates an exacerbation of uncooperative attractiveness policies.

This situation, where markets are emancipated from political control, appears so detrimental to economic development that Rodrik qualifies the European situation as a sort of gloomy "hyperglobalisation":

> After the 1980s, the EU made a big leap into the darkness. It adopted an ambitious single market agenda that aimed to unify Europe's economies,

whittling away at national policies that hampered the free movement not just of goods but also of services, people, and capital. The euro, which established a single currency among a subset of member states, was the logical extension of this agenda. This was hyperglobalization on a European scale.

(ibid., p. 77)

According to Rodrik, the European situation is untenable in the long run. Markets cannot engender sustainable prosperity without some form of political regulation since, in his view, "all successful economies are, in fact, mixed" *(ibid. 131)*. Therefore, Europe should eventually choose either to retreat from economic integration or establish a supranational power of a political nature capable of counterbalancing the regulatory power of the markets. This would imply putting an end to the sovereignty and independence of European nations.

The same problem arises on a global scale. The process of economic integration based on the multiplication of free trade agreements and the supervision of international institutions tends to limit the independence of states by removing their ability to control their economies.[10] But, unlike the European case, there is no question of states giving up their sovereignty entirely. Besides, the institutions that supervise the conformity of trade policies do not have the same force as in the European Union.[11] Thus, even if neoliberal principles impose in theory strict neutrality of public action, many governments do not resign themselves to passivity and behave a bit like cue sport players who, while claiming to respect the rules, blow on the pool balls to deviate their trajectories.

Let's extend the metaphor. In today's globalised pool game, populists are the ones who propose to stop blowing and take pool balls in their hands instead. One can legitimately be offended by this rudeness, but perhaps it would be better – and more useful – to avoid hypocrisy. If very few countries play by the rules, perhaps it is because the rules are not good. What is disturbing about populists is that they do not seem to want to play by any rule. But what is also disturbing about economists and neoliberals is that they pretend to impose rules that no country can follow without risking their economic survival. As a result, one can argue that it would be better to completely change the way we think about globalisation and stop pretending to play pool, when in reality, many have switched to bowling!

Although he does not recant his opinion of the contributions of globalisation and the importance of letting markets organise a large part of the economy, Rodrik proposes some solutions for rethinking the rules of globalisation. Anti-dumping is taken into consideration in the treaties that regulate international trade. A country that subsidises its exports or gains market share by selling its products at a loss with the sole aim of eradicating competing companies may be sanctioned by its trading partners. But, Rodrik points out, when the dumping is social, fiscal, or deals with environmental protection, no retaliatory measures are possible. This situation jeopardises the very basis of free trade agreements and pushes individual countries to promote deadly dumping strategies. Rodrik, therefore, proposes that future trade agreements should consider and condemn social, fiscal, and ecological dumping practices.

This reorientation appears all the more urgent when Rodrik shows how the emergence of populist movements marks the end of the free trade dynamic. Trade agreements should therefore be put back on the table and thoroughly reviewed to incorporate considerations linked to the common good, even if it means reducing the competitive radicalism that is currently at work.

More broadly, Rodrik believes that the requirement of democracy should be placed above that of international trade and free movement of capital (*ibid.*, p. 12). But even with democracy being put forward, many questions remain. Any major change in the rules of international trade risks creating winners and losers. For example, some countries that currently benefit from the absence of rules governing all forms of dumping would lose out if there were to be major changes to trade treaties. Economies that have few resources or lack territorial factors of production, and therefore rely on fiscal and social competitiveness for their development, could be the victims of a globalisation process regulated in the name of criteria that are not strictly economic. There is also the question of the political legitimacy of a profound reorganisation of globalisation. Who will decide on the criteria for fair globalisation? Who will pay any compensation that may be granted to the losing countries? In other words, moving from pool to bowling is likely to raise new questions which Rodrik's general proposals are far from being able to answer. What is certain, however, is that the issue of trade regulation requires a reflection on the relationship between political institutions and the market. As we face an economy that is becoming increasingly integrated globally, should we not be able to organise a form of political regulation on an international scale? This is what economist Thomas Piketty proposes and what we shall now study.

The last supranational temptation of Thomas Piketty

The success of the English edition of *Capital in the Twenty-First Century* (2014) brought Thomas Piketty worldwide renown. This nearly 700-page book, written in an accessible language and benefiting from an extraordinary database that establishes the distribution and evolution of income in many countries, defends a fairly simple idea: capitalism structurally produces wealth inequality. As it perpetuates and increases from generation to generation, this inequality will end up destroying the internal dynamism of capitalism by rewarding inherited wealth more than work and innovation.

Piketty sums up his thesis with the dilemma of Rastignac, a famous Honoré de Balzac character. In the novel *Père Goriot*, Eugène de Rastignac ambitions to join the ranks of the Parisian upper class. His companion Vautrin admonishes him to choose between two strategies: the first one is to continue his law studies, succeed in them, and manage, with a lot of effort, to obtain a fairly well-paid position which might yet not be enough to allow him to become part of the bourgeoisie; the second one is to marry a young heiress, which would ensure that he will effortlessly benefit from her fortune, giving him access to all the privileges of the upper class without taking the slightest risk (Piketty 2014, pp. 238–40).

The question of the "choice" between working and inheriting is at the heart of the problem posed by inequality, Piketty believes. Indeed, a society without any inequality would probably provide no incentive to work and run a business. However, a society in which the bulk of wealth is accumulated and passed on through inheritance does not provide any greater incentive to work. According to the French economist, the natural slope of the capitalist economy, if unregulated, inevitably leads to such an inequalitarian society.

To demonstrate his point, Piketty proposes a concise explanation of the dynamics of inequality as resulting from two phenomena. The first is the pace of capital accumulation, which depends on the rate of savings. Indeed, all savings are inevitably transformed into financial or real estate assets and, ultimately, into productive capital. The second phenomenon is the return on capital. This return (a net return that takes into account depreciation and obsolescence) constitutes the major part of a country's financial elite's earnings. Moreover, the consumption rate of this elite is marginal, which means that the main part of its income is saved. As a result, Piketty explains, the rate of capital accumulation is approximately equal to the net return on capital.

With such dynamics, a country's financial elite is effortlessly allocated an ever-increasing share of national income. This logic of accumulation appears to be unlimited (as capital continues to grow, so does capital income), which poses obvious problems since when income is not directed towards the holders of capital, it is devoted to paying for labour. Thus, offsetting mechanisms must exist to maintain some remuneration for work and avoid a situation where a very small part of the population ends up benefiting from the totality of the income. These mechanisms are of three kinds: exogenous, endogenous, and political. Inflation and war are the main exogenous factors that tend to reduce the amounts of accumulated capital; economic growth, by increasing the total amount of income to be distributed, makes it possible to reduce the relative share going to capital that has been accumulated in the past; finally, taxation redistributes and limits the share of capital held by the wealthy.

In the developed world, where we can hope for the end of high inflation and wars, only taxation and economic growth can thwart the logic of infinite capital accumulation. This is what makes Piketty say that, if no taxation redistributes wealth, inequality increases structurally according to the two parameters of growth, which he designates by the letter "g", and the rate of return on capital, which he notes as "r". More simply, as long as g is greater than r, inequality regresses; if it is r that is greater than g, inequality increases. Since the late 1960s, Piketty notes, the rate of growth has tended to fall structurally, which widens the difference between r and g. Consequently, the only way to prevent inequality from growing to unsustainable levels is to strengthen fiscal redistribution by increasing the progressivity of taxes. But taxation cannot simply tax income. Wealth should also be assessed and taxed, which implies establishing a global "cadastral financial survey" that would allow to quantify wealth precisely and tax it (even at a low rate) in order to limit its accumulation dynamics (*ibid.*, p. 520).

In his subsequent book published in 2020, *Capital and Ideology*, Piketty extends and clarifies some of his analyses. First, he argues that the refusal to tax and to control the dynamics of accumulation is the product of an ideology he describes as "proprietarianism" and which he summarises as the idea that "the primary purpose of the social and political order is to protect private property rights for the sake of both individual emancipation and social stability" (Piketty 2020, p. 189). However, in his view, this ideology – which is intimately linked to the establishment of contemporary capitalism – is deadly and is not based on any natural principle. It has historically justified practices that today appear aberrant and immoral, such as colonialism, censitary suffrage, and the fact that the United States and France, when they got rid of slavery, preferred to compensate slave owners rather than the slaves themselves.

In Piketty's view, fair taxation is necessary not only to finance public services and collective investments but also to avoid the social collapse that natural dynamic of exacerbating inequality inevitably produces. Piketty is far from being anti-capitalist, and the taxation he proposes is not intended to replace the market economy with a new form of socialism. On the contrary, he believes that such taxation is necessary and indispensable to complement the long-term survival of the market economy. Thus, the problem is less about financing additional public expenditure than about avoiding social and economic destabilisation. The tax revenue he proposes is therefore not intended to be accompanied by greater public interventionism but should be returned to economic agents to be maintained in the market sphere. He imagines, for instance, that each person aged 25 years could benefit from a financial capital equivalent to 60% of the average wealth, which would result from the taxation of large fortunes and inheritances.

Piketty has nothing against the market, nor even against the principle of private property. He just wishes to curb the dynamic of unlimited accumulation of wealth, because it is likely to call into question the very foundations of capitalism by creating a class of parasites with no real incentive to invest or work. The problem he faces is that it is nowadays extremely easy for wealthy individuals to hide their wealth and escape the tax system. He, therefore, proposes that supranational assemblies could debate and impose transnational taxation that would prohibit any possibility of tax evasion on a continental and/or global scale. Piketty proposes, in short, to overcome the division of the world imposed by the existence of states and organise a regulation of the world economy through a form of supranational democracy. The European Union could be the vanguard of such a project since it is very far advanced in its economic and institutional integration. In this way, sovereignty would move from what is currently national sovereignty to a form of European and then global sovereignty.

It is not necessary to develop here the obvious theoretical and practical difficulties that the supranational solution proposed by Piketty would inevitably encounter in its implementation. In the current state of the world, states remain the arena of political power and democratic debates, even within the European Union. Whether we are happy or sorry about this, it is a fact that does not seem likely to change in the short run.

What is worth emphasising, however, is the total lack of reflection on the role and effects of the markets in the dynamics of inequalities. Like Emmanuel Saez and Gabriel Zucman, Piketty intends to correct the effects of the distribution of wealth through taxation alone without questioning how resources are organised and distributed in the first place. Moreover, the issue of quantitative inequality in income and wealth is only one of the problems that societies face today. The current tensions in the European Union, which have been analysed in the first chapter of this book, are not only related to inequality as defined by Piketty. The forces of agglomeration and polarisation that empty entire regions of economic resources and agglomerate them into megalopolises where rents become stratospheric are problems that will not be solved by simple fiscal redistributions. The structural imbalances and economic specialisation between countries and regions caused by the division of labour on a continental scale tend to, as we have seen, strengthen regional and national identities and risk destroying the ability to establish the multilateral cooperation Piketty advocates.

In other words, inequalities are not only quantitative and monetary. A worker or a farmer may have the same income, but they do not necessarily have the same vision of the world; working in finance, industry, or public services is not socially equivalent. Thus, the fact that Poland is becoming the territory where the European assembly industry is growing may have an impact not only on its economic development, specialising its population in a particular type of employment, but also on the development of all its social institutions. Market-driven specialisation and division of labour make territories dissimilar, deepen social and political divisions, and structure inequalities that a simple monetary redistribution cannot solve.

Similarly, the creation of a progressive individual carbon tax on consumption that Piketty proposes will not be sufficient to invent new energies and organise the ecological transition of capitalism on its own. Although monetary incentives may be powerful tools, they are not sufficient to take up such technical challenges.

In short, Piketty's reasoning is too quantitative. He is willing to aggregate dimensions that are not necessarily homogenous and thinks that monetary incomes had the same meaning regardless of its origin. But sociology and anthropology teach us the opposite. It is not equivalent to receive money as a compensation for a job and as a social benefit. Similarly, solidarity between people on the same territory is not the same as impersonal solidarity organised by flows of subsidies from foreign territories. Piketty may well state that "there is no essential reason why there should be more solidarity between Bavarians and Lower Saxons or between Greater Parisians and Bretons than between all four and Piedmontese or Catalans" (*ibid.*, p. 1026), but there are many historical, cultural, and linguistic reasons why a person from Ile-de-France feels closer to a Breton than to a Catalan, or why a Bavarian feels more solidarity with a Lower Saxon than with a Piedmontese. The fact that nations are artificial and historically constructed entities does not prevent them from existing. For now, the world without borders dreamed of by Thomas Piketty is pure abstraction.

The abstract and quantitative dimensions of Piketty's analyses can be found in his judgement on inequality. James Galbraith (2016) recalls that capital is not a simple homogenous entity that can be added together as the contemporary economic theory does in its models.[12] A factory is a physical building that has value only as long as what it produces is useful. If a new technology or changes in fashion mean that a commodity is no longer consumed, all the capital that is used exclusively to produce that commodity and that cannot be redeployed immediately loses its value. More fundamentally, the ownership of capital is not a simple patrimony. Galbraith points out that, for Marx, capital is not just a physical factor of production, but represents "the authority to make decisions and to extract surplus from the worker" (Galbraith 2016, p. 113). In other words, capital is primarily the political balance of power in the market and not a mere passive possession of wealth.

It is this political dimension that is sorely lacking in Piketty's analysis. Where does the rate of return on capital come from? In *Capital in the Twenty-First Century*, Piketty claims a world's long run 4–5% rate of profit over a period that includes even the pre-capitalist societies (Piketty 2014, fig. 10.10 and 10.11)! He thus assumes implicitly that the return on capital is exogeneous to any social or economic arrangement. But there is nothing exogenous about this value, which depends on the balance of power within companies and the institutional environment. Karl Marx analysed this perfectly. In his view, the entrepreneur's profit is linked to the employer's ability to generate surplus value from the labour force. However, because workers are in competition and dependent on capital, this surplus escapes them (in this sense, Marx confirms Smith's analysis of the inequality of power relations that structure the labour market). It is therefore conceivable that unionisation, full employment, social rights, and many other measures are likely to strengthen the bargaining power of workers and enable them to obtain better wages, which implies a lower rate of return on capital, and thus generates a reduction in market inequality. Similarly, as demonstrated above, the very logic of neoliberal globalisation implies that states compete with each other to attract capital by promising companies a rate of return that is always higher than the one they can obtain in the neighbouring country.

But is the Piketty solution adequate to break this logic? Instead of creating a global tax on capital, wouldn't it be simpler to prevent capital from arbitrating freely between different countries? In this sense, the most effective way to limit the global circulation of capital would be to re-establishing borders between the national financial markets, as was the case with Bretton Woods. The supranational solutions that Piketty dreams about appear to be easy to implement only in John Lennon's *Imagine* world where "there's no countries".

What economists ignore

The odd thing about Piketty's analysis is the way he draws the line in the debate between him and the conservatives. There are the dogmatists of property on one side (the "proprietarians") and those who, like himself, admit the necessity of redistribution on the other. This is how he makes Friedrich Hayek a pure defender of property, evacuating almost completely the predominant place of the market from his thinking (Piketty 2020, pp. 821–25). In the same way, he largely reinterprets Polanyi's work by turning it into a simple anti-proprietarianism and forgetting that the core of his entire analysis is that of the relationship between democracy and market. In a footnote, Piketty justifies his position as follows:

> Polanyi does not explicitly use the term "ownership society," but that is what he has in mind. In particular, he stresses the quasi-sacralization of private property in the period 1815–1914. Broadly speaking, I think the term "proprietarianism" better captures what is at stake here than "liberalism," which plays on the ambiguity between economic liberalism and political liberalism.
>
> *(ibid., p. 469)*

Indeed, as far as Piketty is concerned, and this is his big difference with Polanyi, the way the market works, the competitive organisation of the economy, the fact that social institutions are subject to market imperatives, do not seem to pose any real problem. He thus endorses the proposal of economist Julia Cagé (2020) who argues that the financing of political life should be organised through "democratic equality vouchers". "In a nutshell, the idea would be to provide every citizen with an annual voucher worth, say, 5 euros, which could be assigned to the political party or movement of his or her choosing" (Piketty 2020, p. 1018). Organising the financing of political life this way would necessarily have important consequences for democratic life. Instead of receiving public funds based on representativeness criteria, as in the majority of contemporary democracies, political parties would receive funding directly through the action of citizens. Such a system would profoundly change the relationship between the public and the politicians since the latter would be forced to organise large-scale promotional campaigns by canvassing the population directly, as a commercial enterprise does. This logic can only, in the long run, strengthen commercial representations and would risk organising political life around a provider/customer relationship. Finally, there is a particular risk that it may not even be fairer than the current situation. In the same way that election campaigns most often result in the victory of the most established parties, fundraising campaigns are likely to benefit the most established and structured organisations, and therefore may not change the financial and political hierarchy between parties.

This way of ignoring the issues raised by the functioning of markets is not unique to Piketty. It can be found among most progressive economists who want to fight against rising inequality. All of them castigate neoliberalism and equating it, as Joseph Stiglitz does, with "market fundamentalism". Rodrik writes, for example, that Milton Friedman "presented government as the enemy of the market" (Rodrick 2018, p. 131). This caricatured view is simply inaccurate. The 1951 text presented at the beginning of this chapter shows that Friedman was not opposed to the role of the state in the market economy. He confirmed this position ten years later in *Capitalism and Freedom*, stating that "the consequent liberal is not an anarchist". Neither Friedman nor Hayek set the state against the market. On the contrary, like all neoliberals, they show that the laissez-faire policy is not enough to protect markets and that markets need a "referee" or a "traffic code" that can adapt to changes in behaviour and technology to allow agents to trade freely. The state is therefore charged with this particular role of maintaining the institutions necessary for markets. Finally, Friedman is not against taxes and he even admits that, in times of crisis, state interventions can be effective.[13]

While caricaturing the neoliberal conception, these progressive economists find it difficult to contradict the principles on which it is actually based. All of them recognise the important role that competitive markets must play in the functioning of the economy. In a collective text, Suresh Naidu, Dani Rodrik, and Gabriel Zucman write:

> Economists study markets (among other things), and we naturally feel a certain pride in explaining the way markets operate. When markets work well, they do a good job of aggregating information and allocating scarce resources. The principle of comparative advantage, which lies behind the case for free trade, is one of the profession's crown jewels—both because it explains important aspects of the international economy and because it is, on its face, so counterintuitive. Similarly, economists believe in the power of incentives; we have evidence that people respond to incentives, and we have seen too many well-meaning programs fail because they did not pay adequate attention to the creative ways in which people behave to realize their own goals.
>
> *(Naidu et al. 2019)*

Later on, they add:

> Economics does have its universals, of course, such as market-based incentives, clear property rights, contract enforcement, macroeconomic stability, and prudential regulation. These higher-order principles are generally presumed to be conducive to superior economic performance. But these

principles are compatible with an almost infinite variety of institutional arrangements with each arrangement producing a different distributional outcome and a different contribution to overall prosperity.

(ibid.)

This text, which seeks to promote an inclusive economy based on the contributions of contemporary economics, is in no way incompatible with the neoliberal precepts as presented earlier. It does not propose a doctrine profoundly different from that of Friedman or Hayek. Like Friedman, the authors consider that markets need public institutions to function. Like Friedman, they admit the imperfection of markets when the full conditions of the competitive model are not met. They conclude that there is a multitude of institutional arrangements that can make markets work better. Here, too, there is nothing new. As we have seen, neoliberals are far from agreeing on the details of their recommendations. The Germans of the ordoliberal school are very attached to an independent administrative authority to defend the competitive order, which Friedman and Hayek refuse to support since they believe that private monopolies are often temporary and generally less harmful than public intervention. However, Hayek and Friedman are at odds with each other on the monetary architecture and have a very different interpretation of the causes of the crisis of the 1930s.

Neoliberalism cannot be market fanaticism because its underlying idea is that market failures exist and public action is necessary to remedy them. What neoliberals do not accept is the questioning of certain fundamental principles: the advantages of free trade, the need for competitive markets to produce an effective price and incentive system, and the rule of law. From these principles, they draw several general recommendations: governments must avoid discretionary intervention, preserve price stability, maintain competition, and guarantee social order.

Most of the proposals put forward by the progressive economists we have just studied contradict these principles only marginally. Of course, Rodrik would like to reconsider free trade treaties to avoid the harmful effects of what he calls "hyperglobalisation". But the addition of the prefix "hyper" shows that he is not opposed to the idea of globalisation. He simply judges that its excesses destabilise the social and political order. He, therefore, proposes an arrangement within the framework: free trade preserved, but attenuated to favour greater social stability and prevent populist chaos. The same reasoning applies to the French economists Saez, Zucman, and Piketty. By affirming their commitment to more progressive taxation, they renounce the strict neutrality of the state in the incentive system. But this is neither new nor profoundly incompatible with the neoliberal architecture. Walter Lippmann proposed progressive taxation and high inheritance fiscality as early as 1937. Other neoliberals have defended the principle of a heavy inheritance tax, notably German economist Alexander Rüstow, who participated in the Lippmann Colloquium and was a member of the Mont Pelerin Society.[14]

Finally, if neoliberalism wishes to preserve budget balances, it is perfectly capable of accommodating cyclical deficits. On Friedman's advice, US President Ronald Reagan did not have much hesitation in pursuing an expansionary fiscal policy based on lowering taxes and increasing public deficit.

The variety of economic policies compatible with neoliberalism is very wide. But it does not admit just any measure. Neoliberalism is neither compatible with protectionism and mercantilism nor discretionary interventionism nor anything that would threaten the rule of law. A neoliberal head of state could not afford to question the independence of the central bank and put pressure on its president as Donald Trump did when he threatened to remove Jerome Powell from office.[15]

Therefore, it is difficult to follow Stiglitz when he states that Trump's economic policy is in the continuity of Ronald Reagan's (Stiglitz 2019a, preface) and would present the dark side of neoliberalism, while, for example, Bill Clinton and Tony Blair would be the representatives of "neoliberalism with a human face" (Stiglitz 2019b). While Reagan, Clinton, and Blair most certainly pursued policies based on the neoliberal framework when they were in power, Trump cannot be placed in the same category. Certainly, the massive tax cuts that Reagan and Trump implemented, and their pro-business bias, may give the superficial impression that their policies are similar. But Reagan had a much more consistent and structured plan than Trump. He let Paul Volker, the chairman of the Federal Reserve, wage war on inflation by raising interest rates dramatically; he played the globalisation game, engaged the United States in free trade agreements, used the American diplomatic and economic influence to reorient international institutions, and impose neoliberalism in the developing world. Reagan did not break with the principles of multilateralism nor with GATT, as Trump did with the WTO.

Donald Trump is not a neoliberal leader. Generally speaking, populist leaders do not have a real economic project. What characterises them is that they offer the temptation to break not only with neoliberalism but with liberalism as a whole; they question the principles of the rule of law and reaffirm the discretionary power of politics in all areas of social life, without exceptions. Their political success rests on the implicit revolutionary promise they make by showing they are not afraid to overthrow the established order and do just about anything. This is why the more they are criticised by editorialists, intellectuals, and the most venerable representatives of the political system, the stronger they become.

The rise of populism is a danger to democracy and freedoms. The populist movements that are arising around the world are the result of the strong social tensions that have grown even stronger since the neoliberal era began. In a sense, they are a product of it. Hence, populism will not be fought by avoiding a substantive attack on neoliberal principles. It will take more than a new tax policy or a softening of globalisation to respond to the process of disintegration that many democracies are currently undergoing.

Economists have an important role to play in redefining the rules on which to rebuild the global economy. However, they seem more concerned with fixing neoliberalism than getting rid of it. Individually, none of the measures they propose is fundamentally incompatible with neoliberalism. But what would happen if all of them were implemented? Imagine an economy with a public health system, a national employment guarantee, very progressive taxation on income and wealth, regulation of finance and trade that would prohibit a country from taking advantage of the loopholes of globalisation to practise social or fiscal dumping, and a monetary policy that would guarantee that states could finance themselves at a moderate cost. It is clear that, in such a system, the regulatory role of the market would be much more limited than it is now. The architecture of incentives would also be very different and market prices would not determine, as they do today, all or almost all of our economic behaviour. The problem is that such a world would be very difficult for a contemporary economist to understand and study. They would have to forget many certainties and certain automatisms of thought.

The paradox is that a process of complete repair of neoliberalism would likely destroy neoliberalism. But no economist seems ready to think of such a world with the tools at their disposal. If economic behaviour is no longer primarily determined by markets, how will they effectively adjust to each other? Such a question is likely to remain unanswered if we start from the premise that markets must be the only regulators of economic activity.

But is this belief in the efficiency of markets based on indisputable results of economic science or on beliefs and preconceptions? It is important to raise this question and discuss it openly. Otherwise, we would be condemning ourselves to indulge in fragile tinkering in the name of the sacredness of markets and their presumed efficiency, when in fact other rules to make the economy work could be imagined.

How economics brought markets into the forefront of its concerns

Rethinking economics involves questioning the centrality of the market. "Economics studies more generally the matching of supply and demand", writes Nobel Prize winner Jean Tirole in his book that presents his conception of economics to the general audience (Tirole 2017, p. 45). Indeed, for most people, the study of market economies can easily be equated with the science of markets. This shared belief makes it possible to invoke the famous "laws of supply and demand" to explain one thing and its opposite. Whether purchases of lemons fall while their prices rise is proof that the laws of supply and demand are validated: demand adjusts to price. Whether purchases of lemons decrease while observed prices decrease is also proof that the laws of supply and demand are validated: prices have adjusted to an overproduction of lemons.[16]

To understand this mystery, it is worth recalling that in contemporary economic thinking the way prices and quantities are supposed to adjust to each other is not based on a single "law" but three. The first is the *law of demand* which states that the quantity demanded evolves in the inverse relationship to the price of a commodity; the second is the *law of supply* which postulates that an increase in price leads to an increase in the quantity supplied; the third is the *law of price adjustment* which assumes that when supply is greater than demand, the price decreases, and when demand is greater than price, the price increases.

These laws pose two basic problems. The first is that their functions and variables are reversible so that they can be made to say whatever you want them to say. In one law, it is the price that is a function of quantities, and in the others, it is the quantities that are a function of the price. This situation creates major problems of internal consistency and explains why two contradictory phenomena can be explained using one "law" or the other, depending on what one intends to demonstrate. The second problem is that the "matching of supply and demand" that is supposed to occur on the markets is not observable in reality. The fact that the number of sales is always precisely equal to the number of purchases says absolutely nothing about the existence of unsold goods or more or less consciously conceived purchase plans that could not be realised. For most commodities, if purchases are measured well, we know almost nothing about demand, and it is virtually impossible to quantify supply precisely at a given time. Anyone who has ever looked at bins in a supermarket can see that a large part of the supply has never been able to match its demand. At most, one can observe that the capitalist system tends to overproduce in order to avoid missing sales, but this structural overproduction only very rarely translates into lower prices, contrary to what the law of price adjustment supposes. In most cases, producers have no trouble discreetly eliminating their unsold goods. It is only in times of severe crises when unsold goods accumulate and sales figures are no longer up to expectations that prices can fall or even collapse.[17]

The reader may be surprised to learn that it is perfectly possible to reason like an economist without putting the market at the heart of economic thinking and without making extensive use of the famous laws of supply and demand. After all, this is what the economists who drew directly on Adam Smith's work have been doing for almost a century.

As we saw in the previous chapter, Smith did not believe in perfect markets. For him, competition is largely driven by industrialists and merchants who do not hesitate to agree on prices, manipulate consumers, and hijack laws and regulations to their benefit. Thus, unlike today's textbooks, which invariably begin with an introduction to markets,[18] Smith devotes the first chapter of the *Wealth of Nations* to the study of the firm and the division of labour. He does this because he believes that, ultimately, the true source of wealth is to be found in labour. This is summed up in the opening sentence of the book: "The annual work of every nation is the fund which originally supplies it with all necessaries and conveniences of life which it annually consumes, and which consist always either in the immediate produce of that labour, or in what is purchased with that produce from other nations" (Smith 1776, p. 4).

As its name suggests, the labour theory of value used by Smith – and subsequently by Ricardo and other economists of the classical school – implies that the exchange value of goods is derived from labour. For economic growth to occur, more must be produced. This can be done either by working more or – this is rather what the classical economists advocate – by making better use of labour through innovation, through the accumulation of machinery, capital goods and skills (what Smith called fixed capital), or finally through the division of labour, which implies a better organisation of production. But there is a limit to these arrangements for improving labour efficiency: the financial capacity of firms. The volume of sales needs to increase in order for the entrepreneur to be able to recruit more workers, innovate more, accumulate fixed capital, and deepen the division of labour. In this way, the firm grows with the size of its market, and the market expands with growth and increased purchasing power.

Classical economics theorises a cumulative growth dynamic based on the existence of increasing returns to scale. The market accompanies this growth, but value emerges from the productive process, not from the market. Changes in market behaviour have therefore no effect on the fundamental value of a commodity; the market price, which is determined by supply and demand, is a cyclical price that only gravitates around value. Yet, the market is not useless. By varying prices, it allows for the adjustment of production incentives and serves to guide investment from one sector to another. If it does not determine value, the market resolves cyclical imbalances and stabilises supply.

The influence of consumer demand and needs is missing from the classical approach. For this approach, value is objective: it is embodied in the commodity itself and not in the use or utility that the buyer derives from it.

In 1871, the English economist William Stanley Jevons published a treatise on economics in which he firmly opposed classical theory. He writes:

> Prevailing opinions make labour rather than utility the origin of value; and there are even those who distinctly assert that labour is the cause of value. I show, on the contrary, that we have only to trace out carefully the natural laws of the variation of utility, as depending upon the quantity of commodity in our possession, in order to arrive at a satisfactory theory of exchange, of which the ordinary laws of supply and demand are a necessary consequence.
>
> *(Jevons 1871, pp. 1–2)*

What are these "natural laws of the variation of utility" that Jevons claims to be the origin of the "laws of supply and demand"? Classical economists rejected utility as the basis for the exchange value by arguing that diamonds, which have a great deal of value, are far less useful than water, which has almost none. "Wrong!" says Jevons, you cannot estimate the utility of a good regardless of how much of it you already own. It is not the abstract utility of a good, in general, that must be conceived but the particular utility of an additional unit of that good to a specific consumer. Rather than conceiving value objectively, it must therefore be conceived subjectively, according to the context in which the purchaser is situated. For example, if water has virtually no value in England, it is simply because the English already have a large natural supply of it. Diamonds, on the contrary, are so rare that although they have little utility of their own, owning one is far more precious than getting an extra pint of water. In other words, utility is not an attribute of the commodity itself, but an attribute related to the needs of buyers. And this utility depends on the quantities of goods already possessed. The more someone is endowed with a good, the less useful it is to obtain one more. This is the law of diminishing marginal utility which means that one must assess value at the margin, according to the relative scarcity of the goods one has.

This way of reasoning opens an entirely new perspective for economic theory, which is why historians of economic thought speak of the "marginalist revolution". By changing the theory of value from labour to utility, economic thought was profoundly renewed and put forward propositions that still seem quite iconoclastic today: value is subjective, it depends on a human desire for possession; scarcity is the source of all value; producing more does not necessarily make one richer. Even more heterodox: the society of abundance is a myth since if everything was abundant, nothing would have any value anymore.

Indeed, Jevons' theory implies a complete shift in thinking economics. With the theory of utility value, the question is no longer whether to produce more and more but rather to distribute better. A world in which all diamonds are owned by one person is a world in which diamonds would be useful to everyone... except to the person who owns them because she would have too many diamonds to really appreciate them. This world would actually be very unsatisfying. How could it be arranged? Well, by the exchange! Whoever has all the diamonds may have needs that other members of society could satisfy. She will be happy to get rid of one of her diamonds, which is of little value to her, in exchange for a good or service that someone else would find less useful to themselves than a diamond.

Now let us imagine that everyone has exactly the same number of diamonds. Should this perfect equality of wealth mean the end of the diamond trade? No, because needs and usefulness are subjective. Each person has different tastes and needs. For some, diamonds will be more useful than for others, even if everyone has the same amount. The law of diminishing marginal utility does not require the utility to be the same for everyone in a given quantity. Moreover, needs may change as circumstances change: "I don't need a diamond now, but if I want to get engaged next year, a diamond would be useful to set into a ring". Overall, the market combines subjective utilities attached to individuals to determine prices; since these utilities may vary, the prices must evolve and adapt according to subjective needs which themselves are constantly changing and adjusting.

What emerges from the theory of utility value is the idea that exchange can intrinsically produce value as long as it is freely accepted by the contracting parties. This puts the market back at the centre of economic analysis. From the end of the 19th century, thanks to Jevons' contributions, economic theory saw its definition and objectives evolve. Whereas Adam Smith saw the aim of political economy as "to enrich both the people and the sovereign" by promising them "plentiful revenue or subsistence", contemporary economists conceive economics as the discipline that should organise an optimal allocation of resources. Thus, in his textbook, Gregory Mankiw offers the following definition:

> The management of society's resources is important because resources are scarce. Scarcity means that society has limited resources and therefore cannot produce all the goods and services people wish to have. Just as each member of a household cannot get everything she wants, each individual in a society cannot attain the highest standard of living to which she might aspire.
>
> Economics is the study of how society manages its scarce resources. In most societies, resources are allocated not by an all-powerful dictator but through the combined choices of millions of households and firms.
>
> *(Mankiw 2017, p. 4)*

Smith's central question: "How can we produce more?" is transformed into a very different question: "How can scarce resources be better allocated?". It is this shift in the focus of economic science that explains the move from a theory centred on labour and production to a theory centred on market and allocation.

The impossible symmetry of the Marshallian theory

Jevons' theory was not immediately accepted by professional economists. At the time when British manufacturing dominated the world, it may have seemed surprising to overshadow productive phenomena. Can the whole economy be summed up as an allocation and market issue? Is utility really the only dimension to consider in the theory of value?

This debate was finally settled a few years later by the English Cambridge economist Alfred Marshall. In his famous textbook *Principles of Economics*, he proposed a synthesis of the two approaches, formulated as follows:

> The nominal value of everything ... rests, like the keystone of an arch, balanced in equilibrium between the contending pressures of its two opposing sides; the forces of demand press on the one side, and those of supply on the other.
>
> *(Marshall 1920, pp. 436–7)*

The Marshallian theory considers both the utility, which characterises demand, and the cost of production, which characterises supply, as the two fundamental dimensions that are supposed to determine value. It relies on the opposition of the two approaches to invent an entirely new theory, the theory of market value. The Oxford economist Francis Edgeworth acknowledged the tour de force of Marshall's proposal. "His predecessors have tilted against each other from opposite sides of the shield of truth: he alone has surveyed with an equal eye both the gold side [of supply], which most attracted Ricardo, and the silver side [of demand], on which Jevons fixed too exclusive attention", he writes in his review of Marshall's textbook (Edgeworth 1891, p. 611).

This theory is the one most freshmen still learn today. It combines the law of supply and the law of demand to graphically establish, at the junction of the two curves, an equilibrium between price and quantity that jointly determine value. This approach is called partial equilibrium because only one commodity, isolated from the rest of the economy, is accounted for.

While it seems to resolve the debate on value by sending each school back to its part of truth, the Marshallian theory was also heavily criticised. Using two contradictory theories, it proposes a model based on a principle of symmetry that forces it to formulate unlikely and problematic hypotheses.

The core of the partial equilibrium analysis is that the equilibrium price is determined by the balance of power between two parts of the market: the suppliers and the demanders. The existence of this equilibrium point rests on two conditions. The first is that there is a point of intersection between the two curves; the second is that neither of the two curves is perfectly horizontal or vertical, otherwise quantities or prices would be determined by only one of the two sides.

Why is the demand curve decreasing? The market demand curve is supposed to represent the aggregation of all consumer demands as a function of the market price. In Jevons' theory, each consumer expresses a specific demand that can be very different from one individual to another (utilities are subjective); but under the law of diminishing marginal utility, as the quantity they obtain increases, their propensity to pay for more decreases. In other words, as consumers consume more and more, they demand lower and lower price for agreeing to buy an additional unit. Thus, all of them have a demand that moves in the opposite direction to the price. Logically, at the aggregate level, the market demand also diminishes as price rises: the demand curve is decreasing as a function of price.

What happens on the supply side is much less clear. At the individual level, a rising supply curve means that suppliers require an increasingly higher unit price to agree to sell off an increasing quantity of commodities. This logic is

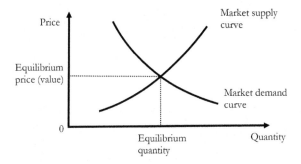

FIGURE 3.3 Representation of a market in partial equilibrium.

also a consequence of the principle of diminishing marginal utility. The lower the stock of commodities owned by suppliers, the more value they place on the commodities they have left. Therefore, the price has to rise in order for supply to do so. The problem is that, in this case, one thinks in terms of given stocks without taking production into account. What happens if, instead of drawing on limited stocks, suppliers become capable of producing? Then the price offered by the market has to be compared with the cost of production. At this point, the theory goes off the rails. The logic of supply is now bound to be very different from that of demand. If the ability to produce has to be considered, there are two possible scenarios. Either the cost of production is greater than or equal to the price, in which case the producers have no reason to produce, and their supply is zero; or the cost of production is lower than the price, in which case the supply is maximum and without limit. As long as the producers can make a profit, they have no reason to stop selling. At the aggregate level, an increase in price no longer has an impact on supply because as soon as the price exceeds the cost of production for one or more suppliers, they start producing at full capacity. The market supply is therefore perfectly elastic, and the supply curve is a horizontal line at the level where the price slightly exceeds the production cost. In this case, the equilibrium price is determined exclusively by the cost of production, and it must be assumed that neither demand nor utility has any effect on the value. This is a return to the classic economic theory of Smith and Ricardo.

For the supply curve to be increasing, a complementary assumption is needed, that of decreasing returns to scale. Indeed, to keep, at the individual level, the property of an increasing supply curve, the marginal cost (the cost of the last unit produced) must increase. Not only must this property be true in the short run, i.e. when the producer does not have time to make new investments, but also in the long run, since the equilibrium price expresses value, that is a medium- and long-term property and not a cyclical situation. This means that when industrialists decide to expand their plant or build a new one, their average unit production cost must increase. Otherwise, they would not have to demand a higher price to produce additional units.

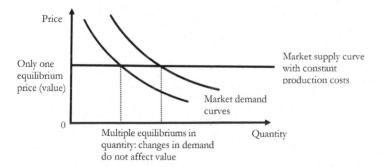

FIGURE 3.4 Partial equilibrium with a constant production cost.

A. Smith's *Wealth of Nations* theorises the principle of increasing returns. It shows how sales increase makes a company more efficient. In trying to work out some kind of compromise about the theory of value, Marshall reached the opposite conclusion: in order to maintain symmetry between supply and demand, returns to scale must be decreasing at the firm level.

Of course, this problem did not escape the attention of economists at the time. As Marshallian theory became popular among economists, voices were raised to challenge its logic, which seemed more concerned with presenting an attractive theory to students than describing reality. In 1922, economic history professor John Clapham referred to the "empty boxes" of Marshallian theory as follows:

> Well, we are building a framework into which we hope facts may in time be fitted. If those who know the facts cannot do the fitting, we shall regret it. But our doctrine will retain its logical – and, may we add, its pedagogic – value. And then you know it goes so prettily into graphs and equations. Besides, in the history of thought analysis has often outrun verification. ... I think a good deal of harm has been done through omission to make it quite clear that the Laws of Returns have never been attached to specific industries; that the boxes are, in fact, empty; that we do not, for instance, at this moment know under what conditions of returns coal or boots are being produced. ... I myself did not appreciate how completely empty the boxes were until I had given a number of public demonstrations with them. And if more acute minds are not likely so to be misled, the rank and file surely are. Unless we have a good prospect in the near future of filling the boxes reasonably full, there is, I hold, grave danger to an essentially practical science such as Economics in the elaboration of hypothetical conclusions about, say, human welfare and taxes in relation to industries which cannot be specified.
>
> *(Clapham 1922, p. 312)*

A few years later, the Marshallian model is attacked by Piero Sraffa, a young Italian economist. Unlike Clapham, Sraffa did not criticise Marshall's theory on its difficulty in agreeing with the facts but on its multiple internal inconsistencies.[19] The whole problem, according to Sraffa, lies in the "fundamental symmetry" on which Marshall's theory is based. "If the cost of production of every unit of the commodity under consideration did not vary with variations in the quantity produced the symmetry would be broken; the price would be determined exclusively by the expenses of production and demand would be unable to have any influence on it at all" (Sraffa 1925, p. 280). To establish that costs vary with quantity, Marshall reinterprets the theories of classical economists by distorting their meaning. For example, the theory of diminishing returns is borrowed from Ricardo's theory of land fertility. According to Ricardo, because of the heterogeneous nature of land – some lands are more fertile and produce more than others – farmers are forced to cultivate less and less productive land to increase production. Yields are decreasing because the best lands are cultivated first.

Thus, the Ricardian theory is based on a fundamental hypothesis: there must be a fixed production factor that is used by the entire sector. It works well for agriculture as a whole because land is a limited and non-reproducible productive asset. But it does not work for manufacturing because it is rare for one sector of activity to exploit all of the production factors on its own. If the factor is shared with other industries, then the increase in production costs may affect every producers that exploit this resource and not just the one that increases its output; diminishing returns are generalised to the economy as a whole and not just to the market that has increased its supply.

As for increasing returns, in Marshallian theory they are only allowed if they concern the entire sector but not the individual companies operating within it. In this case, a firm would risk becoming more efficient than its competitors simply by increasing its production, which would put it in a monopoly situation and allow it to determine its selling price sovereignly.

Finally, and this is where Marshall's theory is inconsistent according to Sraffa, the laws of returns ultimately depends on how the industry is defined, which is unavoidably arbitrary:

> [T]he wider the definition which we assume for "an industry" – that is, the more nearly it includes all the undertakings which employ a given *factor* of production, as, for example, agriculture or the iron industry – the more probable will it be that the forces which make for diminishing returns will play an important part in it; the more restrictive this definition – the more nearly it includes, therefore, only those undertakings which produce a given type of consumable *commodity*, as, for example, fruit or nails – the greater will be the probability that the forces which make for increasing returns will predominate in it.
>
> *(Sraffa 1926, p. 538)*

This arbitrary way of conceiving the market frontier illustrates one of the main limitations of Marshallian theory. By studying markets in isolation, the partial equilibrium approach does not capture the multiple interactions that take place among them. To take just one example, prices are always incomes for some and costs for others. But in both cases, these costs and incomes inevitably have effects on other markets. Incomes will have to be spent somewhere, which should increase demand in other markets; purchases, for their part, decrease the ability of buyers to spend, which should result in lower demand elsewhere. The partial equilibrium model is too simple, its assumptions are too restrictive, and ultimately it fails to demonstrate satisfactorily that equilibrium prices result from anything other than the way Marshall formulated his assumptions.

Deadlocks in the general equilibrium approach

In the 1930s, most economists gradually abandoned the idea of studying the market using the partial equilibrium method and sought a more satisfactory theoretical approach.

The problems of studying markets separately can be addressed by conceiving the equilibrium from the perspective of all markets. In this case, everyone is both a supplier and demander, and everyone decides what to buy and sell by observing not just one price in a specific market but all prices. By construction, this equilibrium considers all interactions that may occur from one market to another. In theory, it is therefore possible that an increase in the price of shoes can either result in a decrease in the demand for fish or in an increase in the supply of bicycles. The way people react to price changes is unique to them, and the result of all these behaviours does not follow a predetermined law. Therefore, the law of supply or demand cannot be established anymore. Through an unlikely interaction effect, it is actually possible that an increase in the price of shoes may ultimately increase the demand for shoes.

This market economy model is known as the general equilibrium. It is presented for the first time by French economist Léon Walras. In his book devoted to "pure political economy", the first edition of which dates from 1874, Walras set out to establish formally how prices emerge and manage to balance supply and demand for all goods. According to Walras, the entire economy could be summed up into a system of equations with three unknowns for each equation: quantities offered, quantities demanded, and relative prices. The mathematical calculation of such a system was, of course, impossible, but Walras claimed that markets would succeed in doing so spontaneously by a method of "tâtonnement" (trial and error) (Walras 1874, p. 127).

At first glance, the relevance of Walras' approach is far from obvious when compared with Marshall's simple and accessible model. The general equilibrium, indeed, allows for greater theoretical flexibility than partial equilibrium. But, on the other – important – side, it does not seem very relevant for understanding phenomena observed in real life because of the extreme complexity of its system of equations.

Walras' successor at the chair of political economy at the University of Lausanne, the Italian economist and sociologist Vilfredo Pareto, acknowledged this shortcoming. If one were to equate the economy of a country with tens of millions of people and thousands of different commodities, it would require a "fabulous number of equations", Pareto admitted. Despite this complexity, however, the market manages, by trial and error and through spontaneous behaviour of individuals, to establish a price system that equates all supply and demand. Hence, the following joke of Pareto when he affirmed that if these equations were to be known it would change the relationship between economics and mathematics:

> In such a case, the roles would be reversed; it would not be mathematics that would come to the aid of political economy, but political economy

that would come to the aid of mathematics. In other words, if all these equations could really be known, the only humanly possible way to solve them would be to observe the practical solution brought about by the market [by means of certain quantities and certain prices].

(Pareto 1909, pp. 117–18)

Despite its incalculable nature, the point of reasoning in general equilibrium is that the question of the economic efficiency can now be answered since the way how all goods are exchanged and distributed can now be studied. For Pareto, an economic efficiency is a situation in which it is impossible to improve one person's situation without worsening the situation of another. He believed market exchange can achieve such an optimality.

Let us take the example of diamonds mentioned earlier. A situation where all diamonds are concentrated not in the hands of one but in the hands of a few is certainly not optimal. Not for a reason of social justice but because this abundance of diamonds in the hands of a few people means that the usefulness of each diamond is, for each owner, very small. Therefore, if they are free to trade, the diamonds would spontaneously go where the buyers are willing to pay the highest price, that is, where they would be most useful, and the usefulness to all would be enhanced. The situation that results from such an exchange is therefore preferable. It may even be described as optimal since if trade stops, it means that it is impossible to improve one person's situation without worsening the situation of someone else.

Sure, but at what price? Where do the prices come from? That is not clear. To solve this problem, Walras, as we have seen, talked about a process of trial and error (*tâtonnement* in French). But that only partially answers the question. In order for a trial and error process to take place, we have to start from existing prices and adjust them as we go along. Who determines from which price system to adjust? And who adjusts it? Walras imagines that the economy works as an organised market, with an auctioneer who collects all the supplies and demands and proposes prices in return. If the supplies and demands are not all equal, new prices are set to which other supplies and demands respond, allowing prices to be adjusted again, and so on. After a long process, a price system eventually emerges that equals all supplies and demands. Exchanges take place. The new situation, Pareto says, is necessarily an optimum. Everybody is satisfied.

Let us be clear. The auctioneer, the process of trial and error, the collection of all supply and demand in all markets … are only fictions that are not meant to describe how the economy actually works. All this model claims to show is that the "pure" economy works and generates effects similar to this fiction. It is a fiction based on two fundamental principles.

- Everyone is free to decide their economic behaviour and tend to maximise their utility in response to prices.

- Competition between suppliers and demanders supresses the ability for an individual agent to have any influence on the market. However, it is the combined action of all agents that determines prices.

The general equilibrium, as presented by Walras and Pareto, resembles, in a more complex and mathematical form, the famous metaphor of the "invisible hand", which is intended to show that any spontaneous behaviour of individuals generates overall well-being. But it should be noted that this is only a conjecture. There is no evidence, not that markets work this way – for it is certain they do not – but that the general equilibrium model can lead to an economic optimality. In order to do so, two questions should be answered:

1. If resources are distributed randomly in an economy, is it certain that there is a price system which makes it possible to equalise all supply and demand?
2. Starting from a random distribution, is it possible to arrive at this price system through a process of trial and error?

In 1954, economists Kenneth Arrow and Gérard Debreu formally demonstrated that, under certain conditions, there is a price system that equalises all supply and demand according to the general equilibrium theory (Arrow and Debreu 1954). This proof of the existence of an equilibrium is extremely important since the authors confirm that this equilibrium constitutes an optimal situation from the point of view of economic agents. Moreover, since an equilibrium exists regardless of the initial distribution, any optimal situation can be obtained by varying that initial distribution. In other words, state intervention in the functioning of the market becomes irrelevant.

The proof of the existence of the equilibrium was done mathematically and based on a number of conditions, such as a situation of perfect competition, a complete price system, perfectly rational and perfectly informed agents, no transaction costs, perfect homogeneity of commodities. It does not prove that real markets function perfectly, but it does give an indication that it would be possible to establish a price system that generates an economic optimality without the state interfering in the choices of individuals. The conclusion that seems to flow naturally from this demonstration is: in order to improve the overall situation of the economic system, it suffices for the state to ensure the proper functioning of markets by improving information, increasing competition, organising the fluidity of transactions ... to improve the overall situation of the economic system. And if, at the end of the economic process, wealth inequality turns out to be too great and socially unsustainable, then rather than intervening and risk losing efficiency, it would be sufficient to redistribute the initial endowments, leaving individuals free to trade as they wish.

The principles of neoliberalism were, in a way, reinforced by science and by the weight of mathematical proof. But what about the second question, the process of trial and error? To make such a process work, it is necessary to be certain that a single equilibrium exists (otherwise, towards what should the price adjustment converge?) and that the gaps between supplies and demands can be filled by a simple rule of change in the price system. To understand the logic of the trial and error process, let us imagine a situation of imbalance. For some commodities, supply is greater than demand; for others, demand is greater than supply. Then, prices must be adjusted. For commodities where supply is greater than demand, the price should fall, while for those where demand is greater than supply, the price should rise. Does this process eventually converge to a single price system?

In the early 1970s, a few mathematical economists addressed this question and answered in the negative. In particular, they demonstrated that it is impossible to predict how the net demand function (i.e. demand minus supply) in a market changes according to price. In other words, if the net demand for a commodity is positive and there is excess demand, then it cannot be shown that a price increase for that commodity reduces the excess demand.[20] Net demand functions can take any form. This result was called Sonnenschein-Mantel-Debreu theorem. It demonstrates that there is no convergence process towards equilibrium, and it implies that there may be several equilibria.

Economic theory has thus formally demonstrated that, under a set of extremely restrictive assumptions, there is a market price system that makes it possible to equalise the supply and demand for all goods; this price system constitutes an optimal situation (in the sense that one cannot improve someone's lot without worsening the lot of another); the trial and error process imagined by Walras to reach this equilibrium does not work.

What can be deduced from these demonstrations in terms of economic policy recommendations? Certainly not that markets alone can spontaneously allow an economy to converge towards an optimal situation. One should even deduce exactly the opposite. Since it has been proven that, even in a situation of perfect markets, there is no spontaneous convergence process, we cannot rule out that some forms of interventionism are likely to improve the situation for everyone. Strictly speaking, the Sonnenschein-Mantel-Debreu theorem should reinforce the conviction of all those who believe that the state should not simply act on the market framework but within it, because there is formal proof that a "perfect" market cannot spontaneously converge towards the social optimum.

The responsibility of political action

This chapter opened with a reference to the dramatic social situation in the United States. Part of this situation is the result of the COVID-19 pandemic, its erratic management, and the abrupt lockdown; another part is the result of a longer process of social segregation between a minority of the population, who have benefited greatly from globalisation and economic growth, and a majority who are in the lower half of the income distribution and whose living standards have stagnated.

The data show that a political and social rupture occurred some 40 years ago. In 1980, American households which belonged to the poorest half of the American population received about 20% of the national income, while the richest 1% received less than 11%. By 2015, the situation had reversed: the poorest 50% received about 13% of national income, while the share of the top 1% had almost doubled to 20% (Piketty 2020, p. 524).

While the inequality situation in the United States appears more serious than elsewhere, all developed countries have been affected by the widening gap between rich and poor. It must be admitted that this development is not the consequence of a natural tendency of the economy to create inequality spontaneously. There is no natural distribution of wealth, nor is there a "pure" economy. How people manage to extract wealth from the market is the product of a political and economic balance of power. However, this balance of power has changed around the world, allowing the rich to extract more than before without benefiting economic growth. Indeed, according to the OECD, the contrary is likely to have happened: the more concentrated the wealth, the lower the growth.

Much has changed in the world over the last 40 years: the end of the communist world, the economic emergence of China, the growth of global integration, and the return of violent economic and financial crises. But something else has changed: the way we think about "good" economic policies. From the 1980s onwards, the economic policy that had to be followed was one that favoured markets, fought inflation, generalised free trade, deregulated financial markets, and stimulated competition. The return of inflation and rising unemployment in the second half of the 1970s was interpreted as proof of the failure of Keynesian interventionism; the economic and political collapse of the Soviet form of socialism ten years later seemed to be the definitive proof that any economic policy that thwarted spontaneous market forces was futile. Following the binary vision of neoliberals, there were only two possible models: either Soviet plannism, which had failed, or the competitive market economy, which was the engine of successful freedom-based capitalism.

Neoliberals believe that markets do not operate spontaneously, and the state is an indispensable tool to create the framework in which they operate. In Europe, competition policy measures took an exorbitant place: former public services had to be liberalised and governments were prohibited from pursuing any industrial policy that could distort competitive dynamics. The Single Market had to be fluid: capital, goods, and workers had to move as smoothly as possible. To facilitate the fluidity of transactions, Europeans created a common currency backed by an independent central bank whose priority task was to preserve price stability.

Neoliberalism took hold all over the world. Free trade treaties were signed frenetically; in almost every country, capital flows were liberalised, and finance was deregulated. Administrations went so far as to organise competition within their own departments. Public services and scientific research moved from a system financed mainly by global grants to a system based on tendering and competition. Evaluation procedures multiplied, increasing bureaucratisation in both the public and private sectors (Graeber 2015). In the hospital and education systems, and even in private companies,[21] the logic of markets was used to stimulate competition and select the best.

Since neoliberalism has conquered minds, political and corporate leaders are driven by the idea that it is possible to design the ideal "machine of government", one that will allow them to pull levers on incentives while leaving it to the market to spontaneously allocate resources in the most efficient way possible. This art of "governance" breaks with the traditional practice of "government". "Where 'government' relies on *subordinating* individuals, 'governance', in line with its cybernetic vision, relies on *programming* them", legal scholar Alain Supiot writes (Supiot 2017, p. 29). We no longer manage people directly and restrict formal freedom, we now deploy a system of incentives based on competition in the hope that the dynamic thus created will alone achieve greater overall efficiency.

This quest for the ideal machine of government is a myth. There is no scientifically proven theory to support the idea that policymakers can simply pull a few levers to allow market forces to spontaneously generate performance. In fact, 40 years after its generalisation, this art of governance appears to have produced a great deal of frustration among populations and little economic efficiency where it was implemented. Populism is the most visible political consequence of this failure. But the emergence of populism is not only the result of the objective situation facing populations. It is also the result of a certain discourse of powerlessness, a rhetoric that makes the markets the sole cause of frustrations experienced and "happy" globalisation the only prospect for humanity.

How, having consciously set up the institutions that have built our world, can political leaders claim they are in no way responsible for the present situation and that the only economic policies imaginable are to make economies more competitive than their neighbours? Why is it so difficult among progressive economists to design economic policies representing an actual break with the present situation?

Populists thrive because they demonstrate that it is possible to reason and make policy without considering the current neoliberal framework as beyond reproach and taking it for granted. But populism is not a constructive programme. It does not say on what alternative principles political action should be grounded. The rise of populism demonstrates one thing without doubt, and one thing only: that the time of neoliberalism is drawing to a close, and that we urgently need to think differently about how the economic system as a whole could be organised.

Notes

1 A. Tappe (2020), "Nearly 43 Million Americans Have Filed for Unemployment Benefits during the Pandemic", *CNN*, June 4, 2020, online.

2 Source: OCDE, https://data.oecd.org/emp/labour-force.htm, consulted on June 5, 2020.

3 The creation of the huge Tesla plant in Fremont, California, is a perfect illustration of how industrial activities have been repatriated to the coasts in the United States in recent decades.

4 The Personal Responsibility and Work Opportunity Reconciliation Act is a Republican law passed under Bill Clinton in 1996. It essentially aimed to limit access to social assistance by strengthening the conditions for receiving it in order to promote inclusion and a return to work. In practice, it resulted in a reduction in access to social assistance and increased exclusion of the most vulnerable populations, particularly single mothers.

5 According to Bruce Western, the 1980s and 1990s were disastrous for Black men in the United States.

> From 1980 to 2000, black men were about six to eight times more likely to be in prison or jail than whites and Hispanics, about three times more likely. ... [I]mprisonment has become a common life event for recent birth cohorts of black men without college education. In 1999, about 30 percent of these had gone to prison by their early thirties.
>
> *(Western 2006, pp. 30–1)*

6 The law of supply states that the quantities offered of a commodity increase with the price of that commodity.

7 See Chapter 1.

8 The BEPS (Base Erosion and Profit Shifting) project was launched in 2012 at the initiative of the G20. It includes a set of fifteen actions, many of which are currently being implemented. An agreement on digital business taxation is currently under consideration. It could lead to a solution by the end of 2020. More information is available on the OECD website at: https://www.oecd.org/fr/fiscalite/beps/actions -beps.htm.

9 In the fifth episode of his television show *Free to Choose: A Personal Statement*, which aired on the US public broadcaster PBS in 1980.

10 Rodrik sums up the problems raised by globalisation as a trilemma that would require a choice between economic integration, democracy, and sovereignty (*ibid.*, p. 5). But the formulation of this trilemma is curious. It gives the idea that it is possible for a country to be democratic without having sovereignty. As Yascha Mounk's sharp analysis shows, such a situation actually implies a kind of undemocratic liberalism, since without economic sovereignty, democratic procedures cannot freely rule the economy.

11 At the time this page is being written, the World Trade Organization is partially paralysed by the blockage of its dispute settlement body due to the refusal of the US administration to appoint appellate judges to replace those whose terms have expired.

12 Galbraith (2016, p. 16) evokes a famous economic controversy of the 1960s, known as the "Cambridge capital controversy", on the relevance of aggregating productive capital that is by nature heterogeneous. In 1966, Paul Samuelson had to admit that it was not legitimate to aggregate capital in a production function. "But then something odd happened: most economists went on doing just that, as if the fallacy of counting up machines by the money spent on them had never been uncovered", Galbraith wrote.

13 See *supra*, note 37, chap. 2.

14 According to Serge Audier, Rüstow advocates "a drastic reduction of the transmission fee. By means of a very considerable – quasi-confiscatory – taxation, situations should be equalised at the starting point" (Audier 2012b, pp. 191–2).

15 J. Smialek, "How the Fed Chairman Is Shielding It From Trump", *The New York Times*, January 28, 2020, online.

16 See Cayla 2018 (pp. 68–72) for an empirical test of the law of supply and demand, and a quantified study of changes in prices and sales of fruit and vegetables in France.

17 On April 20, 2020, oil prices collapsed sharply, even reaching negative levels, as a result of the coronavirus crisis and a sharp drop in demand. The price per barrel for one-month delivery was -37.63 dollars. This exceptional situation was due to many factors, including the high cost of storage, which forced buyers to pay significant charges for any oil acquired, and the technical difficulty of quickly stopping oil production.

18 For instance, the first chapter following the introductory part of Mankiw's manual is titled: "The Market Forces of Supply and Demand" (Mankiw 2017).

19 In 1930, Sraffa expressed this strong opinion about the Marshallian theory:

> We seem to be agreed that the theory cannot be interpreted in a way which makes it logically self-consistent and, at the same time, reconciles it with the facts it sets out to explain. Mr. Robertson's remedy is to discard mathematics, and he suggests that my remedy is to discard the facts; perhaps I ought to have explained that, in the circumstances, I think it is Marshall's theory that should be discarded.
> *(Robertson et al. 1930, p. 93)*

20 Here is how Hugo Sonnenschein describes the consequences of his theorem:

> The importance of the above results is clear: strong restrictions are needed in order to justify the hypothesis that a market demand function has the characteristics of a consumer demand function. Only in special cases can an economy be expected to act as an 'idealized consumer'. The utility hypothesis tells us nothing about market demand unless it is augmented by additional requirements.
> *(Shafer and Sonnenschein 1982, p. 672)*

21 One of the most symptomatic experiences of this period was the early 1990s project of Oticon, a Danish hearing aid company that introduced a hybrid management system based on competitive bidding among its employees to encourage employee involvement and project development. The outcome was partly positive, but the company had to back down in 1996 due to increasing difficulties in managing projects (Foss 2003).

References

Arrow, Kenneth and Gérard Debreu (1954), "Existence of an equilibrium for a competitive economy", *Econometrica*, 22: 265–290.

Atkinson, Anthony, Thomas Piketty and Emmanuel Saez (2011), "Top incomes in the long run of history", *Journal of Economic Literature*, 49(1): 3–71. doi:10.1257/jel.49.1.3.

Audier, Serge (2012a), *Néo-liberalisme(s). Une archéologie intellectuelle*, Paris: Grasset, coll. 'Mondes vécus'.

Audier, Serge (2012b), *Le colloque Lippmann: Aux origines du 'néo-libéralisme', précédé de Penser le 'néo-libéralisme'*, Lormont: Le Bord de l'eau.

Boghosian, Bruce M. (2019), "The inescapable casino", *Scientific American*, 321(5): 70–77. doi:10.1038/scientificamerican1119-70.

Cagé, Julia (2020), *The Price of Democracy: How Money Shapes Politics and What to Do about It*, Cambridge, MA: Harvard University Press.

Cayla, David (2018), *L'Économie du réel*, Louvain-la-Neuve: De Boeck Supérieur.

Clapham, John (1922), "Of empty economic boxes", *The Economic Journal*, 32(127): 305–14. doi:10.2307/2222943.

Edgeworth, Francis, Y. (1891), "Review: Principles of economics, second edition", *The Economic Journal*, 1(3): 611–617.

Foss, Nicolai J. (2003), "Selective intervention and internal hybrids: Interpreting and learning from the rise and decline of the Oticon Spaghetti organization", *Organization Science*, 14: 331–349.

Friedman, Milton (1951), "Neo-Liberalism and its Prospects", *Farmand*, February, 17: 89–93.

Galbraith, James K. (2016), *Inequality: What Everyone Needs to Know*, New York: Oxford University Press.

Galbraith, John K. (1958), *The Affluent Society*, Boston, MA: Houghton Mifflin.

Graeber, David (2015), *The Utopia of Rules: On Technology, Stupidity, and the Secret Joys of Bureaucracy*, New York: Melville Houses.

IMF, Fiscal Monitor (2012), *Taking Stock: A Progress Report on Fiscal Adjustment*, Washington, DC: International Monetary Fund.

Jevons, William S. (1871) [1957], *The Theory of Political Economy*, New York, NY: Augustus M. Kelley.

Lucas, Robert E. (2004), *The Industrial Revolution: Past and Future*, Annual Report, Federal Reserve Bank of Minneapolis.

Mankiw, Gregory (2017), *Principles of Economics, Eighth Edition*, Boston, MA: Cengage Learning.

Marshall, Alfred (1920) [2013], *Principles of Economics, Eighth Edition*, London: Palgrave Macmillan.

Milanović, Branko (2016), *Global Inequality: A New Approach for the Age of Globalization*, Cambridge, MA: The Belknap Press.

Milanović, Branko (2020), "The real pandemic danger is social collapse", *Foreign Affairs*, March 19, 2020, online.

Mounk, Yascha (2018), *The People vs. Democracy, Why Our Freedom Is in Danger and How to Save It*, Cambridg, MA: Harvard University Press. doi:10.4159/9780674984776.

Naidu, Suresh, Dani Rodrik and Gabriel Zucman (2019), "Economics after neoliberalism", *The Boston Review*, February 15, 2019, online.

OECD (2008), *Growing Unequal?: Income Distribution and Poverty in OECD Countries*, Paris: Éditions OCDE.

OECD (2011), *Divided We Stand: Why Inequality Keeps Rising*, Paris: Éditions OCDE,.

OECD (2015), *In It Together: Why Less Inequality Benefits All*, Paris: Éditions OCDE,.

Okun, Arthur M. (1975), *Equality and Efficiency: The Big Tradeoff*, Washington, DC: Brookings Institution Press.

Ostry, Jonathan D., Andrew Berg and Charalambos G. Tsangarides (2014), "Redistribution, inequality, and growth", SDN14/02, IMF Staff Discussion Note.

Pareto, Vilfrido (1909) [2014], *Manual of Political Economy: A Critical and Variorum Edition*, Oxford, UK: Oxford University Press.

Piketty, Thomas (2014), *Capital in the Twenty-First Century*, Cambridge, MA: Harvard University Press.

Piketty, Thomas (2020), *Capital and ideology*, Cambridge, MA: Harvard University Press.

Piketty, Thomas and Emmanuel Saez (2003), "Income inequality in the United States, 1913–1998", *Quarterly Journal of Economics*, 118: 1–39.

Pinker, Steven (2011), *The Better Angels of Our Nature: Why Violence Has Declined*, New York: Viking Books.

Robertson, Dennis H., Piero Sraffa and Gerald Shove (1930), "Increasing returns and the representative firm: A symposium", *Economic Journal*, 40: 79–116.

Rodrik, Dani (2018b), *Straight Talk on Trade, Ideas for a Sane World Economy*, Princeton, NJ: Princeton University Press. doi:10.2307/j.ctvc779z4

Saez, Emmanuel and Gabriel Zucman (2019), *The Triumph of Injustice: How the Rich Dodge Taxes and How to Make Them Pay*, New York: W. W. Norton & Company.

Shafer, Wayne and Hugo Sonnenschein (1982), "Market demand and excess demand functions", in K. Arrow, M. Intriligator (eds.), *Handbook of Mathematical Economics*, vol. 2, pp. 671–693, Amsterdam: North-Holland.

Smith, Adam (1776) [2007], *An Inquiry into the Nature and Causes of the Wealth of Nations*, Amsterdam: Metalibri Digital Edition.

Sraffa, Piero (1925), "Sulle relazioni tra costo e quantità prodotta", *Annali di economia*, II: 277–328.

Sraffa, Piero (1926), "The laws of returns under competitive conditions", *The Economic Journal*, 36(144): 535–550.

Stiglitz, Joseph E. (2019a) *People, Power, and Profits: Progressive Capitalism for an Age of Discontent*, New York: W. W. Norton & Company.

Stiglitz, Joseph E. (2019b), "Neoliberalism must be pronounced dead and buried. Where next?", *The Guardian*, May 30, online.

Supiot, Alain (2017), *Governance by Numbers: The Making of a Legal Model of Allegiance*, London: Hart Publishing.

Tirole, Jean (2017), *Economics for the Common Good*, Princeton, NJ: Princeton University Press.

Walras, Léon (1874) [1926], *Éléments d'économie politique pure ou Théorie de la richesse sociale*, édition définitive, Paris: R. Pichon et R. Durand-Auzias.

Western, Bruce (2006), *Punishment and Inequality in America*, New York: Russel Sage Foundation.

CONCLUSION

"Is there life on Mars?"

A small economic miracle occurred in the United States in the first decades after World War II: real wages grew at exactly the same rate as labour productivity (Stansbury and Summers 2018). In other words, a worker that became 20% more efficient, benefited from a 20% wage increase. This exceptional configuration allowed economic growth to be shared equitably between capital owners and wage earners, thus helping to limit income inequality.

To explain this remarkable consistency, economists most often refer to a balanced power relationship between employers and employees in the labour market. Back then, in the manufacturing industry, the Fordist system of production was widespread. But this mode of working organisation was very sensitive to strikes. On an assembly line, only a handful of activists was needed in order to disrupt the entire production process and force the closure of the whole workshop by going on strike. In order to avoid such events, employers had to negotiate regularly with unions and grant wage increases to all staff. The pay increase then spread to the rest of the economy.

According to this theory, the situation changed abruptly in the mid-1980s when, in response to economic difficulties and the pressure of Japanese competition, the American industry changed its management style. Rather than assigning different tasks to a number of highly specialised workers, as Henry Ford had recommended, teams of multi-skilled, autonomous workers were set up in factories. By giving these teams a sense of responsibility, allowing them to innovate and participate in the engineers' decisions, the entrepreneurial spirit and involvement of workers were strengthened and, as a result, the number of strikes declined. Should a social conflict arise, the polyvalence of workers facilitated the replacement of strikers by non-striker employees. Thus, a handful of activists could not disturb the whole production anymore. This situation profoundly weakened the power of trade unions.

This more flexible organisational model is called "lean management". It is inspired by the methods that made the success of the Toyota company. Deployed first in the automotive industry, then in the rest of the manufacturing sector, it later spread to the entire American economy, and then to the rest of the world. According to economist Philippe Askenazy, this managerial changeover explains both the strong growth of the American economy during the 1990s and the sharp rise in inequality (Askenazy 2002). The empowerment of workers, management by objectives, individualisation of wage increases, and so on subsequently contributed to further weakening the balance of power enjoyed by employees. Combined with the deindustrialisation of the economy, the end of Fordism brought American capitalism into a "neo-Stakhanovist"[1] era based on the intensification of work and the generalisation of the competitive spirit. In this context, the ability of employee representatives to negotiate better wages was significantly diminished; therefore, employers were able to dominate and impose low wages on their employees.

The story is particularly convincing, but it is incomplete. As is often the case, it shows too much confidence in market mechanisms to be completely accurate. While there is no denying that employees and trade unions have been weakened by managerial changes and that the wages of the middle and working classes have benefited little from economic growth since the early 1980s, why is it that the US economy achieved such coordination between wages and labour productivity from around 1950 to the first oil shock?

Why, if workers were in a strong position, would they not have been able to earn more than their productivity growth allowed? In that case, firms would have had to raise prices, which would have led to a surge in inflation. Yet, until the oil shock, inflation in the United States remained subdued. Conversely, if employers managed to maintain their influence on the labour market, why would they not have taken advantage of it to promote wage increases that were slightly lower than productivity growth? This perfect and seemingly spontaneous coincidence between the two values over a period of twenty-five years appears very surprising.

It is probably because the twenty-five-year strict correlation between wage increases and labour productivity is by no means spontaneous, nor an effect of only the market. As economist John Galbraith explains, during the 1950s and 1960s, the US economy was far from being an economy based on competing markets. Most activity, he states, was the result of *planning*. Some of that planning came from the government, which developed industrial policies and sought to promote growth, but most of it came from the private companies themselves: "So far from being controlled by the market, the firm, to the best of its ability, has made the market subordinate to the goals of its planning" (Galbraith 1985, p. 139).

A heterodox economist, Galbraith believed that the predominant role of the "industrial state" in the economy and its global influence over developed countries was minimised if not hidden by mainstream economics. The conventional idea that the economy is controlled by competitive markets and that corporations must obey the law of supply and demand is only a naïve conception of how the economy really works.

> The firm is wholly subordinate to the social edict as so prescribed. So, accordingly, are the people who comprise the firm. They do not impose their imprint on the goals of society. This is a reassuring formula. … If the reader senses that this may understate the social role of such evidently influential and conceivably omnipotent organizations as General Motors or Exxon, General Electric or General Dynamics, he will have correctly guessed the thrust of this book, and he will be receptive to its argument. If he suspects that economics, as it is conventionally taught, is, in part, a system of belief designed less to reveal truth than to reassure students and other communicants as to the benign tendency of established social arrangements, he will also be right. For it is so. Modern economic belief is the servant, in substantial measure, of the society which nurtures it.
>
> *(ibid., pp. 207–8)*

It is clear that a major car manufacturer cannot afford to start production of a new car model without ensuring that it has the necessary supplies of raw materials, components, and capital goods. For technical reasons, and in order to produce efficiently, Galbraith says, the large industrial company is forced to control its market by various means ranging from buying out suppliers or competitors to establishing long-term contracts. This market control also concerns sales. Through marketing and promotion, General Motors was able to condition the consumer to buy precisely what its engineers had decided to produce.

Of course, this planning is often done in consultation with the most influential players in the US economy: other business leaders and the American government. Galbraith, who worked in the price control agency during the Second World War and was a close advisor to President John Kennedy, was very familiar with the workings of the US administration and how the federal government and the industrial sector interacted with each other. In his book *The New Industrial State*, he recounts how the American government came to act as an intermediary between workers and business representatives to restrain the demands of both sides in terms of wages and prices. "In the absence of definition, all parties identified restraint with their normal behavior", Galbraith writes with irony (*ibid.*, 315–6). So in January 1962, Kennedy decided to formally specify the rules that were supposed to apply to wage increases:

> The general guide for noninflationary wage behavior is that the rate of increase in wage rates (including fringe benefits) in each industry be equal to the trend rate of over-all productivity increase.[2]

This is how the joint growth of wages and productivity was organised. But this rule did not satisfy everyone, particularly because it required manufacturers to limit their price increases. Just a few months after its formalisation, in April 1962, the companies in the steel sector collectively decided to raise the price of steel by about six dollars a ton. Kennedy reacted vigorously. The pressure from public opinion and the government was such that the steelmakers were forced to back down. "Thereafter for several years", Galbraith notes, "the wage guideposts, as they came to be called, and the counterpart price behavior were a reasonably accepted feature of government policy. Wage negotiations were closely consistent with the guidelines. Prices of manufactured goods were stable" (*ibid.*, p. 316).

Another economist observed this episode and the ensuing political debate with dismay. Little known at the time, Milton Friedman believed that the manner in which the government intervened to prohibit US steel price increases was an intolerable intrusion into economic life:

> If businessmen are civil servants rather than the employees of their stockholders then in a democracy they will, sooner or later, be chosen by the public techniques of election and appointment. And long before this occurs, their decision-making power will have been taken away from them. A dramatic illustration was the cancellation of a steel price increase by U.S. Steel in April 1962 through the medium of a public display of anger by President Kennedy and threats of reprisals on levels ranging from anti-trust suits to examination of the tax reports of steel executives. This was a striking episode because of the public display of the vast powers concentrated in Washington. We were all made aware of how much of the power needed for a police state was already available.
>
> *(Friedman 1962, p. 134)*

In many respects, Galbraith is the anti-Friedman. Or perhaps it would be more accurate to say that Friedman is the anti-Galbraith. In the 1960s and 1970s, it was indeed Galbraith's theories that caught the attention of politicians and public opinion; it was his books that were in demand by the general public and in academic circles. In 1977, the American, British, and Canadian public television networks joined forces to program a series of fifteen one-hour episodes entirely devoted to Galbraith's thought with the author himself as the star.[3] The program was severely criticised by conservative personalities, including Margaret Thatcher and Milton Friedman, the latter demanding a right of reply and a series of similar programs on the American public television, which he eventually obtained in 1980.[4]

Friedman felt all the more frustrated because he had just been awarded the Nobel Prize in economics. It is thus on the strength of this academic consecration that he chose to lead the battle of ideas by engaging in an almost personal war against Galbraith. In 1977, in response to the broadcast of *The Age of Uncertainty*, he published a small essay for the Institute for Economic Affairs, a British neoliberal think tank. In this seventy-page booklet devoted entirely to Galbraith's thought, he stated: "No scientific studies have validated Galbraith's analysis: it yields no predictions about the behaviour of enterprise, industry or of the economy that have been tested and found correct. The experience of industry in Britain and America is inconsistent with his assertions about the economy" (Friedman 1977, cover). These considerations led him to the conclusion that "Galbraith must be seen not as a scientist seeking explanations but as a missionary seeking converts" (*ibid.*).

Finally, he wondered why Galbraith's theses had been so successful with the public: "Why do his theories find so much more acceptance in the public world than the theories or arguments of persons like myself?" (*ibid.*, p. 36). It is simply because Galbraith's ideas would be "more satisfying to the ordinary man" and "easy to understand". In contrast, "the kind of theories that people like me try to put across is hard to understand. This is a great defect, unfortunately; it has always been one of the great difficulties of getting a market system accepted. The argument for a market is a sophisticated argument" (*ibid.*).

Galbraith's theses, like Friedman's, undoubtedly deserve a critical analysis in the light of the knowledge accumulated over more than forty years. One of Galbraith's theses is that economic planning is a much more widespread phenomenon than claimed in textbooks and recognised by economists. This thesis led him to defend the even more iconoclastic idea that, from the point of view of economic organisation – which excludes any consideration of freedom and democracy – the Soviet system of the late 1960s was perhaps not so different from the American capitalism of the same years.

But perhaps the great question about the Soviet economy that deserves a real answer is that of its survival. How is it possible that Soviet socialism was able to survive for almost seventy years despite all its defects, which were well known to the Soviets themselves? The weight of ideology is undoubtedly crucial in this matter. Convinced that socialism could not be a mistake, the leaders of the Communist Party, up to and including Gorbachev, never stopped trying to patch its most visible flaws. But each reform unbalanced the system and led to the need for another reform. In the end, Sovietism was not possible to reform. It collapsed. And, faced with the evidence, the ideology that had kept it in power for seventy years collapsed immediately after.

From the standpoint of today, is Galbraith's thesis so absurd? Can an economy in which the head of state forbids a large company to raise its prices and imposes a rule on the private sector to determine the evolution of wages truly be called capitalist? In any case, it is certainly not neoliberal. This becomes even clearer when we remember that, at that time, Kennedy launched the Apollo programme which in less than ten years allowed American citizens to walk on the lunar ground. This gigantic state program directly funded the employment of nearly 400,000 people and cost about $300 billion at today's rates.

In 2014, on the 45th anniversary of the mission that sent Neil Armstrong to the moon, a web user asked a naive question on the American website Quora: "How did we lose the technology to go to the Moon?"[5] Robert Frost, a NASA engineer, answered by detailing the technical difficulties that would be posed by a possible return to our natural satellite, such as shut down of the factories, loss of the equipment, relocation of the professional staff. Broadly said, the specific know-how disappeared with the end of the programme. Going back to the Moon would require starting all over again with today's machines, today's engineers and technicians, new software, new processes which would mean redoing practically all the tests and experiments that had been carried out at the time.

But another question arises. Could the United States of today redirect enough of its economic forces to accomplish this goal, as it did in the 1960s? The US economy is more productive, its population much larger and better educated, its science more advanced, and its technology incomparably more efficient, especially in computing and automation. But despite all these facilities, the economic cost seems paradoxically less bearable today than it was sixty years ago. This is because going to the Moon requires another know-how that was lost in the 1980s, that which allowed the government to organise and direct part of its economic system to meet specific needs.[6]

At the time of this writing, we are facing two major global issues: managing the social and economic consequences of the COVID-19 pandemic and transforming our productive system in order to avoid a climate catastrophe. To face these challenges and benefit from an economy where growth is better shared, it seems urgent and necessary to relearn some forgotten know-how related to the way political authorities may take part in the organisation of the economy. There is no doubt that an extremely wide range of collective challenges is in need of concerted and determined action by world leaders. But the latter will not be able to do anything if they are advised only by economists who have become to some extant Friedmanites and who have never ceased to theorise either public impotence and submission to market mechanisms or the art of blowing on pool balls. Likewise, there is a need for politicians who are not constantly responding to the spontaneous impulses of their people but also able to act consistently and implement a longer-term strategy presented clearly and transparently.

Populism and neoliberalism are two sides of the same coin. Neoliberalism theorises a state that is powerless to respond to social discontent and concerned solely with preserving the order of the market; in response, populism generates an authoritarian state obsessed with satisfying the immediate expectations of its electorate. In both cases, it is the capacity to build coherent and ambitious collective projects that is lacking. But these are absolutely necessary. Whether it is the construction of cathedrals, the wish of landing on the Moon or going to Mars to find traces of life, human beings need to undertake collectively, to build works that survive the centuries, just as much as they need to undertake individually and lead their lives in a free and emancipated manner.

Notes

1 "Teamwork is close to the principle of Stakhanovism on two points: communication is horizontal and, above all, both systems seek gains through optimal and flexible use of production factors, in particular by intensifying work" (Askenazy 2002, p. 51).

2 *Economic Report of the President*, 1962, p. 189; quoted by Galbraith (1985), p. 316.
3 *The Age of Uncertainty*, John Kenneth Galbraith, BBC – Andre Deutsch, 1977.
4 *Free to Choose: A Personal Statement*, Milton Friedman, PBS, 1980.
5 Question and answer can be found at the web address: https://www.quora.com/ How-did-we-lose-the-technology-to-go-to-the-Moon-If-it-has-been-built-it-can -be-built-again-cant-it-What-exactly-is-the-problem.
6 Despite the failures of previous projects (In 2004, George W. Bush promised to return to the Moon before 2020), in April 2019, Donald Trump announced that a new manned flight would send an American to the Moon five years later. While it is too early to predict what will happen to this project, it is clear that, compared to the size of the American economy, the means implemented today are considerably smaller than those of the Apollo program of the 1960s.

References

Askenazy, Philippe (2002), *La croissance moderne: Organisations innovantes du travail*. Paris: Economica.

Friedman, Milton (1962) [2002], *Capitalism and Freedom*. Chicago, IL: The University of Chicago Press.

Friedman, Milton (1977), *From Galbraith to Economic Freedom*. Occasional Paper 49, The Institute of Economic Affairs.

Galbraith, John K. (1985) [2015], *The New Industrial State*. Princeton, NJ: Princeton University Press.

Stansbury, Anna and Lawrence H. Summers (2018), "On the link between US pay and productivity", *VoxEU.org*, online.

INDEX

Printed in the United States
By Bookmasters